Aspects of Language and Culture

CHANDLER & SHARP PUBLICATIONS IN ANTHROPOLOGY

GENERAL EDITORS: L. L. Langness and Robert B. Edgerton

Aspects of
Language and Culture

Second Edition

Carol M. Eastman

University of Washington

CHANDLER & SHARP PUBLISHERS, INC.
11A COMMERCIAL BOULEVARD, NOVATO, CA 94949

Library of Congress Cataloging-in-Publication Data

Eastman, Carol M., 1941-
    Aspects of language and culture / Carol M. Eastman. — 2nd ed.
      x + 214 p.; cm. — (Chandler & Sharp publications in anthropology
and related fields)
    Includes bibliographical references (p.) and index.
    ISBN 0-88316-561-9 : $12.95
    1. Anthropological linguistics. 2. Linguistics   I. Title.
  II. Series.
P35.E2   1990
306.4'4—dc20   90-2632
                                               CIP

Edited by W. L. Parker
Book designed by Lisa Nishikawa and Jon Sharp
Cover design and art by Jacki Gallagher
Composition by Page One Graphics / Lisa Nishikawa

CONTENTS

ILLUSTRATIONS

Figures

Tables

Illustrations / Variety

Preface

This book is intended to be a short and general survey of linguistic approaches, methods, and theories with particular attention to their use in an anthropological context. It is a substantially revised and updated version of the first edition published in 1975, intended to be somewhat more comprehensive and detailed than the earlier volume.

Five areas in which linguistics or linguistic influences figure prominently in anthropological inquiry are chosen for discussion, each reviewed in a separate chapter examining issues that impinge on the study of language and culture. As a survey of language and culture, this book naturally relies heavily on a number of prominent sources in the field and makes liberal use of quotations from them. Though I have relied heavily on other works in order to ensure that ideas presented appear as their intender wanted them to appear, I accept the responsibility for my interpretations of them.

A continual merging, separation, and renewed merging of linguistic and anthropological theory and method may be seen in each area of the study of language and culture surveyed in this book. I hope that what is presented in these pages will facilitate an understanding of what is involved in the study of language and culture and anthropological linguistics both from a theoretical and practical standpoint.

I would like to thank Sally A. Ness, Catherine Farris, Lorraine Eckstein, and George Rich for reading a draft of this second edition. I am also indebted to Bill Parker for his fastidious editing, to Shirley Sotter for working on the manuscript, to Bill Seaburg for proofreading the entire book and preparing the index, and to John Jacobsen for dealing with word-processing glitches and periodically retrieving lost chapters.

Seattle, Washington
September 1988

Carol M. Eastman

Introduction

To a great extent, linguistics in anthropology is a matter of describing language use in cultural settings. As such, it is the study of Language and Culture. In contrast, linguistics—strictly as linguistics—is the scientific study of language and has traditionally been concerned with the analysis of language apart from its context of use. Within both fields, however, during the first half of the twentieth century (especially in the United States), description of data was the major task of the linguist. A set of techniques for discovering the significant units of languages— **phonemes** and **morphemes**—was developed. Languages described by such scientific and objective means might thus be made susceptible of comparison with each other. Once the languages of the world were described and compared, it was thought, we would know what various kinds of languages exist in the world and how they are similar and different from each other. Descriptive linguistics was an attempt to solve the nineteenth-century linguists' problem of ensuring that the linguistic data used to classify languages could be productively compared in the interest of arriving at accurate language groupings. Ethnographers interested in cross-cultural comparison and culture classification also developed a descriptive method, using many of the notions of the linguists in order to produce ethnographies that contained accurate and, so all hoped, comparable descriptions of the observed facts.

As linguists described languages hitherto not recorded and not analyzed, it became clear to some that there was more to language than the speech analyzed in a body of data representing utterances of native speakers. **Speech** began to be seen as the expression of an underlying system of the grammar specific to any particular language. Many linguists shifted their attention toward trying to make explicit the elements and relationships guiding the speech of members of various communities in the world. Alongside a descriptive approach to the study of languages, efforts developed to analyze linguistic systems structurally. Interest arose in understanding the nature of the phenomena described—in how languages and cultures operated in giving rise to speech and cultural acts. Thus the structuralist approaches language and culture as logical systems reflecting the logical structure of a community's collective consciousness.

With the advent of the work of the linguist Noam Chomsky, beginning in the

1950s, came the idea that the logical structure of language may be universal, reflecting the unconscious structure of the mind: that the ability to acquire language may be modeled formally. This idea gained credence among linguists, moving more and more outside the field of anthropology. They called this cognitive ability **competence**. Linguists taking such an approach feel that there is a basic structure in all of us which interacts with the cultural reality in which we find ourselves, that the languages spoken in different speech communities of the world share a common base with all languages of the world yet differ in the way various manifestations of the common base appear. In a Swahili-speaking community children use their linguistic competence to acquire the Swahili language; in an English-speaking area English is the child's first language. Language, in this view, is a common human cognitive ability. It is what enables us to acquire the knowledge necessary to communicate with others in our community. The goal of linguists who have this conception of language is to develop a model of the language-acquisition device humans have in the interest of finding out how the mind works.

While many linguists went in such a direction, a number of anthropological linguists developed an interest in the study of how particular language systems are used in particular speech communities. They became interested in language use in its cultural context and sought ways to describe how actual use of language varies with social structure, ethnicity, socioeconomic factors, power, and the like. In the field of anthropology today, the primary concern remains with language in its context of use. Linguistics has developed as a separate discipline that looks exclusively into questions of the nature of language and of the mind and that attempts to come up with a model of linguistic competence as an aspect of cognition. Nonetheless, modern approaches to the study of the structure of language and to the use of language in context continue to draw on ideas developed by linguistics scholars. Some anthropologists have begun to assert that there may also be an underlying common cognitive ability that allows all humans to acquire culture. In the pages to follow, many of the approaches to the study of language, language and culture, and language in culture will be surveyed.

Chapter 1, Anthropological Linguistics, presents the basic ideas of descriptive and structural linguistics from which have been drawn many of the analogies in the study of culture discussed later throughout the book. This chapter describes the methods developed for the description of languages encountered by the anthropologist or linguist in the field. Descriptive linguists, like descriptive ethnographers, seek to replicate the data as accurately as possible. Structuralists developed their approaches to language, in contrast, in order to seek more general and less detailed statements that could account for regular patterns that exist in, for instance, the way sounds interact and meaning is produced.

Chapter 2, Symbolic Anthropology and Generative Grammar, examines the increasing level of abstraction involved in the study of language and culture. It describes the ways in which speech and actual cultural behavior are but surface manifestations of underlying structures that have meaning and that may be interpreted in and of themselves. Structuralists paved the way both for symbolic anthropology as such and for the generative linguistic approach to the study of grammar and of language and culture as cognition. However, what many see as having been a scientific revolution is thought to have occurred with the universalist bent that came on the scene with Noam Chomsky. This chapter describes some attempts by anthropologists to use some of the earlier ideas of the generative linguists and outlines a number of modifications to the theory that have evolved in recent years. As anthropologists begin to seek cybernetic explanations of cultural systems, similarity with the efforts of generative linguists to explain language may be seen.

Chapter 3, Comparative and Historical Studies, distinguishes synchronic and diachronic approaches to language and culture as well as the development and use of various systems for classifying languages and cultures. Approaches to the study of how languages and cultures in contact affect each other are brought in, especially with regard to the processes whereby borrowing occurs from one language to another. What these effects say about the nature of the cultural interaction taking place at the same time is also discussed. Issues regarding the use of linguistic evidence in tracing historical migrations are brought up.

Chapter 4, Language and Culture, considers the relationship of language to culture and of culture to language. Also addressed is the question as to what the studies of language and culture might have to say about how reality is socially constructed. This chapter takes up issues of world view. That is, how are language, thought, and reality related? The study of meaning from both the anthropologist's and the linguist's points of view is examined. Specifically brought in are the kinds of work done by cognitive anthropologists and by discourse, pragmatic, and semeiotic analysts. Brief attention is given to studies attempting to see how language function and brain function interact. Finally, issues of communication in general are taken up with regard to how they relate to language. Nonverbal communication and animal "language" are seen as instances of communicative systems distinct from language. Both humans and animals can communicate but it may be that only humans have language in the strict sense.

Chapter 5, Language and Society, covers the field of sociolinguistics from the perspective of methodology and subject matter. How language and society interact to form ethnic and social identity, social class, sexual identity, and the like is outlined. The ways scholars describe speech events, trace language change within a speech community, and suggest how decisions may be made about choosing languages for national or educational purposes are presented. Finally, what happens in multilingual and multidialectical settings when people need to interact is seen as a matter of accommodating to others, attempting to be polite to them, achieving power over them, or expressing solidarity with them. What ramifications such linguistic negotiations and manipulations have when it comes to learning a second language or to being educated in general are hinted at.

Chapter 1 Anthropological Linguistics

1.0 Introduction

The study of how language and culture interrelate, especially in non-Western societies and cultures, is generally called **anthropological linguistics**. To a great extent, then, most topics covered in this book can be seen as falling into this area of study. What will be done in specific chapters is to survey the activities involved in this study and how the things done in anthropological linguistics have an impact outside the field as well.

The beginning of anthropological linguistics, to a great extent, correlates with the beginning of anthropology in the United States. In the early 1900s Franz Boas had come to realize that for studying the customs of non-Western peoples it is first necessary to be able to communicate with them. He had been trained in physics and geography in his native Germany. When he began fieldwork in North America on Baffin Island, he initially had to rely on help from J. J. Rink, "a Dane who had lived among the Eskimos for a number of years" (Stephen R. Anderson 1985:198) and had analyzed their languages, which were quite unlike the languages of Europe with which Boas was familiar. Before having taken up the study of language as a means to find out about culture, Boas was informally acquainted with European approaches to the study of language. These approaches were based on the idea that the way to describe language structure was to base it on the model of Latin grammar. Philology, before the twentieth century, really was synonymous with linguistics as the scientific study of language. Boas found that the categories of Latin that apply at least to some extent to the languages of Europe (and even to those of classical India) were of little utility in non-Indo-European contexts. In fieldwork he was confronted with languages that had no writing system, for which there were no written records, and whose speakers were not able to translate for him. As a means toward the end of studying the ethnology of non-Western people, that is, of finding out about their beliefs, history, customs, and institutions, Boas recognized that it is necessary both to study language and to study *about* language.

From Boas onward, language has been seen by anthropologists as a part of culture and as the proper study of anthropology. The Boasian tradition began as a way to describe unwritten languages in the field. A particular testimony to that tradition exists in Boas's *Handbook of American Indian Languages* (1911), in which Boas and a number of his students such as the anthropological linguist Melville Jacobs published descriptions of the sounds, word-formation principles, and texts in languages we might know very little about today had it not been for their work (examples are Haida, Kwakiutl, Tsimshian). Each Boasian approached language in the same way. Notebook in hand after a long and weary trip from New York City (where Boas taught at Columbia University) or from the Smithsonian Institution in Washington, the anthropologist/budding linguist would enter a village and find a willing native speaker with whom to work. "Work" initially meant eliciting data, that is, having native speakers speak in the language and then, to the best of one's ability, writing down what the native speaker said. Such recording of speech as perceived sounds is best known as **phonetic transcription**.

The home of Professor Melville Jacobs during the summer of 1927 at Morton, WA, during which he was doing fieldwork on the Taitnapam language. (Photo courtesy of Melville Jacobs and William Seaburg)

In Boas's day, linguists used a set of agreed-upon symbols for certain sounds. Inevitably, agreement was often difficult to come by. To some extent, for example, Boas would hear George Hunt (the Kwakiutl speaker who helped him understand so much about his people and their culture) through German ears and this difficulty undoubtedly had some effect on the way Boas described the Kwakiutl language's set of sounds. When we remember that the texts we have from Boas and his students were also translated into English, it should be clear that the filter from speaker to linguist to us let many variations pass.

To help keep language descriptions as objective as possible from language to language through linguist to linguist, the IPA came upon the scene and was received as a most welcome tool. This International Phonetic Alphabet consisted of a set of symbols guided by the principle that one and only one symbol should be used to write (transcribe) a particular sound no matter in what language it occurs and no matter from what language background the linguist working on the language might originally have come.

Where the ethnologists sought to describe the behaviors, customs, institutions, and if possible the beliefs of a group of people in the most "scientific," that is, objective, terms possible, the anthropological linguist similarly adopted that goal, namely, to describe the speech of a group of people in a uniform and replicable manner. This goal is one of **observational adequacy**. That is to say, a good ethnological or linguistic account of the culture or language of a group of people ought to allow the person reading it to understand enough of the described behavior to be able to act as if s/he were a member of that culture.

Once the anthropologist could understand the language of a people it was then possible to understand their culture. The person who specializes in anthropological linguistics goes further, continuing to be interested in language rather than merely in learning enough of it to find out about the rest of a group's culture. It is the purpose of this chapter (1) to describe what the anthropological linguist does to describe a language in the field and (2) to mention some of the implications the development of this field of descriptive linguistics has had for the study of culture in general.

1.0.1 Descriptive Linguistics

To understand how a language may be described based on what the linguist hears native speakers say, we need to start by making clear certain underlying assumptions guiding this approach to the scientific study of language. First of all there needs to be agreement that by language, in this framework, is meant speech. The second assumption is that speech is hierarchically structured. That is to say, there is a level of sound structure, a "higher" level at which sounds combine to form words, and an even "higher" level where words combine to form sentences. The structure of language defined as speech, then, is describable from bottom to top, progressing through states of analysis called respectively (1) phonemics, (2) morphemics, and (3) syntax. Each type of analysis will be discussed in turn. But first we need a few more words with regard to what it is the linguist in the field is analyzing.

1.0.2 Gathering Data

As is noted above, the first step in describing an unwritten language gathered in the field is to conduct a phonetic transcription using the IPA. Descriptive linguists use the term corpus (Latin, "body") to refer to the set of data they have gathered and on which they base their language description. Indeed, in many ways the body analogy is a useful one since the practice of language description in this framework consists of locating, dissecting, and putting back together the language's various body parts.

The corpus of data itself is transcribed to the best of the linguist's ability so that every sound the linguist has heard the speaker make is represented. Most linguists use the IPA or a modified form of it. Such transcription systems have an **articulatory** basis; that is, they reflect the way the vocal apparatus moves in articulating or producing the sounds. Each symbol represents both a *point of articulation* and a *manner of articulation* (see Table 2, page 14). A point of articulation is the place at which a particular organ of speech (such as tongue, teeth, lips) obstructs the flow of air. The manner of articulation is the way in which the air flow is obstructed. We are able to *stop* the airflow, for example, by closing both lips. In fact, in English we do this quite often, resulting in what the linguist calls a **bilabial** (meaning bi = two + labial = with lips) **stop**. In a phonetic transcription every sound the linguist hears should be written, using the symbol that represents its point and manner of articulation. To indicate that this symbol is phonetic it is conventional to enclose it in square brackets. A bilabial stop then would be represented as [p] or [b]. Similarly, if the speaker doesn't stop the air totally but instead obstructs it by placing the lower teeth against the upper lip and creating friction rather than a closure of the exhaled air the speaker produces what the linguist calls a **labiodental** (lip + teeth) **fricative** represented by [f] or [v].

What the linguist writes, then, are the sounds produced by means of obstructing the airflow generated by breathing. Once that task is done, the linguist needs to find out which of the many sounds transcribed are speech sounds. It should be fairly obvious that we can use our vocal organs to produce sounds that may not be recognized as speech. For example, it is possible to produce a sound by placing the lips together lightly so that the airflow is not totally closed off and thereby creating a sound between [p]/[b] and [f]/[v]. This **bilabial fricative** is considered rude in American society and is referred to as the "bronx cheer" or "razzberry" when used to express displeasure. There is nothing about the sound that is not potentially speech but in American English it does not fit the **sound pattern** of the language, hence when used has this extra-speech effect.

There are other sounds that can be made and are made by speakers of other languages which are not recognized by American English speakers as speech sounds. The anthropological linguist Ward Goodenough has studied the language of Truk in the Trust Territory of the Pacific, noting that a speaker of the Truk language hearing the English words *tap, tab, dap* (as in fishing), and *dab* would perceive all four as minor variants of the same thing. English speakers reciprocally perceived distinctions significant in Trukese as mere variants:

... native speakers of English have great difficulty perceiving the difference in Truk's language among the words *mwáán* ("male, man"), *mwmwáán* ("wrong") and *mwmáwan* ("fermented, soured"), because in English we do not make meaningful distinctions according to the length of time a consonant or vowel is held, distinctions that are crucial in Trukese. (1981:6)

Nonetheless, the first step in describing a corpus of speech data is to write *all* the sounds uttered by the native speaker. As we shall see below, it is the task of phonemic analysis to ferret out what is distinctive (**emic**) in a particular language from that which is nondistinctive (**etic**).

Table 1 presents a sample of speech data in phonetic transcription along with an explanation of the phonetic symbols used and the corresponding orthographic representation of the same material.

Table 1. Sample Transcription and Symbols

Sample Transcription: [ðə græshapɹ̩ pled ɔl sʌmr wail ði ænt wɹ̩kt n̩ sevd wɛn wɪntɹ̩ kem ðə græshapɹ̩ hæd nʌθiŋ bʌt ði ænt kəmplend əv čɛst penz]
Orthographic Representation: The grasshopper played all summer while the ant worked and saved. When winter came, the grasshopper had nothing but the ant complained of chest pains.
Symbols Used: [ ] square brackets enclose phonetic material ə "schwa"—a mid central unstressed vowel pronounced like the "u" in "unkind" ð voiced interdental fricative ("th" as in "thy" as opposed to "th" in "thigh") e mid front tense vowel (pronounced like the "ai" in "bait") ɔ "open o"—as in Easterners' pronunciation of the vowels in "awful," "caught," and "all" ʌ stressed form of schwa as the "u" in "but" ɛ mid front lax vowel (pronounced like the "e" in "bet") æ "ash"—a low front vowel representing the vowel sound in "cat" , the short vertical line under the consonants [ɹ] and [n̩] that represents syllabicity; that is, the sounds are pronounced as whole syllables—[ər], [ən] respectively. ɪ high front lax vowel, as in "i" in "bit" i high front tense vowel, as in "ee" in "beet" θ voiceless interdental fricative (as "th" in "thigh") ŋ "engma"—voiced velar nasal, pronounced as "ng" in "sing" č voiceless alveolar fricative, as "ch" in "choose"

This sample transcription is from Woody Allen's *Without Feathers* as presented in Bissantz and Johnson (1985:77), Language File 36.

It may have occurred to you that if [p] and [b] are both bilabial stops and [f] and [v] both labiodental fricatives, yet any English speaker perceives a difference between words such as "pat" and "bat" or "fat" and "vat," there must be more to the story than describing *only* point and manner of articulation. In such cases, where sounds may appear to share an articulatory structure at least in terms of where and how the air flow is affected, it may be necessary to analyze differences further—especially if it becomes clear that the native speaker perceives a difference to exist. For example, in the case discussed above, Trukese people would hear "pill" and "bill" to be the same word but English speakers would be puzzled by this; English speakers have no idea what difference Trukese hear when they tell you their words for "man," "wrong," and "fermented" are not the same. In fact, an untrained person could easily come away from each society with such erroneous impressions as "people from Truk think of 'man' and 'wrong' and 'fermented' the same way." Or: "Americans don't know the difference between a 'pill' and a 'bill.'"

The distinction between "pill/bill" in English has to do with the fact that when the sound [p] is pronounced by native speakers the vocal cords remain at rest whereas when [b] is spoken the vocal cords vibrate. This difference can be easily demonstrated by putting your fingers up against your Adam's apple and saying "pill" and then "bill." You will feel a vibration of the vocal cords when you say "bill." The linguist says that the distinction between [p] and [b] is one of **voicing**; [p] is, then, a voiceless bilabial stop and [b] is a voiced bilabial stop.

To understand the distinction the language of Truk has that English doesn't, it is necessary to realize that though Trukese do not distinguish voiced from voiceless sounds they do perceive a difference between sounds, either consonant or vowel, that are held for short or long times. Trukese has both short and long consonants and linguists refer to this distinctive feature of the language of Truk as **length**. English speakers learning Trukese need to be trained to notice such differences just as Trukese speakers need to be attuned to [p] versus [b] in English.

In the English word "pill," the initial sound is actually $[p^h]$. That is, the sound [p] is accompanied by ^{h}, the symbol for **aspiration**, meaning a tiny puff of air accompanying the bilabial voiceless stop (occasioned by the lips being opened slightly at the onset of the following consonant). Such an "extra" symbol is referred to as a **diacritic**. Diacritics are used to give detail to a phonetic transcription over and above what using one symbol per sound will allow, particularly where the transcriber is unsure of a sound.

In Hindi there is a distinction between [k] and $[k^h]$, whereas in English whether we say the usual $[k^h ɪl]$ or [kɪl] without aspiration, we mean "to cause to die," "to kill." Thus it turns out that aspiration is not a distinctive feature in English. Furthermore, the occurrence of aspiration in the language follows a pattern: voiceless stops in English at the beginning of words generally occur with this puff of air; when they occur in the middle of words there is no ^{h}, but if the stop is surrounded by vowels, then it makes no difference whether the consonant *in that context* is voiced or voiceless; when voiceless stops are word-final in English they remain voiceless and also unaspirated. Thus, in English it is usual to say [kʰɪl] "kill," possible to say [lɪgɾ] and mean "liquor," and it is expected to say [lɪk] for "lick." We actually have three sounds, [kʰ], [g], and [k] which we "think" are all just "k"! To express this fact, as will become clear below, the descriptive linguist asserts that in English there is the phoneme /k/ with three variant phonetic forms (known as *allophones*): an aspirated form, a voiced form, and a "regular" "k."

The credit for noticing the "psychological reality" of sound pattern in language goes to Boas's student Edward Sapir. In our heads there is just one "k" (psychologically real) even though out of our mouths (physically real) three may emerge. Sapir (author of *Language: An Introduction to the Study of Speech*, 1921) noticed that the phonetic elements which a linguist transcribes do not necessarily coincide with what a native speaker of the language perceives the sounds to be. That is, he realized that native speakers of English may think there is only one "k" sound in words such as "kill," "liquor," and "lick," despite the fact that there are really three. This belief on the part of native speakers was codified by Sapir in the concept *phoneme.*[1] A phoneme is the "minimum unit of distinctive sound feature" in language (Bloomfield 1933:78–79) made up of certain acoustic elements that occur together in "lumps" or "bundles." In different languages some acoustic elements or features are paid attention to that may be ignored in others; these differences give rise to different sets of elements and to different configurations of them into bundles that are perceived by native speakers as their language's sets of phonemes. From the examples seen here so far it should be clear that in English the acoustic feature aspiration (as realized by a puff of air accompanying the pronunciation of a consonant) is not important—that is, it is phonetic but not phonemic. The distinction between everything a native speaker says (*etics*) and what the native speaker perceives to be a sound in his/her language (*emics*) is basic to an understanding of descriptive linguistics. This distinction has been extended to the study of culture as well as applied to the analysis of progressively higher levels of language within the framework of descriptive linguistics. Indeed, once the linguist has transcribed a corpus (body) of data, the entire process of descriptive analysis involves refining this etic material emically.

---

[1]   Sapir was not the first linguist to use the term *phoneme.* The phoneme had figured previously in the writings of some European linguists. For a review of the history of phonemics beginning with Baudouin de Courtenay's *Versuch einer Theorie der Phonetischen Alternationen* (1895), see Kenneth L. Pike (1967:34).

SNAKE TALES

Reprinted by permission of NEA, Inc.

1.1 Phonemic Analysis

It was Sapir's view that languages have constraints that prevent their speakers from recognizing phonetic distinctions (such as aspiration in English) that do not correspond to the sound pattern peculiar to their language. Every different language can be characterized in terms of its sound pattern analyzed as a set of phonemes. The idea follows that the phonemes of a language must be discovered and described in order to understand which sounds a field worker transcribes are actually part of the language being investigated; hence it became necessary to search for **discovery procedures** that could be applied to phonetically transcribed data mechanically and that would determine the distinctive sound units (*emic* elements) in the data. The set of discovery procedures that scholars came up with are collectively referred to as **phonemic analysis**. We will see below that at the higher levels of language, other discovery procedures analogous to those used to analyze sound were also developed.

It is important to understand that descriptive linguistics was the dominant paradigm as American linguistics began to develop. Its beginnings in the twentieth century coincided with the heyday of strict adherence to the scientific method and there was great concern with rigor, objectivity, and verifiability. In his book *Language* (1933), the pioneering descriptivist Leonard Bloomfield made it clear that (1) the gross acoustic or phonetic features (everything we hear) of sounds of a language and (2) the significant or phonemic sound features (what we say we hear) are required in a scientific description of a language. The linguist's task in describing a language is to provide a statement of all the sounds that occur in the language (phonetics) as well as a statement of which sounds are distinctive among all the sounds that actually may occur (phonemics).

Henry A. Gleason's *An Introduction to Descriptive Linguistics* (1961) provides the discovery procedures the linguist needs in order to select out phonemes from a corpus of transcribed phonetic data. Gleason saw the phoneme as a basic unit of linguistic expression, a "class of sounds which: (1) are phonetically similar and (2) show certain characteristic patterns of distribution in the language or dialect under consideration" (1961:261).

To identify the phonemes of a language, once having gathered a phonetically transcribed corpus of data from native speakers, the linguist makes use of a number of procedures for determining the phonemic status of classes of sounds in the transcription. One procedure involves testing to see whether phonetically similar sounds occur in *free variation* or *complementary distribution*.

Phonetic similarity refers to the **point of articulation** and **manner of articulation** of a sound. Sounds may be described phonetically as if viewed on two axes. They may be described on a horizontal axis according to their point of articulation, that is, *where* they are produced in the mouth; and they may be described vertically according to their manner of articulation, that is, *how* they are made. Table 2 illustrates the point and manner of articulation of some of the consonant sounds of English. The sounds are labeled phonetic by their symbols and their features described along two axes. The terms along the horizontal axis indicate where within the oral cavity a sound is produced (that is, at both lips, at the place where the lower teeth meet the upper lip, at the alveolar ridge, at the velum). Thus the term **bilabial** refers to a sound made by air from the lungs striking both lips; **labiodental** refers to one made as air contacts teeth and lips; **alveolar** sounds involve the tongue contacting the ridge in the mouth where peanut butter sticks— the "roof" of the mouth; **velar** sounds are made when the tongue contacts the oral cavity further back of the "roof." The terms on the vertical axis indicate how the sound is made: **stop** refers to a sound made by obstructing the flow of air before the sound is released; **fricative** indicates that there is some occlusion in the passage of air but no total stoppage; a **nasal** sound is released through the nose.

It is interesting to observe in connection with Table 2 that [p], [b], and [m] have the same bilabial point of articulation. The difference between [p] and [b] is that [b] has the "extra" feature of voicing (the vocal cords vibrate as it is pronounced, as was described earlier) and the difference between [b] and [m] is the [m] is released through the nose rather than through the mouth (and thus has the "extra" feature of nasality). Similarly [t], [d], and [n] are all alveolar sounds distinguishable by voicing and nasality. The sounds [k], [g], and [ŋ] (engma) likewise form a set. This observation "explains" why when English speakers have a cold (and their noses are blocked up) they pronounce "nose" as "doze" and "my" as "by." Later we will also see that this observation, made by other linguists, led to an approach

Table 2.
Some Consonant Sounds in English Defined Phonetically in Terms of Point and Manner of Articulation

		Point of Articulation			
		Bilabial	Labiodental	Alveolar	Velar
Manner of Articulation	Stop	p b		t d	k g
	Fricative		f v	s z	
	Nasal	m		n	ŋ

to the analysis of sound in language differing from that being advocated here on the part of descriptive linguistic emicists.

Table 2 illustrates that certain sounds in English are phonetically similar in that they have the same point and manner of articulation (for example, [p] and [b] or [t] and [d]). Because of their similarity, the linguist is led to wonder whether or not native speakers in the language under investigation regard them as distinct sounds (phonemes) or variants of a single sound (allophones). The linguist refers to such sounds that require investigation as **suspicious pairs**. As such, they require special attention by the linguist who seeks examples in the language of forms or utterances in which the suspicious sounds occur and are the only different sounds in those examples. Such examples of word pairs differing in only one sound are referred to as **minimal pairs**. Minimal pairs are used as evidence for phonemic distinctiveness despite phonetic similarity. In English, the words "tin" and "din" form a minimal pair differentiating /t/ and /d/; that is, an English speaker recognizes them as two different words—"tin" is not a variant pronunciation of "din" and vice versa.

If it appears that phonetically similar sounds are not distinguished by native speakers in a language, then the sounds are said to be in **free variation** and to constitute one phoneme. To a native speaker in the case of free variation it does not make any difference which of the phonetically similar sounds is used. In English, some speakers may pronounce the word "tea" in such a way that when saying the initial sound (the "t") the tongue hits the back of the teeth rather than the alveolar ridge ("roof" of the mouth). That is, they may use the sound [t̪] (dental "t") rather than [t] (alveolar "t") and still be understood as saying "tea" appropriately. In a similar vein, it is usual in English to pronounce the initial "t" in "tea" accompanied by a puff of air upon release. That is, the aspirated "t" [t^h] allophone of the phoneme /t/ is the norm at the beginning of a word. But, if there is no puff of air, speakers are still understood to be saying "tea" where in another language [t^{h}i] and [ti] might be minimal pairs. (Observe that [i] is the phonetic realization of the orthographic "ea".)

On the other hand, for an English speaker to pronounce "tea" with the phonetically similar sound /d/ in initial position would not be judged acceptable by a native speaker. The fact that "dea" [di] is not an acceptable pronunciation for the English word "tea" [t^{h}i] is an indication that, despite phonetic similarity—as evidenced by [t] and [d] having the same point of articulation (alveolar) and the same manner of articulation [stop]—the phonetic [t] and [d] are not in free variation and are therefore likely to be assigned to different phonemes.

The class of sounds defined as phonemes may be found to be in **complementary distribution**; that is, each set of features of each class of sounds occurs in a context in which other phonetically similar classes of sounds cannot occur. "Two elements are said to be in complementary distribution if each occurs in certain environments in which the other never occurs" (Gleason 1961:80).

An environment in which sounds occur in complementary distribution is called a **mutually exclusive environment**. Perhaps one of the best ways for westerners to understand the concepts of complementary distribution and mutual exclusivity is to think of Superman and Clark Kent or of Dr. Jekyll and Mr. Hyde. Wherever Superman is, Clark Kent is not; they are variants of a single entity despite being manifest in their separate forms in different contexts. With regard to sounds, in English, for instance, in the word "spin" the sound /p/ after /s/ is pronounced [p] (without aspiration), whereas in "pin," the initial /p/ is realized as [p^h] (with aspiration as is the norm for initial stops in English). An English speaker perceives that both "spin" and "pin" have the sound or phoneme /p/, even though the actual sound produced and heard in each case is different [p] versus [p^h]. In English, [p] and [p^h] are in complementary distribution: unaspirated [p] never occurs initially before a vowel and aspirated [p^h] never occurs after [s]. Similarly Clark Kent never scales tall buildings while Superman does not write for the *Daily Planet*. Their environments are mutually exclusive.

A set of features or a class of sounds that are phonetically similar and occur either in complementary distribution or in free variation with respect to another set or class is said to be an *allophone* of the phoneme. In the example just given, [p^h] and [p] are allophones of the phoneme /p/. It is usual for descriptive linguists to represent the phoneme by the most usual variant of it that occurs, thus /p/. Note that whereas phonetic material is conventionally enclosed in square brackets, phonemic material is enclosed in slashes / /. Allophones are phonetic elements, phonemes are phonemic elements. The phoneme /p/ may occur phonetically as both [p] and [pʰ]. A phoneme is an abstract representation realized in speech through its allophones.[2]

The terms under discussion here—free variation, complementary distribution, suspicious pairs, mutually exclusive environments, minimal pairs, phonetic similarity, point and manner of articulation, and allophone—are all part of the terminology used in carrying out a phonemic analysis. The search for these particular sound situations is the type of discovery procedure that Bloomfield thought necessary for linguistics to become a rigorous science—yielding observationally adequate descriptions of speech. The terms refer to sound situations discoverable through mechanically applicable procedures whereby a linguist may define the significant sounds of a language. They also may be stumbling blocks to many beginning linguists. Since the period of dominance of descriptive linguistics—in general, from 1933 (Bloomfield's *Language*) through 1955 (Gleason's first edition of *An Introduction in Descriptive Linguistics*)—many of the concepts developed within the methodology of phonemic analysis have been extended to broader areas of inquiry, especially in the field of anthropology. This extension will be seen to be the case throughout this book.

We have seen, then, that a linguist in the field, working within a descriptive linguistic framework, begins to describe language with a *phonemic analysis*.

The four steps in phonemic analysis are:

1. Prepare a *phonetic transcription*. Transcribe a sample of the speech of native speakers sufficient to form a corpus of data for analysis. This is no small task if it is to provide enough data to reveal instances of complementary distribution, minimal pairs, and the like. In keeping with the principles set forth by the International Phonetic Association, only one symbol per sound transcribed should be used, with appropriate diacritical markings included.

2. Tabulate all the sounds in the corpus on a matrix according to their point and manner of articulation; that is, classify the sounds as they are physically made. For example, the bilabial stop [b] is articulated at the lips and the flow of air is stopped: the point of articulation is termed *bilabial*, the manner of articulation is termed *stop*. List suspicious pairs, "pairs of sounds that seem to be phonetically similar and hence possible allophones of the same phoneme" (Gleason 1961:275). In cases such as [p] and [b] in English, where the suspicion turns out to be groundless, it is necessary to find out what "extra" feature (of where and how the sound is pronounced) describes their distinctiveness, voicing, for instance. Other "extras" we have seen so far include *nasality, aspiration,* and *tenseness* (with vowels this means the use of more muscular effort resulting in tighter lip rounding or more extreme tongue fronting and the like—tense-vowel counterparts without effort are called *lax* vowels).

---

2   For further details on phonemes and their allophonic forms, see Gleason (1961:Chapter 16).

3. Frame a generalizing hypothesis; for example, if [p^h] and [p] are in complementary distribution, perhaps [t^h] and [t] are also, because they, too, share their point and manner of articulation. What then about [k^h] and [k]?

4. Test the hypothesis by tabulating the distribution of each sound in a suspicious pair. If [t^h] and [t] may be shown to occur in the same environment (for example, before [ɪn] in [t^{h}ɪn]) but are not thought of as separate words by native speakers, then the sounds are *not* mutually exclusive, are not in complementary distribution and thus, do *not* constitute separate phonemes. Similarly, in English, it can be shown that [k^h] and [k] are allophones of a single phoneme /k/.

In contrast, if [t] and [d] may be shown to occur in the same environment (for example, before "in" in "tin" and "din," medially in "la—er" ("ladder" and "latter"), and finally after "fee" in "feet" and "feed" and if a native speaker makes a distinction between them (that is, deems "tin" a word different from "din," "latter" different from "ladder," and "feet" different from "feed,") then the sounds belong to separate phonemes, /t/ and /d/ respectively.

This procedure of organizing and identifying phonemes in the data is sometimes referred to as **item and arrangement** methodology. The centrality of classifying to the method and the emphasis on locating basic units at different levels of analysis from the phonetic to phonemic and upward have also led to descriptive linguistics being labeled *taxonomic*. Phonemic analysis is a process whereby a phonetic transcription is mechanically refined (that is, by locating suspicious and minimal pairs, finding sounds in complementary distribution, and similar details, using techniques of descriptive linguistics) in the process of seeing how sounds distributed in the data compare and contrast with each other, to prepare a transcription representing the significant classes of sounds in a particular language. A re-presentation of the original corpus of phonetically transcribed speech in terms of the phonemes in it shows the sounds distinguished by a native speaker of a particular language. A /p/ phoneme in language X does not represent the same class of sounds as a /p/ in language Y. The process of phonemic analysis amounts to progressively ruling out the variations in speech that do not make a difference to native speakers; different languages differ with respect to just which variations do make a difference. This fact of the noncomparability of phonemes cross linguistically cannot be overemphasized.

1.2 Morphology and Syntax

It is obvious that sound is not the only distinctive part of language. We all know that sounds occur in certain acceptable configurations and that those configurations, expressed in speech, convey meaning. Sound is used in various ways to express ideas. How to describe the meaningful arrangements of sound and how to state what is the meaningful arrangement of sound (as phonemes found in a corpus of phonetically transcribed speech data) is the next procedural concern of the descriptive linguist.

As was mentioned in the preceding section, Bloomfield recognized the need for developing a rigorous methodology for American linguistic science. As part of this rigor, descriptivists developed an inclination to examine only the objectively verifiable aspects of language. For the analysis of sound, such rigor worked well. The descriptive linguists next attempted to adapt the procedures for getting from *etic* data to *emic* entities, so successful in their study of sound, to the analysis of sequences of phonemes in order to describe how spoken words are formed, how sounds are combined to express meaning. The idea was to find out ways in which phoneme combinations compare and contrast in particular languages.

Assuming speech to be hierarchically organized from the bottom to the top, it was further assumed that once all the phonemes of a language were known then the original corpus of data, now rendered phonemically, would provide the body of analytical material at the next higher level of analysis of meaningful phoneme combinations. Indeed, one tenet of descriptive linguists was to fully analyze each level of speech before moving on up to the next one. Further, once having completed the analysis (for example, of sounds as phonemes and allophones), it was taboo to "look back" or to "mix levels." Each level of speech structure was considered to be a system in and of itself—speech was seen to have a (1) phonetic inventory, (2) a phonemic system, and, as we shall see below, (3) a number of phoneme combinations (called **morphemes**) grouped into form classes, according to a set of principles of arrangement by which sentences are formed. To the descriptive linguist the structure of describable speech begins with sound and ends with sentences—each language to be described in terms of the phonemes, morphemes, and sentence types in it as evidenced by the speech of native speakers that was transcribed by the fieldworker. The result necessarily stressed what is unique in each language.

Ironically, Sapir, who is largely responsible for introducing the phoneme to American linguistics, believed the proper area of study for linguistics to be the universality of language and the relationship of language to thought.[3] The descriptivists influenced by Bloomfield steered clear of any attempt to relate language to thought and stressed instead a need to describe the differences between languages

---

[3]   Most anthropologists learn that the father of American Anthropology is Franz Boas and the father of American Psychological Anthropology is Edward Sapir, while linguists hear of these men as equally influential in their other aspects as fathers respectively of American Linguistics and of the phoneme. To a great extent the histories of anthropology and linguistics in the United States go hand in hand with the very real possibility that students of each may get only one side of the story.

rather than the similarities among them. Sapir was interested in what he called an "intuitive formal completeness" of language, which the linguist could not hope to understand without appealing to other fields such as psychology and philosophy. It is only recently that anthropologists and linguists have begun once again to examine language in relation to thought.

Bloomfield, in accord with Sapir and Boas, maintained that ideally linguistics consists of the study of sounds (phonetics) and then the study of meaning (semantics) (1933:74). However, Bloomfield held that descriptive linguistics could not provide a way to link sound and meaning and still be scientific. Bloomfield classified linguists as either mentalists or mechanists. He was a mechanist and the method he was instrumental in developing for a mechanical (taxonomic, classificatory, and combinatorial) analysis of language is the one presented in his book *Language* (1933). The mechanistic view holds that a scientist can deal only with observable fact. Phonemic analysis deals only with what can be observed from regularities discovered in a corpus of transcribed phonetic data (articulatorily classified). Once the descriptive linguist has identified the phonemes of a language, the next and remaining task is to describe how they are used in the language. Again, the methodology developed to do this task requires that only those facts be described which can be observed from the data by employing certain discovery procedures. Still, the goal is an adequate account of a representative corpus of speech—this account contributing to a language description/descriptive grammar.

1.2.1 Morphology

Whereas phonemes, as the minimal units of the distinctive sound feature in a language, are units that distinguish forms with different meanings, they do not carry meaning. Even so, native speakers of a language intuitively feel that certain combinations of phonemes have meaning while others do not. To try to ferret out the minimal unit of meaning in speech, descriptivists proposed the method of **morphemic analysis** for analyzing sound combinations, parallel to *phonemic analysis* for analyzing etic feature combinations into emic units at the lower level of speech's hierarchical structure.[4]

According to Bloomfield, a **morpheme** may be defined as a "linguistic form which bears no partial phonetic-semantic resemblance to any other *form*" (1933:161). It is a unique correspondence of sound and meaning. Conventionally linguists enclose morphemes in curly brackets { } called braces to distinguish them from phonemes / / or phonetic elements [ ].

---

[4]   Before going into this analytical method, it might be useful to discuss the use of the term *descriptive linguistics* here. In much of the scholarly literature on linguistics dealing with phonemes and morphemes, the approach we are labeling descriptive is referred to as *structural* because the focus is on the way speech is structured formally rather than on understanding the nature of language as such. In an anthropological linguistic context, it seems more useful to refer

Gleason (1961:53) defines the morpheme as a basic unit of linguistic expression—the "smallest unit which is grammatically pertinent" and the smallest meaningful unit in the structure of language.[5] Just as we saw the variant forms of phonemes to be allophones, morpheme variants are referred to as **allomorphs**. An allomorph "is a variant of a morpheme which occurs in certain definable environments" (Gleason 1961:62). Above we saw that the variant forms of a phoneme may occur in complementary distribution such that where one form occurs regularly the other does not. Allomorphs are similarly distributed in a language—which variant occurs where depends either on the phonemic context in which the morpheme occurs or on the variant sharing meaning with other forms. Linguists say that allomorphs are either phonologically or morphologically *conditioned*. "Two elements can be considered the same morpheme if (1) they have some common range of meaning, and (2) they are in complementary distribution conditioned by some phonological features" (Gleason 1961:80).

To illustrate this, consider the words "children," "geese," "beds," "cats," "noses." Each word consists of two morphemes: "children" consists of {čaild} + {plural}, "geese" of {gus} + {plural}, "beds" of {bɛd} + {plural}, "cats" of {kæt} + {plural}, "noses" of {noz} + {plural}. It is clear that the plural in English has a number of allomorphs. Just these few examples indicate that there are at least five variant forms used to express plurality.

---

to the school of linguistics that is concerned with adequately describing the minimal units of sound, sound combination, and sentence structure as descriptive linguistics so as not to confuse the approach with that of the structuralist anthropologists and their interest in the more abstract (less concrete) aspects of culture. Transformational/generative linguists most commonly refer to any linguists who work on data from languages for which the linguist has no native-speaker intuition as **structuralists** and they refer to the phoneme, in its sense as an entity described in articulatory terms having its variant forms combined allophonically in the interest of uniformly representing the sound as psychologically perceived by native speakers, as a *structuralist phoneme*. This structuralist phoneme contrasts with what the abstract theorists refer to as the systematic phoneme, seen not as a unitary syncretism of allophones but instead as a bundle of features. The systematic phoneme is a fluid concept, the various features being able to blend and merge in rule-governed ways as sounds combine to form meaning. In essence, linguists who work on language seen not as speech but instead as a cognitive human ability, consider all others who work with the manifestation of this ability in speech as structuralists. For our purposes here it is necessary to distinguish (1) descriptively oriented researchers, who analyze languages that they themselves do not know and for which no grammars exist, from (2) others who work on instances of language use in speech communities of which the linguists themselves may be members, second-language learners, or scholars who have availed themselves of prior research/grammars available. This latter group comprises what I see to be structuralists as opposed to descriptivists, people interested in the underlying grammatical system of a particular language as evidenced by instances of speech use in a social context. This is the position taken below when the distinction is made between speech (*parole*) and grammar (*langue*) as the object of analysis and discussion of the work of Ferdinand de Saussure is presented.

5   Much of the discussion in this section is paraphrased from Eastman (1978).

It turns out that in English, in a number of words the final consonant of the singular form influences the shape of the plural. If the singular ends in a voiceless stop, for example, the plural will be the voiceless alveolar fricative [s] as in "cats" [kæts]; if the singular ends in a voiced stop, the plural will be the voiced alveolar fricative [z] as in "beds" [bedz]; if the singular ends in a fricative or affricate, the plural will have the form [əz] as in "noses"[nozəz]. Such variants of the plural morpheme, whereby the final consonant of the singular and the form of the plural agree, are said to be **phonologically conditioned** *allomorphs*. Where there seems to be no such reason for predicting the plural form yet speakers know that one form means singular and one means plural, the plural morpheme is said to be **morphologically conditioned**. To capture the generalization that native speakers understand that to form the plural in English all that is necessary is to add "s," the usual way the plural morpheme is represented is as {s} even though the linguist discovers that this psychological reality is often contravened by physical reality (much as we saw the situation to be with phonemes as well). People believe that we make plurals by adding "s" in English, just as they believe we say "p" the same way in "pit," "spit," and "tip" despite objective evidence that this is not the case.

The linguist carrying out morphemic analysis is engaged in finding out what the morphemes in a corpus of phonemic material are and how they are distributed in the language. In many ways the method used is analogous to the method used in phonemic analysis. The linguist compares "pairs or sets of utterances which show partial contrast in both expression (sound) and content (grammatical meaning)" (Gleason 1961:66).

Consider the following set of data from Zoque, a language spoken in Mexico (from Nida 1949:21):

ʔəs mpama	*my clothes*	pama	*clothes*
ʔəs ŋkayu	*my horse*	kayu	*horse*
ʔəs ntuwi	*my dog*	tuwi	*dog*
ʔəs mpoco	*my younger sibling*	poco	*younger sibling*
ʔəs ŋkose	*my older sister*	kose	*older sister*
ʔəs ncin	*my pine*	cin	*pine*

Observation leads rather readily to the identification of {ʔəs} as a morpheme which may be glossed as "my." Further, six other morphemes can be identified on the basis of having unique form and meaning: {pama} "clothes," {kayu} "horse," {tuwi} "dog," {poco} "younger sibling," {kose} "older sister," and {cin} "pine." But there is still something not yet accounted for: the nasal consonants at the beginning of ["my" + noun] phrases. Nida explains it by saying "The prefixal forms which occur in this series are m-, n-, and ŋ-. We say that they are assimilated to the following consonant, by which we mean that the alternant m- precedes the bilabial stop p, the alternant n- precedes the dental phonemes t and c, and the alternant ŋ- precedes the velar k" (1949:21).

The prefix denoting a possessed noun has a number of variant forms. The linguistic analysis of this is that there is a single morpheme {n} termed "possessive prefix" which has three allomorphs: /n/, /m/, and /ŋ/. Which allomorph occurs where is determined by the initial consonant of the noun possessed (much as we saw the final consonant in English to condition which variant of the plural is realized). Thus, the allomorphs of the possessive morpheme in Zoque are in complementary distribution and phonologically conditioned: /n/ occurs before nasals, /m/ occurs before bilabials, and /ŋ/ occurs before velars. The possessive morpheme is represented as {n}. What is enclosed in braces as a morphemic representation is an arbitrarily selected symbol comprehending the morpheme and all its allomorphs and ". . . does not directly give any information about pronunciation" (Gleason 1961:63).

Once the descriptivist identifies all the morphemes in a corpus, the task is to arrange them in *structural classes* often referred to variously as prefixes, roots, possessives, suffixes, and the like. By indicating whether morphemes stand alone (are free forms) or go together (are bound forms), the linguist prepares the corpus of data for the next level of analysis, *syntax*—a description of the ways morphemes combine in utterances or sentences.

1.2.2 Syntax

In a linguistic description the next higher level of language structure to be described is the syntactic level. In Gleason's words, "**Syntax** may be roughly defined as the principles of arrangement of the constructions formed by the process of derivation and inflection (words) into larger constructions of various kinds" (1961:128). In keeping with the idea that linguists should proceed from the lowest to the highest levels of the hierarchical structure of speech, syntax ought to be described in terms of morphemes just as we have seen morphemes to be described in terms of phonemes.

The minimal unit of analysis of syntax (which we would expect to be known as the **syntacteme**) is most generally referred to as the **immediate constituent** (IC). "An immediate constituent (IC) is one of the two or a few constituents of which any given construction is directly formed" (Gleason 1961:133). That is, an immediate constituent is a combination of morphemes forming phrases and ultimately whole sentences. Where we have seen morphological analysis to be concerned with the construction of words, syntactic analysis allows us to see how phrases and sentences are put together in particular languages.

To illustrate, we may consider part of the material from Table 1. If we examine the spoken data "The grasshopper played all summer" (now morphologically analyzed): {ðə} + {græshapr̩} + {ple} + {past tense} + {ɔl} + {sʌmr̩} to see which morphemes seem intuitively to go together from the perspective of a native speaker, the following analysis results: "the" and "grasshopper" form a constituent (specifically a noun phrase or NP); "all" and "summer" also form a constituent (specifically an adverbial phrase or ADV). In addition to being able to identify that articles or determiners go with nouns to form NP constituents (articles and nouns are immediate constituents of each other) and that "all" and "summer" are immediate constituents of each other forming a phrase with adverbial function, it is also discoverable that the verb form "played" ({ple} + {past tense}) and the adverbial phrase are also immediate constituents forming a verb phrase or VP. The result of the analysis of morphemes with regard to how they progressively combine to form utterances typifies IC analysis.

The morpheme-to-utterance procedure employed was largely developed by the linguist Zellig Harris and seen "as an attempt to make more rigorous the traditional notion of parsing" sentences (Chomsky 1957:24). Although IC analysis was developed as the next higher level of description of a body of speech data after morphemics and was intended to involve a set of discovery procedures (by analogy to phonemic and morphemic analysis), the results of the analysis seemed to lack the rigor of the descriptions at lower levels. Gleason noted that "the method . . . would be useless to a linguist confronted with a language for which he (sic) lacked a native speaker's feel" (1961:132). Whereas the whole point of descriptive linguistics was to be scientifically objective, in experience, the only way to actually find out what morpheme combinations combine first and then are involved in progressively larger constituents leading up to whole utterances was to have an "intuitive feel" for what goes together in what order. In experience, by the time the descriptive linguist would get to the point of syntactically analyzing a corpus of data, she would have actually learned the language and lost her sense of objectivity. Intuition would have taken over much as native speakers of any language intuitively know how to speak their languages appropriately without having to be taught specifics of pronunciation, word formation, or sentence structure. This point will be seen as largely responsible for what many see as having been a revolutionary change in the field of American linguistics over the past 30 years.

Indeed, even among descriptive linguists, at the very outset controversy surrounded issues regarding whether analysis ought to proceed from "morpheme to utterance" as we have described it here or, perhaps, might best begin from the "top down." Proposals to formalize IC analysis by going from utterance to morpheme rather than morpheme to utterance provided an impetus to the development of transformational/generative grammar. Since phonemics, morphemics, and immediate constituent analysis as procedures for describing a body of speech data normally proceeded from the "bottom to the top" (that is, from the smallest units of analysis to the more complex), not surprisingly the idea of proceeding from the larger complex unit to a formal analysis of its components was considered revolutionary. This innovative approach to linguistic analysis radically changed both the goal and subject matter of linguistic analysis—from (1) observationally adequate descriptions of speech to (2) descriptively adequate accounts of the knowledge of a language's speakers have of what the grammatical sentences are in that language to (3) explanatorily adequate accounts of the human cognitive ability that allows for language acquisition. Indeed, many linguists abandoned the idea of levels of language and of speech being hierarchically structured. In section 1.5 of this chapter, we will discuss how American linguists began to shift their attention from a focus on the speech of native speakers of never-before-described languages in favor of attempting to describe "all and only" grammatical utterances in particular languages.

1.3 Descriptive Linguistics and Ethnography

As was observed in the introductory remarks to this chapter, Boas saw himself primarily as an ethnographer. Prior to Boas's time the field paid little regard to objectivity—". . . virtually anyone and everyone who wished could submit his or her views on man and culture to whatever audiences would listen" (Langness 1987:54). His approach to language, like his approach to culture based on fieldwork experiences, led him to an appreciation of particular languages and particular cultures in their own terms. Indeed, the focus of Boasian descriptive linguistics and descriptive ethnography was on describing the objective manifestations of behavior as unique to certain languages and societies and not comparable across cultures. Just as a /p/ in English and a /p/ in Hindi may have a different set of allophones and be distributed differently in those languages, finding shamans or masks or bows and arrows in a number of cultures does not mean they are the same nor that "they came into being everywhere for the same causes and were everywhere part of the same evolutionary process" (Langness 1987:56).

Descriptivism in the study of both language and culture is often criticized as being nontheoretical. In many ways this criticism is unfair, since the approach sought not to explain human behavior but instead to devise methods for describing it in an objective and verifiable way. Because, Boasians believed, American Indians were rapidly dying out, it was necessary to devise ways to salvage their languages and cultures—leaving theorizing about it all to come later. The theory underlying descriptive linguistics/descriptive ethnography may be seen implicitly in certain methodological assumptions: language and culture are manifest in observable behavior, are hierarchically structured, each with a "unity, coherence, and history of its own" (Langness 1987:58). Inventories of behavioral elements and the way they combine in larger units of behavior (phrases/sentences—rituals/patterns of culture) presented in a systematic way would provide a legacy of linguistic and cultural diversity no longer viable for generations to come.

1.4 Emics and Etics

In the discussion above with regard to descriptive linguistics it became clear that what is *etic* is everything that is out there—all the sounds the linguist hears produced by speakers of a language. What is *etic* is what the linguist needs to gather initially in order to have a body of data with which to work. Indeed, the only thing that is *etic* to the linguist is the initial phonetic transcription done as data-gathering. Thereafter—from the time the linguist has his or her body of data—the rest of the process of descriptive linguistic analysis is the task of finding out what the *emic* units are at the various levels of the structure of speech that the linguist assumes to exist.

Nonetheless, the concepts *emic* and *etic* have received great play beyond descriptive linguistics among ethnographers and ethnologists. There has developed somewhat of a controversy surrounding whether or not anthropologists should best choose *emic* or *etic* approaches to studying cultural behavior.

Recall that to the linguist, the distinction between emic and etic may be viewed thus: **emic** units are functionally significant units among the sounds of the system of language (*langue*; see section 1.6), and **etic** units are the objectively definable entities of speech (*parole*; again see section 1.6). A phoneme is an emic unit. All allophones (all the variant forms of behavior) of a phoneme are etic units. At successively higher levels of description, the methodology of descriptive linguistics involves isolating emic, or functionally significant, units in a particular linguistic system from the etic data of speech.

Kenneth Pike, whose book *Phonemics* (1947) represents the development of the emic approach as applicable to phonological data, attempted to extend the approach used in discovering phonemes in a corpus of linguistic data to apply to a description of human behavior. The response to this attempt will be seen as influential in such areas as cognitive anthropology and the new ethnography (see Chapter 4 below) and also in socio- and ethnolinguistics (see Chapter 5). Pike (1965:55), in agreement with Goodenough (1957:173), sees the problem to which the etic/emic approach is directed as one of how to go from the material world which is infinitely variable (an etic view of the world) to the subjective world which exists in people's minds (through the discovery of emic units).

The anthropologist Marvin Harris refers to the etic/emic distinction as an emic/etic one and sees what he calls "emic statements" to be "distinctions or meanings as they are perceived by the actors themselves—the people themselves, if the reporter is an anthropologist or linguist studying them. Etic statements are those whose meanings can be verified by independent investigators using similar operations—what the people being observed may personally believe about them is simply not relevant to their truth or falsity" (Langness 1987:133). Harris's point in evoking the concepts emic/etic is to assert that ethnographers need to distinguish between the two types of statements when they produce their descriptions of particular societies/cultures (in their monographs) so that readers will be aware of what, in their reading, is "really there" as opposed to "in the heads" of the native speakers/actors and interpretive ethnographers/linguists.

According to Pike,

> Through the etic "lens" the analyst views the data in tacit reference to a perspective oriented to all comparable events (whether sounds, ceremonies, activities), of all peoples, of all parts of the earth; through the other lens, the emic one, he views the same events, at the same time, in the same context, in reference to a perspective oriented to the particular function of those particular events in that particular culture, as it and it alone is structured. (1967:41)

What is emic is specific to a language or a culture. When the emic units of one language are compared to the emic units of other languages, those units are then etic, "since they are divorced from the context of the structure of the language from which they have come, and are viewed as generalized instances of abstract stereotypes, rather than as living parts of an actual sequence of behavior events within a particular culture" (Pike 1967:41).

For descriptive linguistics, with its goal of analyzing a corpus of data into its functionally significant units, etic/emic methodology is appropriate, that is, to go from the units of speech (etic) to the units of the system of a language (emic).

Emic analyses in a descriptive linguistic or ethnographic framework, when compared each to each respectively, yield etic data which tell us about language in general and culture in general. Such comparisons yield cultural and linguistic universals and may be said to employ an emic/etic approach.

It appears that the concepts of etic data and emic analysis, outside the realm of speech behavior, then, have been transformed as two approaches to the study of behavior in general. With an emic approach, the researcher can discover the informant's point of view by analyzing an elicited corpus of data based on the informant's judgments:

> In ethnography, an emic approach to purposes, goals, motivations, attitudes, etc., is premised on the assumption that between the actor and the observer, it is the actor who is better able to know his own inner state. (M. Harris 1968:574)

On the other hand,

> . . . etic statements depend upon phenomenal distinctions judged appropriate by the community of scientific observers . . . an ethnography carried out according to etic principles is thus a corpus of predictions about the behavior of classes of people.

... An emic statement can be falsified if it can be shown that it contradicts the cognitive calculus by which relevant actors judge that entities are similar or different, real, meaningful, significant, or in some other sense "appropriate" or "acceptable." (574)

Marvin Harris, much as Bloomfield was among descriptive linguists, is suspicious of invoking mental states in the analysis of human behavior. It is somewhat ironic that the technique of identifying *-emes* by mechanically segmenting and classifying *-etic* data—an overtly nonmentalist approach—resulted in the discovery of the "psychologically real" units employed in speech behavior (the phonemes, morphemes, and immediate constituents of particular languages). Harris would like to see ethnographic description stripped of psychological terms and assumptions—though such a monograph has yet to be produced. Harris, himself, proposes an *etic* method of investigation in *The Nature of Cultural Things* (1964).

In contrast, the field of cognitive anthropology has developed in the opposite direction—being concerned primarily with the psychological underpinnings (as feelings, thoughts, belief systems, mind states) of members of particular cultures. Cognitive anthropologists, as we will see in more detail in Chapter 4, study *folk models* of behavior. "[A] folk model is a cognitive schema which is intersubjectively shared by a social group" (D'Andrade 1983). That is, people share concepts in a systematic way such that the concepts serve as mental models or schemata of things they define and behave in reference to in their society. Just as in particular languages there are certain configurations of phonetic elements making up phonemes, and certain conventions for word building whereby morphemes combine, people in groups share ways for putting concepts together such that, for example, Americans may view illness in one way, Swahili people in another. The study of folk models as an *emic* approach to the study of culture will be seen to owe much of its methodology to the work of the descriptive linguists discussed above.

1.5 Structural Linguistics

For descriptive linguistics, Gleason's *An Introduction to Descriptive Linguistics* (1955, revised 1961) is generally thought of as its bible; it is so regarded on a practical level in conjunction with its accompanying *Workbook in Descriptive Linguistics* (Gleason 1955) and along with at least three other works—Kenneth Pike's *Phonemics* (1947), Eugene Nida's *Morphology* (1946), and Bernard Bloch and George Trager's *Outline of Linguistic Analysis* (1942). This set of works in part or in full comprised the textual material for courses in General Linguistics during the 1950s and much of the 1960s. This codification of the descriptive linguistic method and technique stands today alongside other schools of linguistics.

In 1951, Zellig Harris (seen above as important in the development of immediate constituent analysis in the descriptivist approach to syntax) published a book titled *Structural Linguistics*. He saw this book as presenting a set of operations that could be performed on a raw corpus of speech data that would lead up to and result in "a compact statement of what utterances occur in the corpus" (1951:361). To Harris, what he called *structural linguistics* referred to methods for doing *descriptive linguistics*. The methods Harris proposed, however, had somewhat of a different effect—they brought the field of American linguistics toward a more abstract representation of language than scholars such as Gleason had in mind for the description of the structure of speech.

Harris defined the **phoneme** as "a unique combination of components" (1951:361). Indeed, Harris saw the **component** as basic to his approach to language. Components are parts of utterances that are not distinct from each other and that can be grouped into classes. Classes of components that occur freely or are in complementary distribution are called phonemes but the important point here is that the phoneme, rather than being seen as a minimal unit of sound structure, is seen rather as a set of components. Components are what define the distinctive differences between phonemes.

To Harris, it became more important to look, for example, at the component of [voice] distinguishing /p/ and /b/, /t/ and /d/, and /k/ and /g/ than at the phonemes /p/, /b/, /t/, /d/, /k/, and /g/ themselves. He also saw the fact of /p/ and /m/ differing in the components both of [voice] and [nasality] to be crucial. In post-structuralist approaches to language (such as that of transformational/generative grammar, which we will discuss in Chapter 2), Harris's components have come to be known as **distinctive features**.

Another change Harris's work brought about was a relaxation of the Bloomfieldian and Gleasonian insistence on the strict separation of analytical levels in describing a language's structure. In general, and as minimal pairs make clear, where there is a phonemic difference in language there is a meaning difference. For example, words such as /pɪt/ "pit" and /bɪt/ "bit", /kəp/ "cup", and /kəb/ "cub" provide evidence for the phonemic distinctiveness of /p/ and /b/ in English. But commonly linguists would come across problems when words with a common range of meaning would have phonemic differences for which the methods of descriptive linguistics could provide no procedural explanation. We saw this earlier when it was necessary with regard to stating the alternate or variant forms of the plural in English to list {fʊt} "foot" as having an "exceptional plural" in {fit} "feet." The words "foot" and "feet" differ in the same way as do "boot" and "beet" but clearly there is something about the way "foot" and "feet" are related that differs from the accident that both "boot" and "beet" are words in English. Indeed, linguists working on English needed a way to account for such phonemic alternations as in "foot"/"feet" to account as well for "took"/"take," "break"/"broke," "sing"/"sang," and so forth. To handle such problems, Zellig Harris introduced the concept of the **morphophoneme** to represent alternating phonemes. The morphophoneme is a class constituted by the "interchange of phonemes or components in corresponding sections of the variant members of each morpheme" (1951:362). The notion of morphophoneme eliminates the problem of having to decide to which phoneme a particular allophone should be assigned. In "feet" {fit}, there is no virtue in saying that the vowel is /i/ because, by so doing, we lose any way to see the morpheme as related to "foot" {fƱt}. The morphophonemic solution is to see the vowel in both morphemes as a morphophoneme /U/. Conventionally morphophonemes are symbolized as capital letters in phonemic brackets. Another example, perhaps providing better evidence of the appeal of the concept, is with regard to the pair "wife"/"wives" [{waif}, {waivz}]. In morphophonemic terms both the singular and the plural would be seen as /waiF/ with the morphophoneme /F/ symbolizing that in the singular it is realized as /f/ while in the plural as /v/ and thereby conditioning the plural allomorph to be /z/.

It is the structural linguistics of Zellig Harris as an extension of methodology in descriptive linguistics that allows a link to be made between linguistics and what has come to be known as structural anthropology. Introducing the notion of the morphophoneme and the component permitted making generalizations about the language being described that might extend even beyond the corpus of speech data at hand. From the analysis of the data, the linguist is able to say that particular sequences of elements occur in the language and other sequences seem not to occur.

> The work of analysis leads right up to the statements which enable anyone to synthesize or predict utterances in the language. These statements form a deductive system which axiomatically defined initial elements and with theorems concerning the relations among them. The final theorem would indicate the structure of the utterances of the language in terms of the preceding parts of the system.
>
> There may be various ways of presenting this system which constitutes the description of the language structure. (Z. Harris 1951:372-373)

The view of language as the object of linguistic description had begun to shift in the work of Harris. His view of language as an analyzable system of relatable elements constitutes a preeminently *structural* approach.

A structuralist approach to data may be contrasted to the view mentioned above, that adherence to the scientific method entailed. Whereas the scientific method that guided descriptive linguists emphasized performing operations on data in order to discover its facts and state them in an objective and verifiable way, the structuralist method involved the prior acceptance of a number of assumptions of another kind. Structuralists subscribe to four assumptions or operational methods underlying their methodological model. The Russian scholar N. S. Troubetzkoy, a noted member of the Prague school of linguistics, set forth these assumptions that characterize the structuralist method as employed by European structuralist linguists and that influenced Zellig Harris (paraphrased from Lévi-Strauss 1967:33):

1. Shift focus from conscious linguistic phenomena to a study of their unconscious infrastructure (for example, focus not on phonemes but on the components or features that comprise them).

2. Do not treat terms (for example, phonemes) as independent entities but instead analyze the relations between terms (for example, [voice]) as a component or feature relating /p/, /t/, /k/, and /b/, /d/, /g/.

3. Consider the object of investigation to be a *system*: that is, assume that the language to be investigated is composed of a finite set of elements that interrelate in patterned or systematic ways and seek to describe language as such a system rather than as a hierarchical structure.

4. Discover general laws: that is, make statements about the way the system works, what is deemed acceptable behavior in it, and what conversely is excluded.

Zellig Harris saw language in these terms. To him a language is a system of relatable elements and the goal of linguistics is to describe the interrelationship of elements within language. This view of language as a system with speech as a representative sample has greatly influenced the study of language and culture. The system of language that the structural linguist seeks to analyze is often referred to as *langue*; the corpus of speech analyzed is often refered to as *parole*.

1.6 *Langue* and *Parole*

As should be clear from the discussion above regarding structural linguistics, the focus of linguistic analysis shifted from speech to the system of grammar underlying speech. This shift was implicit in the work of Zellig Harris, who had come under the influence of ideas widely disseminated in Europe beginning in the 1920s and 1930s, especially in France and Czechoslovakia. The method for describing behavior as a system, the structuralist method, was valuable in the study of myth, kinship, and language. One of the key ideas ascribed to structuralism is that of the "collective consciousness" first defined by the French sociologist Emile Durkheim in 1893 as: "The totality of beliefs and sentiments common to average citizens of the same society." This notion was extended to language by the Swiss linguist Ferdinand de Saussure in a series of lectures compiled by his students in 1916 (1954). Saussure saw language as a social thing, a common set of principles (sounds, grammatical rules, referential terms) shared by the members of a community with a common language (a **speech community**). To distinguish the systematic elements of language that all speakers know to be their language's system from its manifestation in the speech of individuals, Saussure introduced the distinction of *langue* and *parole*. His view was that *langue*

> . . . is a storehouse filled by the members of a given community through their active
> use of speaking, a grammatical system that has a potential existence in each brain, or,
> more specifically, in the brains of a group of individuals. For language is not complete
> in any speaker, it exists perfectly only within a collectivity.
>   In separating language (*langue*) from speaking (*parole*) we are at the same time
> separating: (1) what is social from what is individual; and (2) what is essential from
> what is accessory and more or less accidental. (1966:13-14)

The techniques of descriptive linguistics as outlined above are all means whereby *parole* is gathered and refined as a series of basic units of sound and sound combination with meaning. The resultant description, however, is at best a description of that speech itself—not a description of the language as language. This distinction may be made clear when we consider that a person reading a descriptive linguistic account of a corpus of data can only reproduce the speech in the corpus—a descriptive account does not allow generalizations to be made beyond the corpus in the form of new grammatically acceptable and interpretable utterances recognizable by native speakers as properly in their language. *Parole* represents instances of *langue* only, whereas descriptive linguistic analysis produces what linguists refer to as *observationally adequate* descriptions of those instances.

To Saussure and also to Zellig Harris the science of linguistics should strive to do more—to study the linguistic system that gives rise to speech/*parole* in different linguistic communities. The question to ask, according to the structuralist linguists, is: What are the underlying rules of the grammatical system of French, Swahili, Hopi, or English that account for the way individuals in the French, Swahili, Hopi, or English speech communities use their language? The job of the structuralist is to make claims about *langue* which are borne out in *parole*.

A structuralist account of *langue* is a grammar. The best such account would meet the criterion linguists refer to as *descriptive adequacy*; that is, it would give a "correct account of the linguistic intuition of the native speaker . . . of a language, an intuition shared among all speakers of a particular language" (Chomsky 1964:923-924). To be descriptively adequate, a grammar would account for all the grammatical utterances in a language and also exclude those that are not grammatical.

Structuralism applied to the study of cultural behavior similarly seeks to account for the appropriate behaviors within the kinship, myth, religious, or other such systems enacted in particular societies.

1.7 Distinctive Features

Once it became desirable to look at both language and culture as systems of relational elements, many scholars came to feel that describing a corpus of data based on observed speech or cultural behavior was too narrow a goal. It was felt that facts observed and described in a corpus did not reveal any understanding of the nature of the system behind the data. A person reading a descriptive account of the speech of a native speaker of a language never before described might well be able to sound as if she knew the language by repeating utterances in the corpus. But, if a native speaker were to respond and engage the person familiar with the descriptive analysis in conversation it would become clear right away that *only* the corpus had been described but not the language. The difference between a corpus of speech and knowing a particular language became the interest of structuralist linguists; the difference between the description of myths and what makes a myth appropriate to a particular culture became the interest of structuralist anthropologists.

For any system of behavior examined by a structuralist, the investigator asks (paraphrased from Lévi-Strauss 1967:33):

1. What are the relationships expressed in the system?
2. What connotation does each element of the system express with regard to the relationships within the system? Connotations, that is, how elements function meaningfully, are expressed as positive (+) or negative (−) values.

For example, we have seen that the sound system of English exhibits a relationship between /p/ and /b/, /t/ and /d/, /k/ and /g/ that also may be extended to include other phonemes such as /s/ and /z/. The relationship is one of **voicing**. For each pair of sounds, one is voiced [+voice] and the other voiceless [−voice]; /p/ expresses a negative connotation for voicing with respect to /b/; /t/, /k/, /s/ express the same feature [−voice] with respect to their voiced counterparts /d/, /g/, and /z/. That is, /p/ is to /b/ as /t/ is to /d/, as /k/ is to /g/, and as /s/ is to /z/. The only difference in each of these pairs of sounds is the feature [voice]; each pair shares all other articulatory and acoustic features. Thus [voice] is a **distinctive feature** in English.

N. S. Troubetzkoy and Roman Jakobson, also of the Prague Linguistic Circle, were able to demonstrate that contrasts such as [±voice] form a set of features that are universal. That is, there is a finite set of distinctive features that make up the sound systems of each language among all the languages of the world. The nature of such contrasts in sound (referred to as **phonological contrasts**) is systemic; the structure of the system of sound in any language is a network of binary oppositions of sound difference. The number of such differences of sound is relatively small. One distinguishes consonants as [+consonantal/−vocalic] from vowels which are

[−consonantal/+vocalic]. The terms **consonantal, vocalic, voiced, voiceless** express phonological features of contrastive relationships among sounds in language. The features in a particular language are said to be *distinctive* when their particular plus or minus values serve to minimally distinguish sounds from each other. Distinctive features make what structuralists refer to as *systematic phonemic differences*.

In an effort to isolate the elements of behavioral systems that form infinite combinations with each other to create linguistic and cultural meaning, scholars from a number of disciplines looked toward the Prague School linguists, particularly toward their approach to the systematic study of sound. This approach to language as a system of relationships in opposition, especially in phonology, had a profound impact on both linguistics and anthropology. Marvin Harris (1968:494) claims that for the French structuralist anthropologist Claude Lévi-Strauss this change of approach constituted "a scientific revolution comparable to that which flowed from Copernicus or from the development of nuclear physics." The term "scientific revolution" has also been employed to refer to what has happened to the field of linguistics in post-structuralist years. In his study of culture, Lévi-Strauss saw that the structural approach of the Prague school had a certain appeal in the analysis of kinship systems and systems of mythology. He noted that just as the sounds that are possible for humans to make are almost unlimited, so too are the attitudes people express with regard to interpersonal relationships. There are certain features of behaving (such as [familiar], [authoritative]) whose positive and negative values distinguish important actors from each other; there are certain features of kin relatedness (such as [Bro], [Si], [Fa], [Mo] which refer to "brother," "sister," "father," "mother") that may combine in different ways to express labeled kin terms in different societies. Just as a particular phonological system will select as distinctive only certain features that make a difference, a particular kinship system or social group will likewise select only certain of its attitudes as distinctive in that system. These attitudes may also be seen in structural terms as features of relationships within a system (Lévi-Strauss 1967:38, 43).

The features [familiar] and [authoritative], for example, are used in Bantu-speaking Southern African society to distinguish one's father from one's mother's brother, depending upon whether the society is patrilineal or matrilineal. In Southern Africa, according to a study done in 1924 by the anthropologist A. R. Radcliffe-Brown, both patrilineal and matrilineal societies exist. Radcliffe-Brown was interested in the role of the mother's brother in Southern African society because of the variation he saw existing. Using structuralism, Lévi-Strauss was able to explain the avunculate relationship, that is, how one views one's uncle on the mother's side. Assuming a finite set of possible attitudes with regard to interpersonal cultural relationships, Lévi-Strauss's task was to find out what attitudes are expressed and in what combination in Southern African social groups.

He found two situations with regard to son/nephew (1967:39): (1) where the father represents authority and the uncle (mother's brother) represents familiarity and (2) the opposite. For Lévi-Strauss these two situations represent two sets of attitudes constituting two pairs of oppositions with descent ([patrilineal] versus [matrilineal]) determining the choice of opposition. In a patrilineal society the mother's brother is [+familiar] [−authority], but in a matrilineal society he is [−familiar] [+authority]. This opposition explains why in matrilineal societies of this region one's uncle acts the way in our own society we have come to expect fathers to properly behave. This explanation is similar to the way structuralism allows us to understand why /n/ is pronounced /d/ when we have colds. It is a matter of different values for the features [familiar] and [authority] in the first case, and of the feature [nasality] switching from + to − when the nose is blocked in the second.

To look at kinship or at phonology in this way means to look for attitudes or unconscious features as elements of the system being analyzed. It also means to begin looking at each particular term as a bundle of attitudes (features) that relate in various ways to other terms, similarly composed, within the system.

In his approach to structural analysis in the area of kinship, Lévi-Strauss examines other relationships as well; for in order to arrive at a general law within a kinship system, it is necessary to go beyond correlating only attitudes such as those between father/son and uncle/nephew (mother's brother/sister's son). He sees such a relationship within a kinship system as a correlation that is "only one aspect of a global system containing four types of relationship which are organically linked, namely brother/sister, husband/wife, father/son, and mother's brother/sister's son" (1967:40).

From observing a number of different kinship systems, Lévi-Strauss formulates a general rule to the effect that the "relation between maternal uncle and nephew [in cultures where that relationship is distinctive] is to the relation between brother and sister as the relation between father and son is to that between husband and wife" (1967:40). The claim here is that to know one pair of relations is to infer the other. Likewise, in phonology, if we know the relationship between /p/ and /b/, we can infer the relationship between /t/ and /d/.

This example of the analysis of mother's brother in structuralist terms eliminates the problem faced by a traditional descriptive ethnographer—that of interpreting how a term acquired significance in the culture in which it occurs. The traditional ethnographer could either simply state that there is a term for mother's brother in culture X and then describe that culture as patrilineal or matrilineal and note whether the mother is an indulgent figure and identified with her brother or whether some other situation obtains. Lévi-Strauss's reinterpretation of Radcliffe-Brown's descriptive facts demonstrates that there is no longer a need to describe the occurrence of a special term for mother's brother; mother's brother is a part of all kinship systems whether or not the culture in question uses a kin-term for that relationship. Lévi-Strauss postulates the existence of an underlying structure of kinship (composed of features such as [Mo], [Bro], and the like) from which all societies select certain features in certain combinations and with certain values to express the way people in those societies interrelate. In matrilineal Southern African societies the features [familiar] and [authority] are distinctive, making a difference between mother's brother and father's brother where in American society we have the same attitudes toward [Mo] + [Bro] and [Fa] + [Bro] individuals and use only one term for that individual, namely, "uncle."

From the perspective of distinctive features and their relevance in the study of kinship, it is interesting to observe that as American society has undergone rapid social change in this century owing to the frequency of divorce and remarriage, confusion has developed with regard to what features combine to result in the term "brother," "sister," and even "mother" and "father." It is common for children to have more than one juridical father or mother, hence more than two sets of juridical relatives, and what we see happening is that features available in the universe of kinship relations, never distinctive in the American system before, are being combined with existing patterns to express the changes that have taken place. Indeed, the very [familiar] and [authority] features which interrelate differently in the case of mother's brother in Southern Africa underlie distinctions a number of people make between mother's husband (not ego's father) and mother's former husband (ego's father), distinctions wherein the biological father is much like the Southern African matrilineal society "uncle" who takes the mother's child to the zoo, for burgers, to baseball games, and the like on weekends and wherein the stepfather has become the authority figure. Eventually we should expect English to have terms to distinguish these two fathers—at the current interim stage the [+authority] [−father] spouse of mother is usually referred to as FN (first name) and, ironically, the [−authority] [+father] individual is called "Dad."

Distinctive features show the processual nature of a system of behavior. When languages change, the change involves a shift in value of certain features. We saw this shift to be the case when we noted, in our discussion of morphophonemics above, that when a form goes from singular to plural the shape of the word to be made plural will make the feature [voice] distinctive with regard to the plural morpheme {s}. Language and culture change are a matter of neutralizing certain feature oppositions and introducing others—yet the features are constant and universal, available for use in all languages.

1.8 Discourse

People today who do fieldwork with the intent to describe a language tend to combine descriptive and structural approaches in order to come up with the best account of a language for which the researcher may not have a native speaker's intuition but which the researcher has learned in the process of working on the language and interacting with its speakers. This practical reality has given rise to an appreciation of the fact that speech and behavioral acts express underlying systems of language and culture. Further, a number of scholars have begun to assert that the only way to understand either linguistic or cultural behavior (as the researcher sees each type of behavior expressed) is to study their intersection. Sherzer (1987) has expressed the idea that different cultures create their own systems of *cultural logic* with regard for example to how their members view time, space, and the like, using grammar and lexicon features. The resulting perceived differences among languages have been built up through the intersection of language use and cultural behavior. Language structure provides a set of what Sherzer sees to be potentials that are "actualized in discourse" and which "can only be studied in discourse" (1987:306).

Discourse, in essence, is speech use in a cultural context involving the level of speech structure above the sentence (as descriptivists would have it). It is talk in chunks functioning to construct the shared beliefs of people within a group.

Discourse is a subtopic within the broader study of linguistic communication known as **pragmatics** and concerned with all aspects of language in their cultural context (see Chapter 4 for more detail with regard to pragmatics as an approach to the study of world view). Discourse looks specifically at speech and at *langue* and *parole* in order to see how talk and a speech community's rules for appropriate talk function to create aspects of the culture of that speech community. The essential unit of study in discourse is the *talk exchange* (or "conversation"). Scholars interested in describing conversations in culture see them to be structured and, thus, amenable to the type of analyses which have been of concern in this chapter.

Just as we saw with phonemes, morphemes, and kinship terms, the structure of these "psychologically real" units of behavior is "rarely consciously apparent to speakers" (Akmajian, Demers, and Harnish 1984:415), though all people who know how to participate in a conversation in a particular context can tell when something has gone awry—that is, when some of the basic elements or features of talk have not been applied. Scholars have yet to come up with a universal set of features of talk exchange (analogous to what the structuralists have proposed for sound in language) but some progress has been made in that direction. For example: (1) "any reasonable number of people can participate"; (2) "there are principles that govern how and when people can take a turn"; (3) "there are principles that make certain aspects of the conversation socially obligatory, such as saying hello and goodbye"; (4) "there are principles making contributions to conversations relevant to each other, such as answering questions or justifying refusals" (Akmajian, Demers, and Harnish 1984:415). Participants, turn-taking conventions, obligatory openings and closings, as well as regulations with regard to whether or not one is supposed to answer questions or justify refusing to do something are all features of conversation that may be seen cross-linguistically. Knowing what they are can help explain problems in understanding people from another culture even if, in all other respects, they seem to be speaking our language.

The study of discourse represents efforts by researchers knowledgeable in the methods and theories of descriptive ethnography and structural analysis to say more about language use in a cultural context than has hitherto been possible. Their techniques still involve the description and analysis of data and are avowedly nonmentalist in the sense that the concern is with meaning as socially constructed (rather than as it is cognitively generated).

In general, conversations in English are guided by three principles of turn taking: (1) the speaker determines who speaks next—by asking a question directly, by nodding toward the person expected to take the floor, or by some other signal; (2) the first to talk after a pause becomes the speaker; (3) the speaker continues to speak until finished. These principles go a long way in explaining why interrupters are perceived rude in this culture. Still, even if one understands when to take a turn other features must co-occur for conversation to be judged appropriate. Consider this dialogue from the film *Duck Soup* between Groucho and Chico Marx that illustrates what happens when the culture's distinctive features of conversation are not lumped in bundles in accord with the juxtaposed expectations of our language and culture:

Groucho: Now listen here. I've got a swell job for you, but first I'll have to ask you a couple of important questions. Now, what is it that has four pairs of pants, lives in Philadelphia, and it never rains but it pours?

Chico: Atsa good one, I give you three guesses.

Groucho: Now, let me see. Has four pair of pants, lives in Philadelphia . . . Is it male or female?

Chico: No, I no think so.

Groucho: Is he dead?

Chico: Who?

Groucho: I don't know, I give up.

Chico: I give up too. Now I ask you another one. What is it got big black-a moustache, smokes a big black cigar and is a big pain in the neck?

Groucho: Now, don't tell me. Has a big black moustache, smokes a big black cigar and is a big pain in the—

Chico: Uh—

Groucho: Does he wear glasses?

Chico: Atsa right. You guess it quick.

Groucho: Just for that, you don't get the job I was going to give you.

Chico: What job?

Groucho: Secretary of War.
Chico: All right, I take it.
Groucho: Sold! (Adamson 1973, as quoted in Akmajian, Demers, and Harnish
    1984:419)

Discourse study looks at the structure of such language use where, even though
the phonology, morphology, and syntax are recognizable spoken English, the
resultant sample of speech nevertheless cannot be understood; the reason for
misunderstanding has to do with the internal structure of the patterns of usage (not
with the meaning of the sentences themselves or with the conceptualization
underlying the production of ideas expressed in language). What happened with
Chico and Groucho above (and thus resulted in humor) was that Chico responded
to Groucho's initial question by making it sound as if Groucho had been asked and
was expected to answer. Groucho then went along with this switch, reviewing
details of the question he had put to Chico as if he Groucho must answer it. More
switches and role breaks follow on throughout the entire discourse event.

Linguists concerned with discourse are in the process of making explicit the
principles people follow in conversation in order to arrive at a set of universals of
the way in which social reality is constructed via language use.

A number of these principles have been proposed by the philosopher H. P. Grice,
who has the view that in conversation in any particular language people obey
certain principles that entail certain maxims or rules of pragmatics which "determine how our expectation about conversations, our knowledge about the world,
and our ability to calculate the *sense* of expressions in our language all contribute
to our understanding of sentences as they are used in everyday situations" (Bissantz
and Johnson 1985:182).

For example, a *cooperative principle* and an accompanying set of maxims are
usually in effect when people engage in conversation. The cooperative principle
assumes that speakers make contributions to a conversation "... such as is required,
at the stage at which it occurs, by the accepted purpose or direction of the talk
exchange" (Grice 1975:45). Following from this principle are maxims of *quantity*,
quality, *relation*, and *manner* having to do with the content of what is said. The
maxims amount to conventions "normally obeyed" and may be seen as follows
(after Kempson 1977:69):

Quantity: Be as informative as required but not more so.
Quality: Do not say what you believe is false nor "that for which you lack adequate
    evidence."
Relation: Be relevant.
Manner: Be perspicuous: avoid obscurity, ambiguity, length, and disorder.

When people do not follow these maxims they are said to be flouting them and
much of what is creative in language use amounts to flouting in predictable

ways—indeed humor (as we saw with Groucho and Chico) largely rests on flouting maxims. Indeed, humor at all levels of language use can be found in the "errors" people make, as we saw earlier in the case of phonology (it is a cause for amusement if we mishear "hiss" for "kiss" or "doze" for "nose").

What people do when they obey or flout maxims stemming from the cooperative principle of conversational behavior is engage in conversational **implicature**. "These 'conversational implicatures' of an utterance are, by definition, assumptions over and above the meaning of the sentence used which the speaker knows and intends that the hearer will make, in the face of an apparently open violation of the Co-operative Principle, in order to interpret the speaker's sentence in accordance with the Co-operative Principle" (Kempson 1977:70). We engage in implicature when we make what we hear interpretable within the context of the conversation.

Consider: "The police came in and everyone swallowed their cigarettes." This utterance flouts the maxim of relation but by implicature becomes acceptable. As Kempson (71) portrays this example, once the hearer knows that the utterance occurred in 1976 when police were frequently engaged in cracking down on the illegal possession of marijuana, she would assume that people would swallow cigarettes upon the arrival of police only if the cigarettes were illegal. "Since people smoking illegal cigarettes are generally smoking marijuana (not opium, cocaine, or other drugs) one interprets the sentence as *implicating* that everyone was smoking marijuana."

Implicature depends on recognition of the cooperative principle and its maxims; it is just one possible interpretation of an utterance; and it depends upon a prior understanding of the conventional meaning of the sentence. That is to say, the study of discourse, looking at conversation, provides a way—using ideas developed in descriptive and structural linguistics— to describe appropriate structured speech linked to the context in which it occurs.

1.9 Semantics

What about the meaning of words and the meaning of sentences? We have seen above that descriptive linguistics was concerned with meaning only insofar as it distinguished forms. In keeping with its effort to follow the scientific method and be objective, descriptive linguistics had a **behaviorist** definition of meaning such that the meaning of a linguistic form "was taken to be the situation which preceded the performance of an utterance and the behavior, on the part of the participants in the speech act, which followed it" (Fillmore 1971:273). In a similar vein, yet in accord with their more feature-oriented approach to analyzing speech, the structuralist view of the meaning of a linguistic form was "that feature of the social situation which is shared by all utterances of the form, but not present in the utterances of at least some other linguistic forms" (1971:273). Neither view actually has anything to do with *meaning* in any useful sense:

> The behaviorist definition is a kind of disguised insult; if instead of telling you what a linguistic form means, I tell you something about when people have used it and what happened after they did, I'm not telling you what the form means, I'm asking you to figure out for yourself what it means. The pure structuralist definition is the most hopeless one of all: if we wish to understand the definition, we must presumably know something about the social situations in which language theorists have proclaimed it; but most of us have simply not heard it often enough or in enough contexts to come up with any particularly reliable conclusion. Completely formulaic "definitions" of meaning have never served our discipline well. (1971:273)

Techniques for describing meaning by decomposing forms into smaller features or components have also been proposed but have resulted in problems along the way. Such a structuralist approach would let us discover that the word *wolf* has the features [+physical object], [+living], [+animate] because of its appropriate use in (1) "The wolf fell," (2) "The wolf died," and (3) "The wolf felt it." But if that were the case, why are (4) "The wolf got a divorce," (5) "The wolf didn't get a divorce," and (6) "I accidentally broke your wolf" not acceptably meaningful in English? Semantic analysis needs a way to account both for sentences that have meaning and for those that do not, that is, for those that are semantically *anomalous*. The problem faced by linguists interested in describing and analyzing spoken-language structure or use in context is: What method can be devised to find out what people need to know in order to use forms appropriately and to understand others when the others do so? According to linguist Charles Fillmore, descriptive and structural linguists were asking the wrong question when they tried to find out what forms mean. Asking "What is the meaning of this form?" led them to try to discover "the external signs of meanings, the reflexes of meanings in the speech situation, and the inner structure of meanings" (1971:274).

In Chapters 4 and 5, we will see that **sociolinguists** and persons interested in the study of world view (as **pragmatics** and including much of what discourse analysts study as well) are now asking about linguistic and cultural knowledge necessary for appropriate behavior. In seeking this knowledge, it seems that mechanical discovery procedures and guesses about the context of use in the absence of any universal set of features of meaning are being forsaken.

The study of meaning in language and culture requires focusing not on the forms themselves (words, sentences), nor on the features of which they are composed, but instead on some understanding of the knowledge people have that results in appropriate behavior. This idea in pragmatics has resulted in **speech-act** theory and in **sociolinguistics** is referred to as the study of *communicative competence*.

Before these abstract approaches to language use and their analogies in the study of culture will be taken up, we need to see how the whole field of linguistic science, on the part of some of its practitioners, shifted away from the analysis of speech to the study of the abstract underlying system of knowledge that results in language acquisition. Indeed, the theories of language use adopted by *speech-act* theorists and *sociolinguists* in some sense may be seen to complement nondescriptive, nonstructuralist linguistics.

1.10 Summary

In this chapter, we have seen that anthropological linguistics developed largely in response to the need to describe non-Indo-European languages never before described yet encountered in fieldwork settings. Descriptive linguists believed that by describing the levels of speech structure in a corpus of data they had a description of the language itself that would enable others to learn the language. What they didn't realize was that by doing their fieldwork on the language, as they moved to ever higher levels of analysis of their data, they were acquiring the language in the process. By the time a linguist is ready to describe how morphemes combine to form utterances, intuition about the language accounts for how the linguist knows what morphemes go together in what order.

The structuralist contribution to linguistic analysis was to allow the linguist to be more flexible in terms of levels of analysis. Speech, rather than being assumed to be a hierarchical structure, was seen to be a system of behavior shared by speakers in a social context. But this systems approach could not replace descriptive linguistics as a first-encounter approach in field situations. The structuralists' task, beyond providing a recapitulation of the speech of native speakers, was to describe the relationships of linguistic elements underlying all grammatical instances of speech use in a particular language.

Both descriptive linguistics and descriptive ethnography had an emphasis on replicable data when the task was to document behavior never before encountered and likely to die out. Scholars sought observationally adequate descriptions of behavior. With structuralism came a new interest—finding out what constituted the rules guiding shared behavior in language and culture. The goal of such studies was to produce descriptively adequate accounts of behavior—analyses that account for all appropriate behaviors in a particular society while ruling out inappropriate (ungrammatical) ones. Neither the approach nor the goal made much progress in the realm of the study of meaning—though scholars interested in discourse are using some of the methods and procedures of the descriptivists and structuralists to account for appropriate talk exchanges as expressions of appropriate cultural beliefs.

The culmination of structuralist ideas, building upon the concepts of *langue* and *parole* and *distinctive features*, may be seen in Noam Chomsky's *Syntactic Structures* (1957). To Chomsky, a student of Zellig Harris, a grammar was seen to be ". . . a device of some sort for producing all of the grammatical, and none of the ungrammatical, sentences of a language" (Dinneen 1967:360). That is, Chomsky envisioned formalizing the structure of language in the hope of moving toward a theory of Language (as opposed to accounts of languages). Chomsky believes that the grammar of a particular language is but a subset of the grammar of Language— that is, each language's phonological system, rules of syntax, and even semantic system is a reflection of Language as a system of human knowledge. If we know the features selected and the manner of combination into meaningful units in one language's sound, syntactic, and semantic systems and if we compare them with the features and combinations in all other languages, we will be led to universal grammar. The goal Chomsky set for this post-structuralist approach to language is referred to as **explanatory adequacy**. Explanatory adequacy refers to the goal met by a theory that provides "a principled basis, independent of any particular language, for the selection of the descriptively adequate grammar of each language" (Chomsky 1964:923-924) in the world. This goal of linguistic theory requires a radical shift in the task of the scientific study of language—especially from the perspective of the anthropologist whose whole justification for being rests on examining behavior in particular languages and cultures not independent of them.

Thus, within anthropology people interested in the expression of behavior continue to avail themselves of descriptive and structural approaches. Indeed, structuralist anthropology has progressed in a number of directions, including a move toward reflexivity and interpretation using a number of ideas originally seen in descriptive approaches to semantics. This development will be our concern in the next chapter as we also look at the consequences of the Chomsky revolution for the field of linguistics in particular. We will devote some discussion, as well, to the impact of the cognitive approach of Chomsky on the study of culture. Cognitive anthropology, as discussed in Chapter 4, will be seen more as an outgrowth of descriptive/structural linguistics than as having come under the influence of the Chomsky "intuitivists."

Chapter 2 **Symbolic Anthropology and Generative Grammar**

2.0 Introduction

The view of linguistic and cultural analysis in this chapter does not imply that linguists and ethnographers are no longer concerned with expressed or observable behavior—as Basso and Selby (1976:3) have noted: "On the contrary, an understanding of behavior is essential." As we saw at the end of the previous chapter, the question is not with regard to the structural description of observed behavior but with regard to the knowledge necessary to understand it. Both anthropologists and linguists have begun to search for a theory of what behavior means: with respect to the behaver on the one hand and with respect to what cognitive ability the behavers have that allows for the behavior on the other hand. In this chapter, we will look at efforts by anthropologists to understand the social meaning of expressive behavior (including language) and by linguists to understand the cognitive ability responsible for the fact that all humans acquire language (and culture).

We will see that anthropologists are pursuing their task proceeding from the "premise that a satisfactory understanding of meaning in speech depends upon the recognition of a plurality of sign functions or 'modes of signification'" (Basso and Selby 1976:5, citing Michael Silverstein). How behavioral expressions or "signs" refer and are interpreted in context constitutes much of the work of symbolic anthropologists.

In contrast, linguistic theorists are shunning the expression side of language—seeing the study of language use or performance to be premature. They believe with Chomsky that the primary goal of linguistics is to come up with a theory of Language as the cognitive ability that accounts for human language acquisition. Such a theory of this ability, known as **competence**, is necessarily prior to a study of **performance** or the expression of competence complicated by the effects of the context in which it is manifest.

In the first part of the chapter, we will discuss symbolic anthropology, broadly defined as the analysis of symbols, as it applies to the way anthropologists pay attention to language use. In the second part of the chapter, the work of linguists examining linguistic knowledge as distinct from language use will be discussed with regard to the influence that the ideas such noncontextual theorists may have had on current thinking in anthropology.

2.1 Symbolic Anthropology

As "[A]n approach that attempts to analyze cultures as systems of meaningful symbols that enable human beings to organize their lives and survive" (Langness 1987:227), symbolic anthropology may be seen as somewhat akin to structural linguistics as described in Chapter 1. This is most clear in the work of the anthropologist Claude Lévi-Strauss, who was directly influenced by Prague School linguistics. Lévi-Strauss made it respectable, in the analysis of culture, to go beyond the objectively verifiable data of observed behavior and attempt to describe what lies behind the surface data. His approach (as discussed in Chapter 1 above with regard to his analysis of the relation between mother's brothers and sister's son in Southern Africa) demonstrated how the structure of a society's kinship system described in terms of the relationships of the elements within that system offers a descriptively more adequate model of kinship than does a description of the elements or features of the system alone.

Lévi-Strauss sees social activity (as manifest in kinship roles) and social expression (as manifest in myth) as similar to language in that each is (1) a type of communication, (2) a form of expression, (3) a system of behavior structured by unconscious laws. The structure of social activity and expression, thus, is amenable to analysis much as the linguist analyzes language (George and George 1972:xxv). We will see in this chapter that as the linguist's approach to language has changed, so, too the anthropologist's way of studying social activity and expression is also changing.

2.1.1 Paradigmatic and Syntagmatic Relations

Extending Lévi-Strauss's structural view beyond kinship to myth brought forward the view that it is of little value to describe a myth as told by a native speaker or as it appears in written form. Instead, the analysis of myth must lay bare the myth's structural features (in terms of oppositions such as right/left; male/female; high/low) and their interrelationships from one section or **gross constituent unit** to the others in sequence and across versions. This approach, according to Lévi-Strauss, reveals the meaning of a myth.

Myth, like language, has both a structural side composed of a finite set of elements or features (akin to *langue*) and a statistical side such that there may be infinitely variable combinations of features expressed, reflecting the underlying structural system (akin to *parole*). Lévi-Strauss argued that it is necessary to add a third dimension to the study of language, especially if we wish to study language use in larger forms such as myth. This third dimension is *time*. Where systems of behavior are seen as both structured and variable (in terms, for instance, of *langue* and *parole*), they are also enacted both simultaneously and linearly.

This notion of simultaneously occurring features (occurring in bundles as we have seen with phonemes and kin terms) combined into larger meaningful units with a beginning and an end (as morphemes combine to form sentences) makes use of a distinction between synchronic and diachronic dimensions of a system. The word **synchronic** means "at the same time"; **diachronic** means "through time."

Expressive behavior is at once synchronic and diachronic insofar as its elements occur in association as larger units that then sequentially occur together forming even larger units. One gross constituent unit of a myth will have bundles of oppositions of meaning arranged in one way only to be followed by a unit revealing features comprising different oppositions (and values) arranged in another way. We saw this phenomenon in language when we considered that /s/ is a bundle of distinctive features of sound pronounced at once (synchronically). When /s/ occurs after /d/ in English its set of features changes somewhat so that [−voice] becomes [+voice]—thus, in a diachronic or sequential arrangement a synchronic or simultaneous configuration may systematically change.

The synchronic/diachronic distinction with regard to how elements of a system behave has more generally come to be known as a matter of *paradigmatic* versus *syntagmatic* relations.[1]

A syntagmatic relationship exists in the opposition which units (as bundles of features) in linear sequence have in relation to units that come before and after them. For example in *bit* /bɪt/, /b/ stands in syntagmatic relation to /ɪ/ and /ɪ/ to /b/. Moreover /ɪ/ has a syntagmatic relation to /t/ and vice versa. Paradigmatic relations occur at a more abstract and simultaneous plane. For example, in /bɪt/ the /b/ may stand in a paradigmatic relationship with /p/ since both sounds share many features and can occur before /-ɪt/. Conceivably, a listener might ask, "Did you say *bit* or *pit*?"—not "Did you say *bit* or *rag*?"

Syntagmatic relations are overt, surface, and *autonomous*; paradigmatic relations are covert, deep, and *systematic* (Saussure 1916:123). Lévi-Strauss saw the need to locate the systematic elements of the unconscious systems of human kinship, myth, and linguistic expression and the simultaneous need to see how they are expressed syntagmatically in the autonomous enactment of expressive behavior.

---

[1] People who study comparative historical linguistics also use these terms. To them, synchronic studies are those that look at a language solely as it exists at the time it is being spoken; diachronic studies compare the state of a language over time to see how it has changed. See Chapter 3 below for further discussion of this usage in the work of both anthropologists and linguists interested in comparative and historical work.

2.1.2 The Meaning of Myth

To Lévi-Strauss, myth exists in a culture as the culture's way of resolving certain contradictions between the culture bearers and nature. Mythology appears to have no logical continuity, yet it has correspondences, much like sequences of sound have one meaning in one culture and another meaning in another.

To analyze myth, Lévi-Strauss proposed discovering where both paradigmatic and syntagmatic relations within one gross constituent unit appear throughout the myth at different and separated intervals. The idea was to group these sequentially occurring bundles of relations together—to retell the myth in terms of structure rather than content. Thus a myth is reorganized

> according to a time referent of a new nature corresponding to the prerequisite of the initial hypothesis, namely, a two-dimensional time referent which is simultaneously diachronic and synchronic and which accordingly integrates the characteristics of the *langue* on one hand and *parole* on the other. (Lévi-Strauss 1967a:207-208)

Essentially, the structuralist retells the myth as a series of recurring relationships among its structural units and thereby discovers its structural meaning as distinct from the narrative sequence. Indeed, what a myth's structure says it means is quite different from what the teller is heard to mean.

A myth's structure consists of **sequences** and of **frameworks** (each framework constitutes a **schema**). Sequences represent the content of the myth and are chronological; that is, they occur in order. Sequences occur within frameworks. In his analysis of *The Story of Asdiwal*, a myth of the Tsimshian Indians of Northwest North America, Lévi-Strauss (in Leach 1967:1-47) perceived four frameworks in which the meaning of the myth could be found; a geographical, a sociological, an economic, and a cosmological framework.

Each framework/schema is seen to have a code which may be discovered to reveal a message. The interaction of the messages of the schema codes is seen as the structure of the myth's message. To get at this, the analyst looks among the frameworks for pairs of oppositions which need to be resolved, that is, for instances of features that are in conflict. For example, in a myth literally involving animals, oppositions among them that show up in the narrative may reveal meaning at the underlying level of the myth's structure. Keesing and Keesing (1971:311) noted the case of a myth with a sequence involving antelope and lion and another sequence with hyena taking part. From these the opposition herbivore (antelope)/carnivore (lion) may be seen to emerge.

This opposition needs to be resolved for the myth to convey meaning. The analysis would indicate that hyena neutralizes or mediates the opposition between antelope and lion. At the abstract level of meaning, one of the paradigmatic features of meaning within the feature bundle hyena is that hyena is neither +herbivore nor +carnivore and thus cancels out the distinction set up between antelope and lion. Hyena eats meat but does not (usually) kill the meat it eats. As neutralizer of the distinction between antelope and lion, hyena serves to deny the contradiction expressed in the opposition that emerged between them.

This kind of analysis, drawing on the intuitions of the analyst with regard to what features and oppositions come to mind, is certainly a far cry from the objective observationally adequate efforts of scholars concerned at the outset with the structure of language and the structure of culture. Carrying the analysis further to find out what the antelope/lion/hyena sequences actually mean, the structuralist would find that the myth at hand functions to "mediate the gulf between life and death" (example elaborated from Keesing and Keesing 1971:311):

antelope : life :: lion : death
(The antelope is to life as the lion is to death.)

In these pages it is impossible, without recounting a myth and going through the analysis step by step, to demonstrate fully how a structural analysis of a myth operates. The important aspect to note is how this approach compares methodologically with that in structuralist phonology. One might envision an analyzed myth on a feature matrix with the rows representing the sequences of the narrative and the columns representing the feature composition of each gross constituent unit. The rows would then represent the diachronic/syntagmatic relations of the myth as they represent the beginning, middle, and end of a word; the columns would represent the synchronic/paradigmatic features of the units, be they systematic phonemes with [±voice] and the like or antelopes, lions, and hyenas with /+/, /−/, values for the feature [carnivorous]. The pluses and minuses on the matrix represent the resolutions and oppositions from which the meaning of the message is extracted. Table 3 represents a matrix of the partial feature composition of /bɪt/ *bit*—imagine the /b/ + /ɪ/ + /t/ as mythic as well as phonological sequences; imagine the /b/, /ɪ/, /t/ separate systematic phonemes as bundles of mythic oppositions as well as bundles of distinctive features; the analogy should be clear.

Table 3. Partial Feature Composition of /bɪt/ *bit*

		Segments		
		b	ɪ	t
Features	vocalic	–	+	–
	consonantal	+	–	+
	high	–	+	–
	back	–	–	–
	low	–	–	–
	coronal	–	–	+
	voice	+	+	–

Myth, to Lévi-Strauss, permits intellectual solutions to events that can be resolved in no other way. ' The oppositions uncovered in analyzing a myth are paradoxes of which the culture bearer is unaware. The message of a myth uncovered by such an analysis occurs at all levels of the myth in a symmetrical pattern. The structuralist argues that both conscious and unconscious social processes are at work in areas such as language, kinship, social organization, myth, religion, magic, and art. The nature of the phenomena is not important; instead the relations among phenomena and the systems into which relations enter hold the key (Lévi-Strauss 1967a:ix).

2.1.3 British and American Symbolic Anthropology

The above discussion, in brief, accounts for the outlines of what has become known as the French Structuralist approach to symbolic anthropology. In essence, structuralists such as Lévi-Strauss may be seen as symbolic anthropologists because the analysis of symbols (features of meaning) is central to their approach.

"Lévi-Strauss believes that certain binary concepts are just naturally part of the human condition: left and right, male and female, nature and culture, up and down, and the like. These natural sets come to be infused with cultural significance and thus can symbolize good-bad, permitted-not permitted, sacred-profane, and the like" (Langness 1987:153). Everything in nature can, thus, be imbued with symbolic significance—indeed, systems of symbols such as kinship, myth, and language may be seen as mediating the overarching distinction between Nature and Culture.

In Chapter 5 we will see that this approach to the study of symbols in use is being used by people who are interested in language use in context. The new approach to language in conversation appeals to the work of Pierre Bourdieu as an extension of a number of Lévi-Strauss's ideas (compare Bourdieu 1977). Lévi-Strauss's background interest in the linguistics of Saussure is also shared by scholars of language in context who see cultures as systems of symbols and meanings. The approach to language use known as discourse has roots in structuralist views.

Perhaps more an extension of descriptivist than structuralist views regarding social expression is the approach to symbols taken by British scholars—indeed Victor Turner claims to have "observed" symbols "in the field" which "were, empirically, objects, activities, relationships, events, gestures, and spatial units in a ritual situation" (1967:19). Departing from the descriptivist insistence on describing observations only, Turner saw that it was also necessary to have those observations interpreted by culture bearers and to have the context described by the anthropologist. The meaning of symbols can be understood by observation and questioning.[2] As such, meaning, to symbolic anthropologists, is similar to what structuralist and descriptivist linguists were able to get at by asking native speakers whether transcribed forms in a corpus of data were considered by them as the same or different. Meaning in symbolic anthropological terms is akin to the psychological reality of the linguist—meaning locatable in a system's structure rather than meaning as the reflection of a cognitive ability. In the second part of this chapter we will see that the next generation of linguists, the generativist, is interested in understanding meaning as the ability people have that allows them to interpret syntactic and phonological structures—a system of semantic knowledge.

To Lévi-Strauss, Victor Turner, and other symbolists, meaning in anthropology is communicative behavior in context. Turner's insistence on context as important in addition to form and structure is a *semiotic* stand. In structural linguistics, Saussure made the same point. In addition to his *langue* (underlying grammatical rules of language) and *parole* (individual speech acts) distinction used in the study of cultural systems by Lévi-Strauss, Saussure referred as well to *langage* (individual speech acts plus the rules of language). *Langage* represents the inclusion of context as a necessary component of the study of language if the goal is to analyze language considered as a system of communicative behavior.

Linguists following Saussure, until recent years, chose to examine the structure of *langue* as exemplified by *parole* to the exclusion of *langage*. This practice may have been done largely for methodological reasons; there were no discovery procedures allowing for the integration of language structure and speech acts. We will see in Chapter 5 that sociolinguists are proposing procedures for integrating the description of language and society. In Chapter 4 we will see that

---

The discussion of symbolic anthropology in France, Britain, and the United States follows that of Langness (1987: Chapter V, "The Ethnographic Present," pp. 139–164).

anthropologists interested in *world view* are proposing cognitive structures that they see to be "mapped" onto social reality. The important point here is to understand that anthropologists in France and Britain became interested in studying cultural systems and social behavior in the same way linguists study grammatical systems and linguistic behavior.

By focusing on *langue*, structuralist linguists and Lévi-Strauss among anthropologists were able to come up with descriptively adequate accounts of all grammatical or rule-abiding forms of systematic behavior manifest in sentences, or kinship systems, or sets of cultural myths; however, they did not account for actual behavior with regard to language use, the use of kin terms, or the content of myth. These real uses of systematic knowledge can be looked at only if we understand the context in which the knowledge is used. Victor Turner and Saussure knew this—the problem, however, is: Is it possible to include context in the study of structural systems in the process of trying to understand the system's structure? Saussure (and Chomsky as we will see below in the study of language) chose to advocate the study of *langue* as necessarily prior to the analysis of *langage*. Lévi-Strauss similarly adopted a noncontextual approach in the study of culture. In contrast, Victor Turner and others in Britain felt that a triadic approach to cultural behavior was possible and desirable, as opposed to the hitherto dyadic approach. This view received attention in the United States on the part of anthropologists but has been largely eschewed in the 1980s by linguists. Linguists who do look at form and structure in context have essentially departed from the separate field of linguistics—working, instead, within the broad field of anthropology as sociocultural anthropologists of language. They study language as a cultural system much as political anthropologist study political activity, as economic anthropologists look at exchange, and so forth.

Most American anthropologists of language or politics or economics who see their approach to be a symbolic one operate with a working definition of culture coined by the anthropologist David Schneider. To Schneider, culture is a "system of symbols" that include language and words and also objects and things. The anthropological task is to gain an understanding of the systems of symbols and their meanings that constitute the culture of a group of people. More empirically based anthropologists have a problem with this goal of "understanding" symbols and meanings: How do we know the anthropologist's understanding is what the culture is all about and how do we test the results of such a study, let alone replicate it? This same problem, of course, bothers critics of Lévi-Strauss and descriptive linguists who see the proper work of linguistics to be observationally adequate analyses of speech.

Clifford Geertz goes a step further than Turner in adopting the Saussurian triad, emphasizing that in his view culture is neither patterned behavior nor something located in the mind but rather is a context for the description of social events

(1973:14 as in Langness 1987:161). Geertz calls for "thick description" of ethnographic detail by (1) ethnographically describing the detail, (2) finding out what the native's view is regarding what such detail means, and (3) describing the ethnographer's own interpretations of that detail. Unlike a descriptive ethnography or grammar, a Geertzian analysis of context does not allow the reader to recapitulate the data (it allows the reader to find out what the Geertzian thinks in some sense); unlike a structuralist analysis of *langue* or myth, it does not allow the reader to know what the rules of the underlying system of behavior are (though many would say such knowledge was not useful either, since the resulting behavior does not directly reflect the rule system governing it). Nonetheless, a Geertzian semiotic approach to behavior in context, including the anthropologist's own interpretations, roots culture as a concept in the broadest possible sphere—in the mind of the culture bearer, in the mind of the cultural analyst, and in the context of behavior in which both operate. Even though this view is descriptive, it seeks to describe intuitions as well as actions and will be seen to have some connection to current views espoused by post-structuralist linguists examining language seen not as a system of symbolic behavior but as a cognitive ability.

2.2 Generative Linguistics

While structuralist linguistics was having a dramatic effect on anthropologists who began to look at rules and patterns of cultural behavior shared by members of particular societies, the field of linguistics underwent what many scholars see as a scientific revolution. The revolution began in 1957 when Noam Chomsky published *Syntactic Structures*. Chomsky was trained in the techniques of descriptive linguistics and was a student of Zellig Harris's structuralist methods.[3]

Largely in response to problems that Zellig Harris identified in attempting to describe a language's grammatical structure by describing levels of the structure of speech, Chomsky decided that it was necessary to try to "construct a formalized general theory of linguistic structure" (1957:5). The unique significance in Chomsky's approach to language is that an understanding of language comes not from structural features, but rather from determining and describing the properties of the system of rules that underlies the features and relationships of language. These "rules of grammar" make explicit the principles of organization of a grammar and also of language.

On the face of it, Chomsky's 1957 approach to language was quite similar to the goal Lévi-Strauss had for the study of systems of cultural behavior. Where

---

[3]   It is interesting to note that a chain of influence is directly observable in the history of American linguistics. In a sense Boas begat Sapir, Sapir begat Harris, and Harris begat Chomsky.

Lévi-Strauss saw meaning in culture to emerge from the features and relationships they enter into, Chomsky's insistence on viewing language as an abstract *rule-governed* system represents quite a different tack. The two notions of *rule* and *grammar* represent a departure from structuralism. The term *grammar* to Chomsky refers to a theory. A grammar of a particular language is a theory of that language and a subcomponent of a general theory of *Language* (of language writ large), a theory encompassing all the particular grammars of all the languages of the world.

In order to produce a general theory of linguistic structure, Chomsky added to linguistic science (post-1957) a *rationalist* dimension (compare the continued empiricism of the structuralist linguists and anthropologists). He observed, following the philosopher Descartes, that language use has a creative aspect that is an indicator of a human innovative ability underlying diverse linguistic behavior. To Chomsky, a general theory of language

> requires the postulation of a "creative principle" alongside of the "mechanical principle" that suffices to account for all other aspects of the inanimate and animate world and for a significant range of human actions and "passions" as well. (1966:6)

Chomsky's theory aims to account for this "creative principle" of language with the central doctrine of his approach to linguistics—that "the general features of grammatical structure are common to all languages and reflect certain fundamental properties of the mind" (1966:59).

2.2.1 The Innateness Hypothesis

Another important feature of this approach, focusing on the creative aspect of language and on the relationship of language to mind, is the assumption that all people share an innate capacity to acquire a linguistic system—that all human beings come into this world with an innate cognitive ability that allows for language acquisition. And indeed, all humans acquire language. This *innateness hypothesis*—the idea that the structural properties of language, as a skeletal linguistic system, are inborn and universal—has caused quite a furor.

What language a person learns is a subset of Language (with a capital L); generative grammar as a theory of Language aims to account for descriptively adequate grammars of *all* languages. The innate structural base, in the process of language acquisition that all humans go through, has added to it the fully specified system (descriptively adequate grammar) used by the members of society with whom the language learner will be interacting. The goal of generative grammar— to come up with a principled basis from which descriptively adequate grammars of all languages may be derived—is referred to as **explanatory adequacy.**[4]

---

[4]   An understanding of the *principle of three adequacies* involved in the various goals of different
       approaches to linguistics (and by extension to the study of culture) will be useful throughout this
       book. According to Chomsky, a grammar of a language is *observationally adequate* if it gives
       an account of the corpus of data. A grammar is *descriptively adequate* if it gives a "correct account

The anthropological linguists (specifically descriptive linguists), as we saw in Chapter 1, sought to describe speech data in the interest of achieving observationally adequate accounts; structuralists were attempting to come up with descriptively adequate analyses of the grammatical system shared by members of a speech community. They wanted to be able to account for what constitutes a grammatical utterance in language X and also what would be ungrammatical in that language. Generativists want to go beyond descriptive adequacy and produce a theory of Language that is sufficiently abstract and general that it will account for the way the human cognitive capacity for language acquisition works. It is Chomsky's view that observationally adequate grammars (such as those aimed at by the descriptive linguists) emphasize the development of procedures for rearranging and reorganizing data. He feels that the more productive path to take is one attempting to account for the knowledge of people who have language. Further he believes that this uniquely human capacity for language acquisition, that the linguist ought to seek to characterize, is innately specified.

As Andrew Radford explains it (1984:27):

> . . . only if we assume that grammars contain a highly restricted set of principles of a highly restricted set of types, and that the child is born with this knowledge (i.e., genetically pre-programmed with a "blueprint" for language), can we explain the rapidity of language acquisition in children. In other words, Chomsky assumes that the child is innately endowed with the knowledge of what are "possible" and "impossible" linguistic rules, so that his task in learning a language is thereby vastly simplified . . .

It may not be necessary to "buy" the innateness hypothesis; that is, we do not have to adopt Chomsky's "Philosophy of Mind" in order "to go along with his views on the goals of linguistic theory, the nature of linguistic structure and rules and so forth"(Radford 1984:28). However, it is useful if we expect the rest of Chomsky's approach to logically follow.

2.2.2 Rules of Grammar and Universals of Linguistic Theory

Aside from its theory about the innateness of the human ability to acquire language, Chomsky's approach diverges from structuralism in its emphasis on a rule-governed system in which the rules of grammar attempt to account for linguistic competence, that is, for what people know unconsciously about their language. The linguist's rules attempt to determine the rules that a language learner (for example, a child) uses in the process of building an actual speaking and hearing ability in one language (for instance, a first language) onto an innate language

---

of the linguistic intuitions of the native speaker" (that is, if it accounts for what is grammatical in a language and rules out what is not); and, finally, a grammar is *explanatorily adequate* if it is a *theory* seeking to "provide a principled basis, independent of any particular language, for the selection of the descriptively adequate grammar of each language" (1964:923-924).

structure common to all humans and serving as the basis for all human languages.

> A grammar of a language purports to be a description of the ideal speaker-hearer's
> intrinsic competence. If the grammar is, furthermore, perfectly explicit—in other
> words, if it does not rely on the intelligence of the understanding reader but rather
> provides an explicit analysis of his contribution—we may (somewhat redundantly)
> call it a *generative grammar*. (Chomsky 1965:4)

This theoretical approach to language differs in one major respect from both descriptive methods and from structuralism. Both the structuralist and the descriptivist are interested in finding out about language and culture from directly observable data. The descriptivist's main focus is on producing adequate descriptions, on the assumption that one may abstract from the data to the language or the culture. The structuralist focuses on the systematic nature of language and culture and seeks to describe each system in terms of relationships within it, as found in data, assuming that systematic relationships reveal an understanding of the system itself. On the other hand, the generative grammarian proceeds from theory, using data to check the applicability of rules.

One byproduct of this generative view is that, since the theory aims to account for sentences not yet produced as well as those one might be able to elicit from a native speaker, the best data are often those provided by one's own intuition. Generative linguists tend to be their own best informants. In order to test a theory of language acquisition, the linguist needs to know if a rule results in an utterance of language. If the rule applies to the linguist's language and if it works the linguist will know that it does according to his or her own native-speaker intuitions. This assumption is responsible for most generativists' working to produce descriptively adequate accounts of their own first languages in the belief that any such account (as a theory of a particular language) represents a proper subset of universal grammar. If all languages of the world were represented in terms of descriptive adequacy—that is, if we knew the rules for generating grammatical and meaningful sentences in all languages and for excluding ungrammatical anomalies—then a superset of rules accounting for them all would constitute an explanatorily adequate theory of Language (capital L). Certain rules would be shared by all languages and would constitute **universal grammar** while others would be language-specific and be associated with particular speech communities.

Accordingly, a generative grammar aims to describe formally the competence (knowledge) of an ideal speaker-hearer in a language, in the interest of coming up with a formal theory of Language as a human cognitive ability.

In language there are both **absolute** and **relative** universals. That is, "an absolute universal is a property which all languages share without any exception; a *relative* universal represents a general tendency in languages, but one which has some exceptions (which might in turn be attributable to other universal principles)" (Radford 1984:28-29). Both relative and absolute universals are **substantive**. That is, they refer to linguistic facts (substance), making the claim that "items of a particular kind in any language must be drawn from a fixed class of items" (Chomsky 1965:28). The distinctive features proposed in phonology represent substantive universals. Phonological theory states that all languages select their distinctive sounds from a universal set of features of sound including such features as [consonantal], [vocalic], [nasal]. In absolute terms it is safe to say the feature [consonantal] is universal; the feature [nasal], on the other hand, while part of a universal set of features from which all languages choose their own set, is not chosen by all languages. Furthermore, languages which do select [nasal] will select it in relative terms. In English, for example, [nasal] is a distinctive feature of consonants only /m/, /n/, /ŋ/; but in French, [nasal] is also a feature of some vowels. Linguists have found out that no language will have a [+nasal] vowel if that language does not also have the same vowel with the feature [-nasal]. This implies that [-nasal] is the usual value for vowels in all languages.

Formal universals, in contrast to substantive, involve "the character of the rules that appear in grammars and the ways in which they can be interconnected" (Chomsky 1965:29). Substantive universals may be seen to deal with the content of language while formal universals literally have to do with the form or structure of the model of language the theory generates.

Formal universals of language determine the structure of grammars and the form and organization of rules. The conventions used in writing rules of grammar are examples of formal universals while substantive universals of language "define the sets of elements that may figure in particular grammars" (Chomsky and Halle 1968:4).

2.2.3 Markedness

The distinction between the usual and the unusual has become increasingly important in the study of both language and culture. In the preceding section we mentioned that there is a relative substantive universal in the theory of Language as being espoused by generativists to the effect that no languages will have nasal vowels if they don't already have the corresponding oral vowels. To express this universal one may say the feature [nasal] is *marked* in contrast to the feature [oral]. Within what linguists refer to as *markedness theory*, "An *unmarked* phenomenon is one which accords with general tendencies in language: a *marked phenomenon* is one which goes against these general tendencies, and is hence 'exceptional' in some way" (Radford 1984:29). In Chapter 5 we will see that the notion of markedness is being used by sociolinguists and discourse analysts to describe the process of achieving status and identity in various social contexts using language. Perhaps the clearest example of markedness and its relation to linguistic and cultural process and change may be seen by considering certain pairs of words, such as poet/poetess; doctor/woman doctor; man/woman. This very small data set graphically reveals what until recently (and still in some places) was the view in the United States of the usual occupier of the role of rhyming, curing, and even being. In order to indicate that the usual is not the case we need to mark one form as unusual by, for example, a suffix *-ess*, an extra word *woman*, or the seeming prefix *wo-*: this is similar to adding the feature [nasal] to vowels in French—marking them unusual and not the norm.

Chomsky feels that the innate cognitive structure may be a set of unmarked rules for natural language—a kind of genetic head start (compare Radford 1984:30). Learning one's first language, then, amounts to learning the marking conventions of the speech community in which the incipient speaker-hearer will be participating. Language learning amounts to finding out what the not-usual rules are that are necessary if we are to use our linguistic competence to interact with others.

In a like manner, learning a second language amounts to finding out what the marking conventions are in another speech community (still building on the unmarked rules with which we may have entered the world). Becoming a member of another culture may likewise (as sociolinguists and discourse-oriented scholars are beginning to think) involve acquiring that society's marking conventions—learning to do the unusual things they do. It will be interesting to see if scholars interested in language and society will be tempted to relate their use of the theory of markedness[5] to notions of linked universals of Language (capital L) and Culture (capital C). Later in this chapter, we will talk about some gentle leanings in this direction by espousers of what is known as the **new ethnography**.

The sum of all the immutable principles—comprising grammar, sound, and meaning especially—built into the human language capacity via the genes constitutes **universal grammar** and contemplates the **language organ** as discussed in the section that follows. This totality makes it possible to speak and learn human languages and impossible to learn a language that violates those principles. The options that are chosen (the selected marking conventions) in particular languages are like selections from a menu that lets you choose only one item per course—thus if you get soup then you can't have salad. In Chapter 3, we will see that languages may be classified on the basis of selections made—there are groups of "soup" languages and groups of "salad" languages, so to speak.

---

[5]   The notion of markedness may be traced back to the Prague structuralists, who saw a *mark* as the feature distinguishing two phonemes from each other. Thus the mark [voice] distinguishes /p/ and /b/ in English. The marked member of an opposition such as that between /p/ and /b/ is the member characterized by the presence of the feature of opposition. It is the member manifesting, in this case, the feature [voice], namely, /b/. Thus /b/ is marked with respect to /p/, much as a nasal vowel is marked with respect to an oral vowel and "poetess" is marked with respect to "poet."

2.2.4 Competence and Performance

In Chapter 1 we saw that descriptivists made headway in the analysis of speech, using a distinction between everything a speaker says and what is psychologically real in that speaker's language (referring to the *etic/emic* distinction). Structuralists distinguished the grammatical system underlying speech in particular languages (via the *langue/parole* distinction). With generative grammar appeared the distinction proposed by Chomsky between *competence* (the human cognitive ability to acquire language) and *performance* (what humans do with competence in language-use contexts). Competence is the unconscious linguistic knowledge of the ideal speaker-hearer as opposed to performance or "the actual use of language in concrete situations" (Chomsky 1965:4).

The competence/performance distinction is akin to Saussure's *langue/parole* distinction but it is important to understand how these distinctions differ. *Langue* and *parole* refer to socially constituted rules and their use respectively. *Competence* refers to a cognitive structure whereas *performance* has to do with the way competent humans (who all have, as humans, this cognitive structure or "language organ" much as every human has a heart and a liver) use their language-acquisition ability to behave appropriately in social and cultural contexts.

To Chomsky:

> The theory of language is simply that part of human psychology that is concerned with one particular "mental organ," human language. Stimulated by appropriate and continuing experience, the language faculty creates a grammar that generates sentences with formal and semantic properties. We say that a person knows the language generated by this grammar. Employing other related factors of mind and the structure they produce, he can then proceed to use the language he now knows. (1975:36)

Chomsky is not concerned with the performance aspects of language. In Chapters 4 and 5 we will be primarily concerned with scholars from whom performance takes precedence over competence—scholars interested in the way language and society covary and in language use as it functions in the constitution of social reality and cultural beliefs.

Generativists feel that to explain performance is beyond the scope of their field until an adequate theory of competence is available. In general, linguistic theorists seeking to work within a generative-grammar framework remain skeptical of approaches to analyzing intent through the study of language use. Where Saussure "conceived of linguistics as a branch of social psychology," Chomsky began to think of the scientific study of language as more akin to the natural sciences:

> Just as physics seeks to specify precisely the class of physical processes and biology the class of biological processes, it followed that a task of linguistics would necessarily be to provide "a precise specification of the class of formalized grammars." (New-

meyer 1986:3, quoting Chomsky 1962:534)

In an interview for *Omni* magazine, Chomsky likened language acquisition to what happens when birds acquire wings. Just as bird embryos grow wings, human embryos grow languages. Birds aren't trained to grow wings; humans aren't trained to grow languages. Our language organ interacts with early experience and matures into the grammar of the language we speak. Thus, if we experience Japanese, our language organ's structure is so modified; if we experience English, the organ is modified for it. If we don't experience language at all, our ability to acquire it may atrophy ("use it or lose it") much as limbs will atrophy in disuse. Thus, competence does us little good unless performed.

2.2.5 Syntax and the Chomskyan Revolution

In both structuralist and descriptivist linguistics most success was achieved in the analysis of sounds—perhaps because sound, as a physical signal present in the world, is objective and socially recognized data. We saw that efforts to look at the structure of sound combination in larger hunks of speech such as sentences and phrases defied analysis on the basis of mechanical procedures for discovering their basic elements. In recognition of the fact that sentence construction relies to a great extent on sentence users having some degree of native-speaker intuition, generative grammar has been able to make its greatest contribution to the scientific study of language. As Newmeyer has stated, "By focusing on syntax, Chomsky was able to lay the groundwork for the explanation of the most distinctive aspect of human language: its creativity. *The revolutionary importance of the centrality of syntax cannot be overstated*" (1986:3) (emphasis added).

In a generative grammar, language is thought of as a set of sentences "each with an ideal phonetic form and an associated intrinsic semantic interpretation. The grammar of the language is the system of rules that specifies this sound-meaning correspondence" (Chomsky and Halle 1968:1). The exact form of a generative grammar is a matter of issue and debate among linguists and the theory of generative grammar since its beginning has gone through a number of changes. The centrality of syntax and the importance of syntax for understanding the creative principle underlying language has remained constant.

There has been a great deal of discussion regarding whether or not Chomsky's work in linguistics, emphasizing the centrality of syntax and focusing on language as thought, really amounts to a scientific revolution in the sense of Thomas Kuhn (1970). Newmeyer cites Larry Laudan's argument that it does:

> . . . a scientific revolution occurs, not necessarily when all, or even a majority, of
> the scientific community accepts a new research tradition, but rather when a new
> research tradition comes along which generates enough interest (perhaps through a
> high initial rate of progress) that scientists in the relevant field feel, whatever their

own research tradition commitments, that they have come to terms with the budding research tradition. Newton created the stir he did because, once the *Principia* and the *Optiks* were published, almost every working physicist felt that he had to deal with the Newtonian view of the world . . . (Laudan 1977:137 as quoted in Newmeyer 1986)

In the event, linguists have had to decide whether to accept or reject Chomsky's views. This has been particularly the case for persons who see themselves as linguists in a descriptivist or structuralist tradition. Indeed, any scholar who works on field languages (languages for which the researcher does not have a native-speaker intuition) is at a disadvantage when it comes to generative grammar. How can a person in the field gathering data assess linguistic competence? Indeed, the theory of generative grammar would have all data amenable to field research in the realm of performance rather than that of competence and would eschew data-driven analysis altogether.

One manifest effect of Chomsky's ideas has been the development since the 1960s of a number of independent departments of Linguistics at American universities, with an emphasis on linguistic theory to the exclusion of language descriptions. Work on language use is often done by linguists trained in descriptive and structural approaches in Anthropology departments and, as was mentioned earlier, this work sees language use as socially constituted and inextricably linked to the context of its use. At the end of this chapter we will say a few words about the glimmerings of an analogous revolutionary approach to the study of culture—but these glimmerings remain only faint. The study of actual behavior remains paramount in efforts to relate language and culture. Meaning, as it obtains in form rather than in substance, interests scholars of linguistic and cultural communication who prefer to focus on the social- rather than natural-science aspects of their subject matter.

In the remainder of this section we will provide a brief description of what generative linguists see a theory of language to be,[6] mostly as a way of showing how far afield their interest in language as thought and their philosophy of mind are from what anthropological linguists are generally about.

Chomsky's *Syntactic Structures* (1957) made the point that linguistics ought to focus more on theory construction than on methods for describing languages. The first phase of generative grammar is characterized by a formal model accounting for sentences as the result of a set of *Phrase-Structure Rules* and a set of *Transfor-*

---

[6] There have been so many changes in syntactic theory since the publication of the first edition of this book that the reader will see very little similarity. For example, the distinction between deep and surface sentence structure has lost importance and the idea of an autonomous semantic component has become controversial. Modern approaches too have essentially abandoned the need for transformations, preferring to generate "transformed" sentences in the base component of "core" grammar (compare Radford 1981 and Sells 1985).

mational Rules. The phrase-structure rules yield basic sentential elements expanding the notion S (sentence) from the top down.

For example, consider a simple set of PS (phrase-structure) rules:

$$
\begin{aligned}
S &\rightarrow NP\ VP \\
NP &\rightarrow (Adj)\ N \\
VP &\rightarrow V\ NP
\end{aligned}
$$

This set of rules generates a number of possible sentences in English. To understand the generation it is necessary to know what the category symbols stand for: S (sentence); NP (noun phrase); VP (verb phrase); ( ) an optional category—that is, one which may or may not be selected; Det (determiner or definite article), Adj (adjective), N (noun), V (verb). A phrase-structure (PS) grammar is said to consist of an ordered set of rewrite rules such that one progressively expands the symbol S into its component parts (thus, PS grammar is a formal model of top-bottom immediate constituent (IC) analysis; see Chapter 1 above). Linguists represent the structure of sentences generated by a PS grammar on tree diagrams, as in Figure 1.

Figure 1. Tree Diagram Representing a Sentence's Phrase Structure

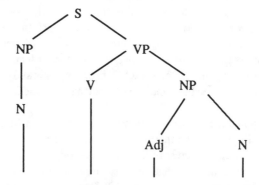

Depending upon what lexical and grammatical choices are made to represent the category symbols generated by PS grammar, different yet grammatical sentences may be produced. The last line of the tree diagram was seen as the underlying or **deep structure** of a sentence [in Figure 1, the deep structure would be N V Adj N]. This deep structure is what receives semantic and phonological interpretation (that is, it is submitted to the other two components of a generative grammar).[7]

---

[7]   A generative grammar as a theory of linguistic competence has three components: (1) a phonological component, (2) a syntactic component, (3) a semantic component.

The notion of deep and surface structure as central to syntax is associated with Chomsky's view of language expressed in his *Aspects of a Theory of Syntax* (1965). The idea was that the elements of deep structure are submitted to the system of phonological rules for interpretation there and simultaneously to the semantic component for interpretation as a sentence. Each component was seen as a rule-governed system. As Figure 1 indicates, the PS rules generate declarative sentences (referred to as **kernel sentences**). In English (as is also the case in other languages) such a base structure is just one possibility. In English there are sentences with added parts, deleted parts, substituted elements, and other details. When we ask questions, we rearrange words (for example, as in "Did Chomsky revolutionize linguistic theory?"). We also express sentences in the passive (as in "Linguistic theory was revolutionized by Chomsky"). Generative linguists felt that such **operations** performed on kernel sentences did not change the content of a sentence but did have an effect on its form in a meaningful way—that is, these **transformations** are syntactic. Thus, a set of **transformational rules** was seen by linguists to be additional to the PS rules as necessary in a theory of language. Transformations map deep structures onto the surface structures that receive phonological interpretation. In more recent versions of generative grammar, the need for transformations has become a matter of controversy, as we shall see below. The important point for our purposes here is to note that symbolists in anthropology and generativists in linguistics are both interested in how communicative behavior receives interpretation. For symbolic anthropologists the emphasis is on how communicative behavior receives social and cultural interpretation "out there" whereas for generative linguists the emphasis is on how human cognitive linguistic ability integrates sound, grammatical structure (syntax), and meaning (semantics) so that sentences may be interpreted mentally "in there." This divergence of interest between empirical approaches in anthropology and rational philosophy in linguistics has brought about the situation today where most of what we see to be involved in the study of language and culture (that is, linguistics "out there") is done by persons who see themselves to be anthropologists (specifically anthropological linguists as discussed in Chapter 1 and ethnolinguists or sociolinguists who will be the focus of Chapters 4 and 5).

In a report of the Chomsky revolution in linguistics, John Davy of the *London Observer* made the following analogy:

> It is as though students of cookery were to turn their attention away from analysing various species of cake and time and motion studies of pastry cooks, to discover the principles of cake-making lying behind the activities of cake-makers, the rules they are following, and the complex structure of the concept "cake" which guides their operations. This concept can be transformed by following the rules, into a number of confections, all of which are digestible. (August 10, 1969, p. 21)

The rules of syntax account for human knowledge of sentence structure much as phonological rules account for how we bundle and manipulate sounds. They generate (according to rules) *phrase markers* that "account for our ability to recognize sentences that are structurally ambiguous" (Fromkin and Rodman 1983:234). For example, the sentence "The horse is ready to ride" is open to at least two interpretations in English: (a) the horse is in a trailer in which it will ride to the track, (b) the horse is ready for someone to ride it. If we were to diagram this sentence purely with regard to its surface structure it would look like diagram (1).[8]

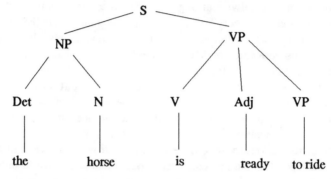

But if we interpret the sentence to mean that the horse is ready to become the rider in the trailer, we get the deep structure as in (2).

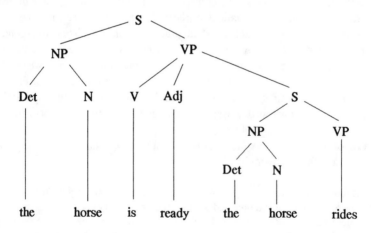

---

8   The examples and structures in diagrams (1), (2), and (3) are adapted from Fromkin and Rodman (1983:235–236).

The deep structure of the sentence meaning that the horse is prepared for a rider has the form of (3).

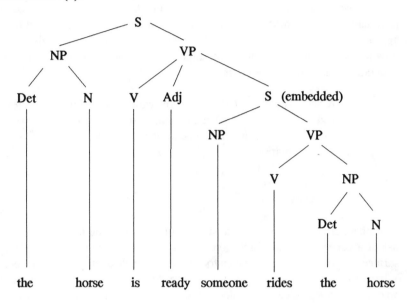

Transformational rules relate the deep structures (3) and (2) to the surface structure (1). In (2), the rules permit inserting within the kernel sentence a sentence having "horse" the subject of "ride(s)" and under the resulting interpretation the horse will do the riding. In (3), the **embedded** sentence has "horse" the object. To get from deep structure (3) back to surface structure (1), transformational rules then delete the final NP "the horse" and the pronoun "someone" and reorganize "rides" as "to ride." The processes such as insertion, substitution, deletion, and movement as shown here that allow us to see how more than one phrase marker (2), (3) may represent a single sentence (1) are known as **transformations.**

In Chapter 4, we will see that this notion is beginning to be used by cognitive anthropologists to account for different structural arrangements of behavioral activity that, on the surface, appear the same (see Randall 1987). Where generative linguists see syntactic rules as modeling the structure of language as cognition, some cognitive scientists interested in language and culture are using the notion of rule to describe patterns of action (Randall's *routine action plans*) reflecting cultural cognition.

It is important to understand that for Chomsky, syntax refers to rules of sentence *formation.* It is solely structure that accounts for the two meanings of "The horse is ready to ride." If the sentence were "The horse is afraid to ride" its deep structure would be (2), its surface structure (1), and the difference in meaning would be a matter of semantic interpretation not syntactic structure.

Chomsky's ideas about language still dominate the generative approach but have undergone a number of changes and are increasingly being joined by other approaches—particularly with regard to what a syntactic theory ought to be and how it fits into an overall theory of language. As Radford (1981:362) sees it, a generative grammar must contain:

1. A base—containing PS rules (now called categorial rules), a lexicon, and rules for plugging lexical items into surface-structure categories—that is, for lexical insertion
2. Transformations
3. Case-marking rules
4. Deletion rules
5. Surface structure

Rather than positing a set of transformational rules, modern generativists make use of a generalized transformation known as *Move-alpha* that relates deep and surface structures. Alpha is "understood to be a variable over syntactic categories." What Move-alpha does is alter a structure "in any way by 'moving anything anywhere'; independent principles will dictate just what can move and where it can move to, allowing the transformation itself to be stated in a maximally general way" (Sells 1985:21).

Where earlier generative grammar (then called transformational generative grammar) had specific transformations known for instance as *passive, question formation*, or the like, generative grammar in the current **government-binding** **(GB)** mode introduced by Chomsky in 1981 (see Chomsky 1981) does not.

> The GB point of view is not that movement to the subject [in the case of Passive] must be specified, but rather that movement to any other position must be prevented. Thus the GB analysis of passive is that Move-[alpha] moves anything anywhere, and that other independent (universal) principles and constraints rule the example out unless the movement happens to be from object to subject position. So passive is the epiphenomenal result of the interaction of various aspects of the grammar, these aspects being direct functions of properties of Universal Grammar . . . What we find in Universal Grammar, then, is not a rule of Passive, but rather more abstract things like constraints on movement applying across the language as a whole. (Sells 1985:22-23)

A Base generates a class of deep structures (now known preferably as D-structures) mapped onto surface (S-)structures by transformations. Then, a set of **case rules** applies to all NPs (nominative, genitive, objective) depending upon their position in the generated sentential string. What case a NP is assigned has to do with the lexical category governing it (that is, whether V, P, N, or A(dj) labels the node above the NP on a phrase marker). If a NP is immediately dominated by another category (as by S or NP), then the NP is unmarked for case. Case rules are of the form "NP is marked nominative if the subject of a tensed S" (Radford 1981:324). Such a rule indicates, for example, that "she" in "She reads Chomsky" is nominative. NPs are objective if dominated by a transitive V or P (preposition), genitive if governed by a POSS (possessive).

Thus, base rules, transformations, and case rules generate case-marked surface structures, which then undergo a set of phonological rules (now seen as **deletions** and **filters**) that organize the case-marked structure into a [proper] surface structure that is then mapped onto "an initial representation of their meaning," to which Chomsky refers as **logical form** (LF). Thus a generative grammar as envisioned by Chomsky in what is referred to (expanding on his earlier work in *Syntactic Structures* and *Aspects of a Theory of Syntax*) as his *Extended Standard Theory* may be schematized as follows (adapted from Radford 1981:363):

The case-marked surface structure (syntactic component) is input to both the

Table 4. Schematic of Chomsky's Extended Standard Theory

CASE-MARKED SURFACE STRUCTURE	
Syntactic Component 1. Base Rules 2. Transformations 3. Case Rules	
SURFACE STRUCTURE (PF—Phonetic Form) Phonological Component 4. Deletions 5. Filters	LOGICAL FORM (LF) Semantic Component 6. Semantic Inter- pretation Rules

phonological component (deletions and filters) and the semantic component (semantic interpretation rules). So, in skeletal form, the theory of language espoused by Chomsky can be seen in relation to its original guise. Syntax remains central and mediates the opposition between sound (surface structure) and meaning (logical form).

This form of generative grammar, referred to as **government-binding** (GB) theory, is so called because of the importance of which category dominates or "governs" another (as we have just seen in our discussion of case-marking rules) and because of the introduction of the notion of indexes or **binding conditions**. What binding conditions do is constrain overgenerated sentence interpretations. An overgenerated interpretation would be, for instance, "I_2 like yourself$_2$" where "I" and "yourself" are co-indexed (by the subscript 2), meaning they are coreferential. The sentence is overgenerated in the sense that the indexing requires it to have an interpretation it cannot have. To avoid this, Chomsky has devised conditions to state what, for example, proper pronominal coreferential relations may be. "I" and "yourself" may not be assigned the same index because they do not match in number, gender, person. In contrast "I_1 like myself$_1$" is fine. Binding conditions and government (via case marking) constitute recent innovations in generative grammar, though the theory still seeks to provide an explanatorily adequate account of the intuitions of native speakers' language-acquisition ability.

Generative theorists are seeking to factor out as much as possible "of the grammars of particular languages" and put it into the "theory of grammar—or universal grammar" (Wasow 1985:196).

Some scholars working within generative linguistics, but not as GB theorists, are doing research as if observational and descriptive adequacy are their goals (forgetting perhaps that the theory is intended as a model of competence and also seeking to inform universal grammar?). Notable are pursuers of approaches known as GPSG (**generalized phrase-structure grammar**) and LFG (**lexical-functional grammar**). We will say just a few words here about those approaches as they contrast with GB theory, primarily because what they advocate may be of use to language and culture scholars for whom those goals remain paramount.

Generalized phrase-structure grammar pays attention to actual "explicit grammar fragments, which are evaluated on the basis of the acceptability of the strings they generate" (Wasow 1985:198). This approach is akin to what Chomsky was doing in *Syntactic Structures*, that is, seeking a rigorous and formal model to account for "all and only grammatical utterances" of language X. GPSG, unlike the approach by Chomsky in the early years which excluded semantic considerations and his GB view where semantics (logical form) remains separate from syntax, sees semantic analyses as "an integral part" of linguistic theory and "inseparable from . . . syntactic proposals" (Wasow 1985:199). GPSG appears to be primarily motivated methodologically rather than by a concern with either language acquisition or universal grammar. Using notions such as ID (immediate dominance—discussed as "mother-daughter relations") and LP (linear precedence—discussed as relations among "sisters"), generalized phrase-structure grammar syntactic rules are formed. Further, each syntactic category has a unique type of denotation (in terms of how entities are related to truth values). For a discussion of GPSG in detail see Gazdar and others (1985).

Lexical-functional grammar is so called partly because it represents grammatical functions such as subject and object among others and is concerned with the role the lexical items assigned such functions play in a sentence.[9] Further, functional structures (f-structures) are seen as functions in the mathematical sense. Thus in the sentence "Fish swim" "fish" is the subject of the predicate "swim"— also there is a function which gives the value *fish* when applied to the name SUBJ (subject). Whereas GB sees each component of a grammar as having the same sorts of representations (rules and constraints), in LFG different levels of language have different kinds of representations and separate constraints. In addition to functional structures (f-structures), LFG makes use of constituent structure (c-structure) where cross-linguistic variation can be seen (c-structure may be roughly likened to phonetic form in GB theory and surface structure in GPSG). Lexical rules relate, for example, passive to active forms of verbs; all lexical items are inserted into c-structure in their fully inflected form.

For linguists working on languages other than their own these more data-driven theories may be of use. Since Chomsky came on the scene, linguistic theory has had little to say to the scholar working on non-Indo-European language data, especially trying to describe languages never before described or actual instances of language use in a speech community. See Eastman (1978, Chapter 4) for a discussion of efforts by descriptive and structural linguists in the 1960s to try to adequately handle syntactic and semantic levels of language (for instance, using approaches known as *tagmemics, stratificational grammar*, and early efforts at *machine translation*).

2.3 The "New" Cultural Anthropology

Influences such as structuralism (see Chapter 1) and generative grammar have begun to have ramifications in cultural anthropology. In 1964, the anthropologist Ward Goodenough came up with the concept of culture as an ideational order "composed of ideal forms as they exist in people's minds, propositions about their interrelationships, preference ratings regarding them and recipes for their mutual ordering as means for organizing and interpreting new experience" (1964:11). This idea of culture as having an underlying structure sees culture to be much like *langue* and amenable to description by rules (ordered recipes) and judgments of acceptability (with regard to whether or not the rule set results in behavior

---

9   GPSG owes much of its semantic approach to philosophical ideas of Montague (1974) and "Extended Montague Grammar" (see Gazdar, Klein, Pullum, and Sag 1985). LFG is an outgrowth of Relational Grammar associated with Perlmutter (1983).

acceptable in that particular culture). Roger Keesing (in Keesing and Keesing 1971) outlined ideas regarding how a model of culture (as a theory of an ideational code) might develop. In this section we will look at that approach and also at some examples by anthropologists who have attempted to describe cultural behavior as a rule-governed system. In our discussion of **cybernetics** here it should be obvious that some of the terminology is akin to that of the formal, now philosophical, linguists.

As has been seen throughout the discussion so far and as will be seen in following chapters, linguistic analogies are very tempting to apply in the study of culture. Roger Keesing drew a parallel between culture/competence and behavior/performance. He proposed that certain insights as to the nature of language might also apply to the nature of culture.

The ideational code of culture is to be distinguished from its enactment in behavior, just as our linguistic competence is distinguished from performance. Keesing urged cultural anthropologists to take up the study of the ideational code even though it cannot be directly observed, in addition to the traditional pursuit of analyzing the patterning of observable behavior.

A theory of a culture's ideational code aims to account for the creativity of behavior just as a theory of linguistic competence has as its goal an accounting for the creative aspect of language. Such a theory of code in culture is seen as a system of rules. Cultures are expected to vary greatly in content and in particular rules, yet all cultures, like all languages, are expected to be similar in overall design. Keesing suggests that for culture we might hope to arrive at a set of universal distinctive features of behavioral acts which would enter in various ways into the rules governing behavior.

Just as Chomsky assumes that the ability to acquire language is innate, so too the general outlines of cultural design may be deemed partly or largely built in. In culture, humans continually produce behavior sequences, as in language they produce speech sequences, that they have never experienced before. New combinations of familiar elements of behavior are continually being generated.

For culture, as well as for language, the scientist is shifting away from an attempt to show how an analysis has been reached; that is, efforts to make discovery procedures explicit are not as important. More important, if the object of study is culture's ideational code, is whether or not the theory proposed works—whether it accounts "for the intuition of the people under study" (Keesing and Keesing 1971:81). Discovery procedures in both language and culture fail to provide systematic ways of going from linguistic data to a theory of Language, from behavior to a theory of Culture.

Just as in linguistics a theory of linguistic competence may be seen to slight the study of performance, an analogous approach to culture through a theory of the ideational code might be said to slight the use of culture—the actual behavior in a cultural context.

Roger Keesing believes that, despite these possible analogies of language to culture, linguistic models have only limited applicability to the study of culture (ideational code and behavior). Culture—seen as what people know about what they can do or what can be done to or for them (ideational code), and as which is actually done (behavior)—occurs in a broader framework than that of the behavioral act. Anthropological linguists, too, are beginning to argue that the sentence as the basic unit of linguistic theory is perhaps too narrow. Scholars doing research on discourse and other aspects of language use in context hope that efforts to include the situations in which linguistic behavior takes place will lead to a better understanding of both language and culture.

Keesing called for a broader science of communication which will "have to be a study of messages, not simply sentences; of nonlinguistic as well as linguistic communications; and of contexts and networks as well as codes" (Keesing and Keesing 1971:85). In addition to anthropological linguists (doing sociolinguistics, ethnolinguistics, and/or discourse analysis), communicational anthropologists (owing much to the work of Gregory Bateson), and students of nonverbal communication, proxemics, and gesture (spurred on by Edward T. Hall and R. L. Birdwhistell) deal with the way culture (including language) interacts with the environment. Much of this work takes us well beyond the scope of this volume. Yet, it should be clear that Lévi-Strauss, too, saw this need to go beyond language in the study of social systems, especially in his analysis of myth, wherein he drew on such communicational notions as message and code.

2.3.1 The Structure of Residence, Address-Term Choice, and Routines

In 1969, Robbins Burling applied the approach of transformational/generative grammar to cultural anthropology to data on household composition among the Garo of Assam, India. He came up with rules that account for the varied array of dwellers found there. Using the linguist's approach to "rules of grammar," he stated "rules of household composition can be said to constitute a theory" (1969:822). The rules do not specify the configuration of any particular household, but account for the range of alternatives of household composition in Garo society. The system of rules Burling set forth predicts not only what occurs in the data, "but also predicts additional data in the form of other household types that were not included in the original sample" (1969:822). Burling does not justify the rules with reference to any particular method used; that is, he does not make explicit any discovery procedures. The rules of household composition, as rules of grammar, are checked insofar as they account for the data.

Burling had ten rules that generate all possible households among the Garo

(1969:821). By way of illustration consider just three (in paraphrased form):
1. A married couple lives together.
2. Children live with their mother.
   a. If their mother is married, therefore, they also live
      with her husband—usually their father.
3. One daughter, after marriage, *must* continue to live with her parents.
   a. From Rule 1, we also know that this married daughter's
      husband lives with his in-laws.

Just as in language a sentence's surface structure may have two underlying deep structures, the application of different sequences of household-composition rules might produce superficially identical households.

These rules of household composition are a kind of syntax of the Garo ideational code. Each individual Garo household conforms to the rules, and so would any new household. Burling maintains that rules which account for the data are more satisfying than traditional ethnographic accounts describing the diversity among households.

Since 1969, a number of studies have appeared attempting to describe cultural knowledge with rules that can be assigned a cognitive interpretation, much as syntactic theories have sought to describe the underlying rules of linguistic knowledge that would then undergo semantic interpretation.

Where household composition and kin-term or address-term choices tend to be representable in terms of arrangements of elements (people in a house, features of relationship or status), humans perform on a routine basis a number of other activities that consist of a sequence of categories which may have subsequences within them and which may also admit variability. People engage in occupations (such as fishing; see Randall 1977), compose music (see Jackendoff and Lehrdal 1983), make music (see Feld 1984), and perform other activities in their societies. Culture-bearers know when these behaviors are done appropriately (grammatically), what variation is allowed, and what sequences of behavior are prohibited. Moving beyond representing the structure of behavior, much as linguists represent core grammar via phrase-structure rules, to account for the routine yet nonritualized activities we all perform has led a number of scholars to admit rules to their analyses which rearrange the way categories or elements of behavior are ordered, substitute some elements for another, add certain elements and delete others.

Randall found that Philippine fishermen usually head for a certain place *unless* "word strikes [that] the scad are really biting" at another place; and they *usually* buy number 24 hooks "*unless* they 'happen to hear' there are number 25 hooks in stock" (1977; quoted in Randall 1987:48). As seen in discussions both above and in Chapter 1, PS (phrase-structure) rules account for the usual—the unusual in respect to the usual is marked. Transformations usually handle the marked forms of behavior in language and are now seen as useful in the analysis of sequences of nonlinguistic action as well.

Indeed, marking allows for behavior to be variable and also creative. Composers generally follow base rules, in writing symphonies for example—it is the culturally permitted variability and the way it is used that distinguishes an outstanding piece of music from one that is just acceptable. In this study of Philippine scad fishermen, Randall showed that exceptions to the usual routine "result either in *deleting* a usual sequence, *inserting* one, *replacing* one (deleting then inserting), or *reordering* a routine sequence (deleting an activity and inserting it subsequently)" (Randall, 1987:49).

Not only are such processes similar to the transformations of early formulations of generative grammar, but they are also reminiscent of computer programming. Attempts to model both language and culture this way may be seen as tending toward the analysis of the underlying knowledge people have that is enacted in their occupational, musical, or linguistic behavior. Randall and other cognitive scientists working in anthropology, in contrast to generative linguists, hope to root their analyses in a context of goal-realizations sensitive to both ecological and cultural factors. Most transformations of the routine to handle the exceptional arise in order to overcome obstacles and the unavailability of familiar means for getting the task accomplished. That is, when one thing won't work—given the behaver's goal—something else (culturally appropriate) is tried. Whether the behavior is fishing or composing, creativity is equally possible

> . . . adult fishermen have, at several points, been forced, through the unavailability
> of routine means (such as certain sinkers or shoals) to try unknown means. These
> turned out to be improvements, and subsequently became routine among all fisher-
> men. (1987:54)

I recently carried out research among four groups of nomadic people in Kenya in order to do a comparative study of the process of transhumance (moving from one place to another). Using Randall's idea of the *routine action plan*, it became clear that the woman placemaker in each case followed essentially the same routine when it came to dismantling a domicile, packing up, and moving to a new location where she would construct another structure. Variations, seen as transformation processes, revealed a continuum from nomadism to sedentarism whereby the number of pack animals decreased, building materials ceased to be transported, containers once functional became symbolic, and so forth.[10]

Much as we saw in early generative grammar (as in *Syntactic Structures*), it was considered productive to study the structure of kernel sentences:

---

[10]   The research was carried out in conjunction with LaBelle Prussin on a National Science
Foundation pilot project (August–November, 1985, fieldwork) examining the role of women as
placemakers in a nomadic African context (see Eastman 1987a and 1987b).

In the early stages of plan research, it may have been productive to study tightly bounded problems such as nail hammering, chess playing, address terminology, or restaurant eating. But if we want to explain planning as we actually observe it, then models must be developed which incorporate the full hierarchy of goals people actually use. (Randall 1987:57)

Perhaps the need to address cultural knowledge as well as linguistic knowledge might lead to an approach in the study of culture addressing the kind of philosophical issues we have seen to be of concern to Chomsky and other generative theorists. For the moment, however, most scholars of language and culture continue to work in other cultures and do not have the intuitions necessary for them to know when to apply a transformation in order to keep behavior on track toward the basic goals of behavior. It is only possible to "infer from the structure of observed sequences the planning rules generating the sequences" unless and until culture-bearers themselves become interested in developing a theory of culture.

Cognitive scientists interested in modeling cultural behavior along these lines, like generative linguists, are also interested in the acquisition of cultural behavior by children. Geohegan (1973:184-205, 322-335) found that with regard to behavior surrounding use of address terms by the Samal people of the Philippines (the same group Randall worked with in his fishing study), children first acquire the distinction between *adult* versus *child*, next comes a distinction between adults who have reached puberty with regard to whether or not they are *married*. The feature *gender* enters the picture next so that by the age of six, Samal children "would have five alternative pronames; two for children of each gender, two for adolescents of each gender, and one for adults" (Randall 1987:66) and the process continues.

When such an approach is taken to cultural behavior in an empirical context, one must be aware of the possibility of uncovering (via innovative transformations and extensions of meaning) a culture/symbolic new dimension of meaning accompanying the more basic functional set. This became clear in the study I participated in, revealing the process whereby nomadism is giving way to a more sedentary form of constructing the environment. As the woven basket container for storing and transporting water was replaced by the tin watering trough, when doors come on the scene, what used to be does not disappear but becomes imbued with a different kind of meaning (the water basket becomes art, the doorway takes on a meaning of safety and protection). This cultural meaning, too, as we saw in the first part of the chapter, must also be considered—both ecological and cultural dimensions of cultural knowledge are as important to a theory of Culture as they are to a theory of Language.

2.3.2 Cybernetics and Parallel Distributed Processing (Connectionism)

Much of the discussion in this chapter has used vocabulary that the anthropologist Gregory Bateson (1967, 1972) saw to be associated with **cybernetic explanations**—especially when the concern is primarily with the form rather than the substance of behavior: ". . . cybernetic explanations deal in the relations between things rather than in what actually composes or makes up the things" (Langness 1987:204). Meaning is derived from the structure, with the information that emerges from the ordered set of rules. Indeed, meaning in myth as analyzed by Lévi-Strauss is exactly meaning in this sense. Similarly, the meaning that comes across via the ordered string that results from the application of PS rules (that is, the last line of a tree diagram prior to semantic and phonological interpretation) is also meaning in this sense. We know for example that an N is preceded by Det and Det + N precedes a V which may have another NP after it, so we know that, if this is the case, it is likely that the "something or other" acted upon "something else" just as we know that certain oppositions in myth are interrelated but we don't know what the sentence says nor can we retell the myth.

It is important to understand that the same message can mean different things in different contexts (recall that the phoneme /p/ in English is not the same as the phoneme /p/ in Hindi; see Chapter 1 above). As Bateson points out (1972: 408), without context there is no communication; the cybernetic explanation serves to indicate the "restraints" (note that linguists use the term "constraints" to refer to the same idea) that order behavior. Bateson (1972:406) likened "restraint" to factors determining the fit of a particular piece in a jigsaw puzzle—features such as color, shape, edge orientation, puzzle boundary, and the like, though they guide the puzzle solver, nonetheless "From the point of view of the cybernetic observer they are *restraints*" (Bateson 1972:406). Likewise, PS rules restrain or constrain the generativist's theory of language and permitted routine actions constrain the cognitive anthropologist's view of what Samal fishing is, yet both the rules of grammar and the routine of fishing allow maximal creativity to the sentence producer and to the fish getters in "solving" their respective puzzles of communicating and earning a living.

As scholars of language and culture turn their attention to cognition, the age-old debate between rationalists and empiricists continues to be important. Where Boas, Bloomfield, and Gleason called for linguistics to be an empirical science, the generative linguists see it as a rational philosophy. In the tradition of empirical research, symbolic and cognitive anthropologists are concerned more with how learning linguistic (or cultural) behavior takes place in a social context. Both approaches, nonetheless, are concerned with language acquisition, ". . . the jewel in the crown of cognition. It is what everyone wants to explain" (Kolata 1987:133, quoting Stephen Pinker of the Massachusetts Institute of Technology). Research in the field known as PDP (**parallel distributed processing**) is providing an alternative to the "rules" approach to modeling cognitive abilities. This view essentially holds that language acquisition, as defining what it means to be human, operates according to "ruleless systems" called **connectionist networks** by which analogies are formed. The debate has to do with whether, for example, when children learn a language they learn a "rule" for forming the past tense or whether they form it by analogy. When children learn a language they overregularize by associating one past-tense form with another. We think we just add -*ed* to everything. But first, connectionists say, children learn the irregular forms such as "brought" or "went"; later they switch to "bringed" and "goed," based on analogy with the usual -*ed* forms such as "laughed" and "talked." After that they "relearn the correct irregular forms" (Kolata 1987:133). Whether we learn by association or by rule, whether the behavior is cultural or linguistic, will continue to keep empiricists and rationalists debating for years to come.

The PDP/connectionists take issue with the idea that concepts such as N, V, and others are somehow part of linguistic cognitive ability and play a role in language acquisition. Instead they feel that children learn languages by deciding that "this word sounds like that word" (Kolata 1987:133). Evidence for this claim is provided by research having to do with ruleless computer systems. In particular, one model developed by David Rumelhart of the University of California, San Diego and James McClelland of Carnegie Mellon University suggests that children acquire English by means of a connected network of processes resembling analogies. Rumelhart and McClelland (1987) believe that the ability to correctly respond to new situations is more analogical than rule-governed. Further, connectionist models (ruleless computer systems) attempt to formulate how this ability occurs.

Opponents of this view feel that the process of child language acquisition and the computer model of English acquisition are quite different: the computer overregularizes because its world changes—its input is given increasingly more regular verbs after initially learning irregular ones, whereas

> The proportion of regular to irregular verbs in children's vocabularies stays at 50-50 over a period of several years. But during this time, the children start to over-regularize. The explanation lies not in the environment but in the head of the child. (Pinker and Prince 1987, in Kolata 1987:134)

2.4 Summary

In this chapter we have seen that a number of approaches to the study of language and culture, once structuralism appeared on the scene, have become quite abstract. Social activity and social expression may be seen as manifestations of an underlying structure much as *parole* or speech is a manifestation of a particular language's grammatical structure *langue*. We have seen that in structure there is meaning which may be uncovered if the object of study, whether myth or language or a set of kin terms, is analyzed as a system of interrelated elements. Such structural meaning reveals patterns that explain how the system itself operates. For example, the English language uses the feature [voicing] to distinguish stop consonants; in American kinship, no distinction is made between [MoBro] and [FaBro], so important in other cultures to explain the nature of the *uncle* relation. A number of anthropologists are looking at how systems of behavior function in context in an effort to accomplish "thick description." They seek to describe the structured behavior itself, the perspective of the behaver, and also to interpret the behavior in context (Geertz 1973). Where anthropologists are interested in how the systematic structures of language and culture operate in context, linguists have become more interested in accounting for the acquisition of language (both structure and expression) and in modeling Language as a common human cognitive ability. The ideas of Noam Chomsky and his followers have led many linguists to seek rules common to all languages (*universal grammar*) as well as language-specific rules (the concern of the structuralists).

A number of ideas from structural and generative linguistics have attracted the interest of cultural anthropologists. From the structuralists came the notion of *markedness* (section 2.2.3 above). The idea of Culture as *ideational code* is akin to the idea of Language as *competence*.

In this chapter, some detail was provided regarding the way generative linguistics has been changing in recent years. The notion of *transformation* and even *rule* has come under scrutiny. Yet for people interested in describing rule-governed behavior either as *action plans* (Randall 1987) or as appropriate household composition (Burling 1966)—such notions, originally intended to account for grammatical structure, have been most useful. The autonomy of *syntax* as a component of grammar continues to be central to the theory of Language espoused by Noam Chomsky. His work has profoundly affected the entire field of linguistic research—turning from a focus on the data of actual language use to a concern with the process whereby language as a cognitive ability is acquired. Perhaps the linguistics of Chomsky has had the most to say to anthropologists with regard to what it has in common with cyberneticists' efforts to model cultural behavior. There is a meeting ground where research seeks to understand cognition and the nature of linguistic and cultural behavior. The meaning of such behavior in context and issues regarding how best to interpret and describe it are left to the symbolic anthropologists (semeioticians) and sociolinguists (see Chapters 4 and 5 below).

Chapter 3 Comparative and Historical Studies

3.0 Introduction

In Chapter 1, we looked at the development of descriptive methods for analyzing languages, focusing on a concern for rigorous attention to data, for ways to identify units within the data, and for the resulting adequate descriptions of the data. We also saw that such an approach applied as well to efforts to produce scientific ethnographic descriptions of social behavior.

A shift in focus—away from identifying units of behavior toward an emphasis on describing the structural systems that instances of behavior reflect—called for looking at linguistic and cultural behavior as sets of features interrelating in patterned ways (via rule or analogies). Structuralist efforts to analyze the elements of particular languages and specific forms of cultural behavior in terms of relationship sought to arrive at general statements with regard to how languages and cultures work. These "rules of grammar" and "rules of behavior," as well as descriptions of actual language use and behavioral acts, tended to focus on behavior at the time it is being behaved—at a specific point in time—the time being represented by the data. That is, both structuralism and descriptivism are **synchronic** approaches. The symbolic anthropology and cognitive studies (seen at the beginning and end of Chapter 2) are also synchronic whereas generative grammar, reliant on intuition and seeking to make statements about universals in language and about cognitive ability, is both ahistorical and asynchronic.

In the study of language and culture, over the years, attempts have been made to delve into the question of history. In this chapter we will look at those attempts and also see what current work is being done.

3.1 Comparative and Historical Method

Attempts have been made to reconstruct the history of particular languages by examining earlier descriptions of the languages or by setting up a hypothetical earlier form of related languages through a comparative method known as **historical reconstruction**. Using this method, **historical linguists** seek to show how language changes over time. We will see in Chapter 5 that language change is also amenable to study within living speech communities. The idea is that variation in the "actual speech habits of the members of the community . . . provides the key to the mechanism of language change" (Bynon 1977:198–199). Historical linguistics as such is primarily concerned with the actual facts of change rather than with its mechanics and also determines the facts of change by comparing forms at one point in time to their counterparts at other times.

Interest in the facts of change and in the comparative method is important too in **ethnohistory**. Ethnohistorical studies seek to describe and observe culture change much as the goal of historical linguistics is to study language change. Ethnohistory makes use of oral and written traditions that reflect earlier time stages of a culture, and attempts to reconstruct cultures—not in order to demonstrate progress, but rather to note and observe change.

There are other linguists who also compare language descriptions or parts of descriptions in the interest, not of writing history, but of establishing relationships among languages. Such **comparative linguists** analyze correspondences in sound, meaning, and other aspects of a set of languages, with the goal of showing relationships among those languages, that is, of producing language classifications.

The comparative method itself derives from nineteenth-century anthropological *evolutionary* views which assumed that present-day "primitive" cultures represent versions of past cultures. It was thought that many "exotic" societies were in an earlier stage of development than modern "civilized" ones. Observing certain cultural forms or traits in these "uncivilized" societies, such as marriage and religious practices, would allow the anthropologist to see how those same traits existed earlier in the civilized ones. This form of the comparative method claimed to demonstrate cultural evolution by comparing existing cultures with respect to stages of development of common traits within them.

This evolutionary bent of the comparative method was largely discredited. It developed in anthropological studies in two directions. First, the comparative method may be seen today in cross-cultural comparison studies in which existing cultures are compared on one or another particular dimension. In such studies no claim or assumption is made that one culture in the comparison represents a higher or lower, earlier or later form with respect to the others. Such comparison is often used in culture classification. In this sense, then, cross-cultural comparison and comparative linguistics are analogous.

The comparative method seeks to make generalizations about sociocultural systems by comparing descriptive analyses of data from different cultures with each other. The generalizations specify what is common to language and what is common to culture wherever found in the world. If a generalization applies to all known instances, it is known as a universal (see Chapter 2).

In addition to the goal of discovering cultural and linguistic universals, the comparative method is used for making cross-linguistic and cross-cultural comparisons in order to establish relationships among languages and among cultures. The comparative method is the approach used to establish language family trees. For example, the Indo-European family of languages to which English belongs was established through the comparative method in linguistics.

Along with comparing data from language to language and from culture to culture (synchronic comparison), it is also sometimes possible to compare descriptions of sociocultural systems made years apart. This type of comparison allows the scientist to discover instances of change in the system. The comparative method applied to data for the purpose of analyzing change over time is known as diachronic comparison. Practitioners of synchronic comparison in linguistics are generally known as comparative linguists; those who practice diachronic comparison are known as historical linguists. Scholars who examine linguistic variability within a particular speech community as evidence of the mechanism of language change see change as a social process, correlated with such variables as class and status, and see themselves to be sociolinguists (their approach, as exemplified in the ideas of William Labov and others, will be discussed in Chapter 5).

In this chapter, we will not be dealing with the nineteenth-century development of the comparative method except to note that the evolution of the method in Europe coincided with the beginnings of linguistics and of anthropology as sciences. The comparative method predated the focus on descriptive method in both anthropology and linguistics; in fact, the comparative method gave impetus to the development of rigorous descriptive techniques. As cross-cultural and cross-linguistic comparisons were beginning to be made, it became clear that a uniform method of data description for the ethnographer and linguist would facilitate later diachronic and synchronic comparisons of the data.

The evolutionist anthropologists of the nineteenth century noted the need for detailed synchronic studies; they wanted to trace the evolution of sociocultural systems through time, but had at their disposal only "documentary accounts about native cultures written by travellers, missionaries, etc." (Carmack 1972:227). Indeed, Boas's main interest was in language classification. He hoped to set up the language families of North America but saw the need, first, for developing a uniform methodology for the gathering and describing of linguistic data. In order to classify the languages of the new world, he would have to compare them to each other. He needed a way to ascertain that the data used in his comparisons were actually comparable.[1]

In Europe, where the problem of unwritten and unknown languages was not as

---

[1]   Ironically, the development of descriptive linguistics and its methodology of arriving at *emic* units that were "psychologically real" resulted in descriptions of data that were solely in terms of the particular language being described and not amenable to cross-linguistic comparison!

acute, data often existed in a form that was, to some extent at least, valid for comparison. However, for both language and culture the results of comparison are only as valid as the descriptions of the languages and cultures being compared.

In this chapter, we will briefly outline the field of historical linguistics as it contrasts with attempts to deal with culture history and then shift our attention to the comparative method and how it has been used in linguistics specifically with regard to various systems of language classification. Comparative studies in linguistics, in recent years, have undergone a resurgence of popularity, particularly from the perspective of setting up *typological classifications*—those based on structural features shared from one language to another. Linguists remain concerned with efforts to show sound and meaning correspondences across languages (that is, in setting up *genealogical classifications* in the form of language family trees). A third concern of the comparative approach to language is the study of the process of *borrowing* from one language to another—*areal classifications* of language group languages according to principles of *diffusion*. The idea is to study what linguists refer to as *language spread*, that is, "an increase over time in the proportion of a communication network that adopts a given language or language variety for a given communication function" (Cooper 1982b:6). Where areal classifications traditionally are a concern of comparative and historical linguists, language spread is seen, in a broader context, as a branch of sociolinguistics (and in that connection will also be discussed in Chapter 5).

How the comparative method has been used to classify cultures will be discussed as well. Brief mention will be made of the controversial approach known as *glottochronology* and its associated technique of *lexicostatistics*, which attempted to provide a means, based on comparing linguistic data in a number of different languages, for determining when languages diverged from a common ancestor.

3.2 Historical Linguistics

When one hears of university courses such as "The History of the English Language" or "The History of German," reference is to studies of English and German from the earliest days of written records until the present time. Such studies compare grammatical and lexical data. In the history of English, for example, Anglo-Saxon, Old English, Middle English, and Modern English are compared. The purpose is to uncover regularities and significant relationships among these various time states of English. In this way, much of what seems random or unexplainable about modern English may be explained. The relationships noted between and among elements of English at these various historical periods are stated as generalizations with regard to the systematic process of language change. If a sound in Old English occurs in Modern English as another sound in a single lexical item, the same shift will be observed throughout the language. Thus if Old English /p/ appears as /b/ in Modern English whenever the sound is surrounded by vowels, then all instances of OE /p/ = Modern English /b/ between vowels. If regular correspondences at different stages of a language's history could be found, then such regular agreement is taken as evidence of the way the language has changed over time. To document the history of an entire language, it is necessary to look for correspondences in both vocabulary and grammar. In the next section of this chapter we will see that this same approach applied to different languages reveals correspondences which provide evidence that those languages are genetically related to each other.

Regular correspondences both within a language and across languages, in the absence of written records instancing their existence, may be hypothesized as reconstructed forms using the technique of historical reconstruction. Such hypothetical forms are marked by an asterisk (*), indicating that they are purely hypothetical yet based on what present linguistic evidence indicates the prior form may have been.

Bynon provides the example of the reconstructed Proto (Hypothetical)-Indo-European forms *mrtró- and *mrtó- as ancestors of the word "murder"in English. The Proto-Indo-European forms are formulas from which we can trace sound and meaning equivalents in each language of the IE (Indo-European) language family. Interestingly, in Latin the word appears as *mori* "to die," and is related to *mors*, *mort* "death" whereas in German it is realized as *Mord* "murder" much as it is in English. The sound and meaning correspondence from the hypothetical PIE ancestor language is regular; but there have been both sound and meaning *shifts* such that in the Germanic branch of the language family (where English and German but not Latin belong) the meaning has become more specific as "the premeditated and unlawful killing of a fellow human being" (Bynon 1977:62).

A **proto**language is the total set of reconstructed hypothetical forms to which present-day forms in a language may be traced back. Each form that is traceable back to a protolanguage is referred to as a **cognate**. Thus "murder" is derived from PIE *mrtró-* and related to *Mord* and cognate with both.

For any two languages, if change is regular in both lines of descent from a common protolanguage, then there should be regular correspondences observable between forms in one language and cognate forms in another and those correspondences ought to be statable systematically. One such statement is what is known as **Grimm's Law**, as formulated by Jakob Grimm (one of the Grimm brothers of fairy-tale fame). Grimm's Law accounts for the correspondences in consonants between languages in the Germanic branch of the Indo-European family with consonants in the rest of the IE languages. For example, Grimm observed that whereas in Greek and Latin there are voiceless stops (/p/, /t/, and /k/), in English they appear as /f/, /θ/, and /h/ respectively. Thus we have Latin *piscis* cognate with

English *fish*; Latin *tres* cognate with English *three* [θri], and Latin *cornu* cognate with English *horn*.

In historical linguistics, linguists have chosen to look diachronically at the development of language over time as we have just discussed. This approach was largely that of nineteenth-century scholars known as **neogrammarians**, who like Grimm assumed that "language change must have order and thus be amenable to systematic investigation" (Bynon 1977:24). In addition to the process of **phonological change**, neogrammarians saw *analogy* as important in language history as well. Analogical changes depend on grammatical structure with regard to whether or not they take place and thus may serve to explain apparent ir-regularities in sound change. As we saw analogy as a counterexplanation when "rules" appear not to work (at the end of Chapter 2 in our brief mention of **connectionism**), neogrammarians saw regular sound change as the usual case in phonology but saw analogy as playing more of a role in grammar. Analogy may be seen in child language when forms are produced such as *tooths* for teeth, *foots* for feet, and *goed* for went. Analogy works to let us know what a form is where phonological change might have rendered its grammatical role opaque (see Bynon 1977:44). Thus, in common verbs, irregular past-tense forms that conform to phonological rules of change may survive whereas in less common verbs analogy pushes for the regular -*ed*. The child learns all verbs as uncommon and hence can handle the irregularity; but as his/her language learning (development of language) proceeds the irregular, in consequence of their frequency of use, need not conform to the analogical forms whereas rarely used and new forms must.

> . . . in English for instance nouns like *tooth, foot, mouse, man, woman,* and verbs like *to be, go, eat, drink, will, can, do*, etc. . . . may be said to be members of so-called *basic vocabulary* which would appear to be the sector of language least influenced by cultural change. . . . All that may be predicted in their case is what would be their likely form were they to undergo analogical change . . . . (Bynon 1977:43)

Descriptive/structural and generative linguistic approaches have also had some-thing to say about the history of language—essentially elaborating upon the work of the neogrammarians (see E. H. Sturtevant 1917 for a full account of that approach, which remains essentially in the same form today as it was in Sturtevant's day). Still, as our conceptions of what language is have changed over the years, changing views have had an effect on historical linguistics.

> With the insight provided by this new structuralist approach neogrammarian "atomism," the tracing through successive language states of individual sound segments and of grammatical or lexical forms without any attempt to make explicit at each stage their status in the synchronic system was no longer acceptable. (Bynon 1977:76)

Historical linguists shifted to looking at change in linguistic structure and focused on how a change in one part of a language's sound or grammatical system relates to other changes in phonology or syntax. For example, interest centered more on how the system of language changes and less on the actual changes that occurred. What is interesting with regard to Grimm's Law, from a structuralist perspective, is what motivated for example the change in Germanic to /h/ from /k/ in PIE, to /f/ from /p/, and so forth. Structuralists assumed that phonological and grammatical systems change systematically, constrained by phonological and grammatical structure. The Latin voiceless stops /p/, /t/, and /k/ in initial position are unaspirated as well—a structuralist view of change would posit that the stops acquired the feature [aspiration] and then the feature **[continuant]** whereby $/p/ \rightarrow /p^h/ \rightarrow /f/$; $/t/ \rightarrow /t^h/ \rightarrow /\theta/$; and $/k/ \rightarrow /k^h/ \rightarrow /s/$. Aspiration in pre-Germanic was a nondistinctive feature of voiceless stops; the introduction of the feature [continuant] resulting in voiceless stops in PIE surfacing in Germanic languages (such as English and German) as voiceless fricatives is one manifestation of the "replacement of aspiration by continuance," one change (which with others such as the introduction of [voicing] as distinctive in these sounds) "ultimately led to the reorganization of the system as a whole" (Bynon 1977:85).

Structuralists differ in how they account for systematic changes in language. The example just given is regarded as a **drag-chain** interpretation, that is, one feature shift precedes another in chronological order, each change making the next one possible. **Push-chain** explanations, in contrast, hold that sound and grammatical shifts arise in order to avoid mergers: /t/ shifts to /θ/ so as not to merge with $/d^h/$, which was simultaneously losing its feature [aspiration]. In the process, again simultaneously, [voice] was becoming a distinctive feature to keep /t/ and /d/ distinct. These two structuralist approaches to change differ in that drag-chains assume chronological states in a systematic change (a *syntagmatic* view) while push-chains see shift to be a simultaneous reorganization of features (a *paradigmatic* view). Bynon feels that drag-chain explanations rest on a stronger theoretical basis than do pull-chains and that "An optimal phonological system will ... be one which, with the minimal number of distinctive features, obtains the maximum number of distinctive segments" (1977:88). That is, linguistic systems are *economical*; they change on the basis of the opposition between "the requirements of communication" and "human inertia" (Martinet 1955, cited in Bynon 1977:89).

It is important to keep the distinctive-feature inventory small but also to be sure that necessary distinctions are made. In English the distinction between /θ/ "theta" and /ð/ "eth" keeps a relatively small set of words apart, such as "thigh" and "thy," yet for English to merge the sounds (via eliminating the distinctiveness of the feature (±voice) would serve no purpose since the feature (±voice) is necessary to distinguish a number of other pairs of sounds and lexical items in the language. "[T]his fact would account for their continued differentiation in spite of the low functional load carried by their opposition" (Bynon 1977:89).

The generative linguists' view of linguistic history focuses on the fact that language changes via rule changes. Their concern is not on shifts in forms (as the structuralists would have it) but on the underlying rules of grammar generating the forms. "The addition of a new rule has the effect of systematically modifying the phonetic representations generated by the grammar so that they differ from those generated by the previous grammar in which the rule is lacking" (Bynon 1977:114). King (1969:80f) provides an example of language change as interpreted within a generative framework as follows: Suppose English speakers pronounced *witch* and *weather* with an initial [w], while using a voiceless labiovelar fricative [ʍ] in *which* and *whether*. At some later period in the history of English, speakers of some varieties of the language use [w] in all four words. This pronunciation change "will be represented in the grammar by the addition of a rule which modifies the feature specification of /ʍ/ so that it matches that of /w/" (Bynon 1977:115). The child acquiring English as a first language hears nothing providing a clue that *witch* and *weather* are different words from *which* and *whether* so the child's grammar of English will have only an underlying /w/ while that of the adult will have both /w/ and /ʍ/. "The addition of a rule in one generation has thus led to the restructuring of underlying representations and the elimination of the added rule in the following generation" (Bynon 1977:115).

From the above it should be clear that language change over time may be accounted for as a change in forms, in structural relationships among systematic elements, or in rules of grammar, largely depending upon the researcher's idea of what definition of language and what epistemological approach to studying it is guiding the research. Just as we have seen the study of culture to have been influenced by descriptive and structural approaches to the analysis of language, scholars interested in the history of cultures likewise look at change from a number of perspectives. It should be noted here, however, that linguists, for the most part, have avoided any of the problems that anthropologists have had in the study of social and cultural change. The taint of evolutionism has remained remarkably slight in linguistics—owing largely, perhaps, to a focus on change rather than on any notion of progress from the primitive to the civilized and also owing largely to much of what we know as linguistics today having had its roots in the work of Boas, who was acutely aware of the need not to confuse history and evolution. Still, even during the heyday of evolutionism in anthropology when the neogrammarians held sway, little effort was put into saying that languages changed from the simple to the complex. Indeed, the methodology of historical reconstruction, whereby hypothetical proto-forms were set up as abstract underlying formulas from which present-day forms could be derived, did much to indicate that ancestor languages were as rich in their sound and grammar and lexical systems as are their children.

Early twentieth-century linguistics and anthropology were primarily concerned with providing adequate descriptions of linguistic and cultural behavior based on data gathered in the field whereas nineteenth-century researchers tended to be more of the armchair variety, using available written records. We have noted earlier that these twentieth-century descriptive approaches are *synchronic* in that they deal with a particular state of a language and culture at a particular point in time. The distinction between *synchronic* and *diachronic* studies in the study of culture was made early on by Clyde Kluckhohn, who sought to discover in different societies what behaviors (in each society's own terms) resulted from psychology, biology, and constraints on social interaction. From describing the differences across cultures, perhaps common and universal categories of culture may be found (see Kluckhohn 1953). Diachronic studies, rather than showing how we have progressed, now seek to document the history of a culture by using the evidence of oral and written traditions, archeological findings, and what linguists have found out about language changes over time. Documented culture histories may shed light on changes within specific systems of culture—indeed, it seems clear that different versions of a myth from different times in a group's history will reveal systematic changes in mythic structure.

For much of the work that has been done, however, diachronic linguistics and diachronic anthropology have tended to differ with regard to the interpretation of results. Little work has been done in culture history by scholars who regard culture as a system. Linguists who regard language as a unified system consider changes within its sound or grammatical system to be interrelated. The elements of a phonological system and the elements of a grammatical system are finite. Language change involves a rearrangement of features of the system whereby new configurations may be created but the features of language themselves are immutable. Reconstructed forms are regarded as strictly fictions—not primitive in any sense nor intended to be instances of language at all. PIE (Proto-Indo-European) was *not* the language of any supposed set of real speakers. Although linguists note language change over the years and recognize certain forms as having derived from "earlier" ones in an abstract sense, the results of linguistic reconstruction are not seen as indicating that the modern language has either progressed or regressed—simply that it has changed over time in a patterned way.

The distinction between synchronic and diachronic studies, which we noted earlier as having been introduced by Saussure, implied that diachronic descriptions would presuppose previous synchronic analysis of the different states or time stages through which the languages have historically gone (Lyons 1969:49). The descriptive linguists from Boas through Bloomfield sought to make their analyses of speech uniform in the interest of comparability both across time (though, as we have noted, as the method developed the progressive ruling out of etic variability made this goal impossible). Marvin Harris is one who saw the implication of this synchronic/diachronic distinction for anthropology. He felt that the comparative method can be valid only where the ethnographies compared are comparable and adequate (1968:156), recognizing further that *emic* analyses render making comparison impossible.

3.3 Language and Culture Classification

The comparative method is used not only to trace the history of a language but also to set up various types of language classification. The most familiar form of language classification is that to which we have already alluded whereby a language belongs to a particular family and within that family to a particular branch. Within a branch, a language may also have a number of sister and daughter languages as well as a set of parents. This kinship vocabulary refers to what linguists call **genetic classification**. Language classification uses the methods of comparative linguistics in order to show the degree of relationship of languages to each other—whatever the criteria of relationship happen to be. According to criteria of relationship, there are generally considered to be three basic modes of language classification: (1) genetic or genealogical—using sound and meaning correspondences (*cognates*) as criteria; (2) areal classification—using borrowing from one language to another as evidence for grouping languages together; and (3) typological classification—using structural features of languages as the basis upon which to link them. Culture classifications are generally done on an areal and typological basis. Some attempts using genetic language classifications as evidence have been made to propose genealogical relationships among groups of people.

3.3.1 Genealogical Classification/Language Families

Genealogical classification compares languages in order to discover parental and sibling relationships among languages and to construct language family trees. The classification is based totally on resemblances arising from a genealogical historical connection among the languages, regardless of where the languages are located geographically or temporally. Languages are classified by historical relationship and descent (demonstrable or hypothetical) from a single ancestor.

In a language family tree representing such a classification, every node or branching point represents a language, whether or not it is known from written records. All languages descended from one such node on the tree constitute a genetic group. For example, all Indo-European languages belong to a single genetic group because they all descend from one node, Proto-Indo-European (Greenberg 1968:121). The Germanic languages within the Indo-European genetic group constitute a genealogical subgroup (see Figure 2).

Figure 2. Family Tree Diagram: An Example of Genealogical Classification Showing the Relationship of English to Indo-European (adapted from Sturtevant 1947:157-158)

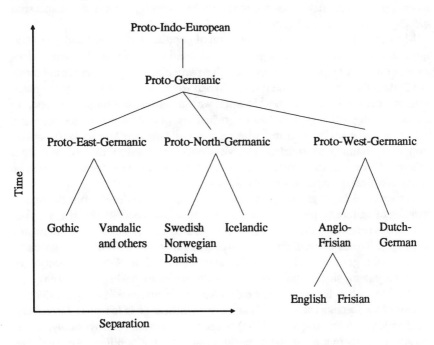

Genealogical classifications result from comparing languages in terms of sound and meaning correspondences in grammar and vocabulary. The findings that the method reveals about linguistic change from language to language establish the relative degree of relationship among languages. That is, sound and meaning correspondences between languages tell us how close, for example, Danish is to Norwegian and how far apart these languages are from English.

The variables of time and separation (the arrows on Figure 2) account for the use of genealogical language classifications by anthropologists to infer that migrations have occurred. For example, scholars have attempted to trace the migration of Bantu-speaking peoples in Africa (see Collins 1968:57-113). The idea is that if two languages share a large number of cognates, it is likely that their speakers were in contact relatively recently; if two languages have little in common (are far apart cognatically), then their speakers probably separated (diverged) a relatively long time ago. Indeed, with regard to the Bantu-speaking people of Africa and in the absence of any direct historical written records or strong archaeological radiocarbon, *only* linguistic evidence and historical inferences could be used to trace the migration of Bantu people throughout the continent. The anthropologist George P. Murdock noted that since all the Bantu languages are closely related according to comparative evidence, they must have diverged from a single ancestral speech community relatively recently (1959:272).

Most scholars interested in the question of population dispersal and migration agree that the establishment of genealogical relationship among languages does provide one type of evidence to indicate that particular groups of people did move in a certain direction at a certain time. When we move we do take our language with us—even if once at the new location we may abandon it for another one. In addition to linguistic evidence (with a gradual loss of cognates between languages indicating dispersal from an area where a common language was spoken), data on crop introduction and archaeological evidence are used to discern migration patterns. Once migration patterns are set up, it is possible to suggest likely degree of genealogical relatedness among cultures.

For anthropology, genealogical language classification can aid in the understanding of culture by providing facts about a time when people shared a language and about a time when they subsequently separated and spoke different but related languages. To some extent different languages imply different cultures, especially in terms of a genealogical relationship and classification. Further, some of the vocabulary items shared and later lost provide an idea as to what physical environment existed where the languages were spoken at various times (Swadesh 1959:39).

One of the foremost scholars of language classification is Joseph H. Greenberg. His *Language in the Americas* (1987) suggests, somewhat controversially, that in the Americas there are just three genealogical language families: Amerind, Na-Dene, and Eskimo-Aleut. Greenberg feels that this assumption, along with archaeological and historical evidence, indicates "at least three major migrations from Asia to the Americas over a Bering land bridge thousands of years ago . . . . [T]he oldest must be represented linguistically by Amerind . . . since that group covers a far more extensive territory than the others, centers to the south of them, and shows far greater internal linguistic differentiation" (Paul 1987b:6). The Na-Dene are thought to have arrived next, followed by the Eskimo-Aleut. Greenberg is working on data that he feels will support the claim that there are only 15 genealogical language families in the world. Though scholars differ in their analyses with regard to each other's reconstructions and cognate comparisons as well as interpretations of data, it is generally thought that the setting up of language families using lexical and grammatical comparative data will answer a number of questions regarding among other things the peopling of the world.

As is clear from the above, genealogical classification may reveal only *relative* chronology with regard to when languages diverged from a common ancestor. As Bynon noted: "If no points on the tree are datable on the basis of external evidence the entire construct will then remain uninterpretable in terms of the real time in which historians are used to operating" (1977:226-267). In order to try to fix real dates for language divergence, Morris Swadesh proposed a technique for *absolute* dating based on the approaches of the archaeologists using dendrochronology and carbon-14 dating. The **glottochronology** argument, in essence, contained the assumption that the longer two languages have been separated the greater the degree of difference between them would be. Thus it should be possible to quantify such degree of difference to "provide a means of determining the length of time during which divergent development had taken place" (Bynon 1977:267).

The means or technique devised to establish linguistic time depth (that is, to establish glottochronology) is known as **lexicostatistics**. Lexicostatistics makes use of the established genealogical variables of time and separation to compare percentages of cognate items retained in pairs of languages. The technique assumes: (1) that some parts of the vocabulary of any language are less subject to change than other parts; (2) that the parts of vocabulary which are unlikely to change are retained constantly through time; (3) that the rate of loss of items from this basic core vocabulary set is 19 percent per thousand years in any and all languages; (4) that if we know the percent of cognates among basic core vocabulary for any pair of languages, we can calculate the amount of time which has elapsed since those languages diverged from a common parent (paraphrased from Gudschinsky 1956:177-178).

The basic core vocabulary consists mainly of assumed culture-free items such as pronouns, numerals, body parts, and the like. The idea is that certain objects and situations occur in all societies despite cultural and geographical differences and there would be no need to acquire a new word to express something that is always with us. All humans, for example, have the same body parts and kinfolk, the argument goes, and all humans label them; hence we can expect that in related languages the words for "hand," "leg," "mother," "uncle," and so forth will be cognate and in unrelated languages they will not be.

Only cognate items are acceptable evidence for establishing genealogical relatedness and time of divergence. The procedure to follow in glottochronology is: (1) collect lists of culture-free vocabulary in the languages to be compared; (2) find out which are cognates and which are not, via establishing sound and meaning correspondences as outlined above in the discussion of linguistic reconstruction; (3) compute the time depth by solving for t in the equation

$$t = \frac{\log C}{2 \log r} \; ;$$

(4) compute the range of error by means of another equation. The mathematical procedures in steps (3) and (4) constitute the *statistics* part of the approach while

the linguistic procedures in (1) and (2) are what make the overall technique one of *lexico*statistics. In the time depth formula (step 3), *t* refers to time: *C* is the fraction of corresponding cognates in the two languages and *r* is the percentage of cognates assumed after a thousand years (that is, 81 percent). Languages or dialects that show little difference in time depth may be assumed to "have been closest geographically and longest in cultural contact" (Gudschinsky 1956:207).

Glottochronology and the lexicostatistical method of dating language divergence have been controversial topics since their inception. Especially controversial has been the concept of culture-free vocabulary. Questions regarding synonyms arise—how can the linguist know that the appropriate form has been compared? What about languages in which the range of meaning of labeled vocabulary items do not overlap? For example, in Bantu languages such as Swahili the several concepts "hand," "arm," "elbow" are all referred to by a single word (for instance, *mkono*) because the separate labeled distinctions that English makes do not apply. It would make little sense to try to compare *mkono* with *all three* source vocabulary items. Swadesh eventually modified his proposed 200-item basic vocabulary list to 100 items, dropping words such as "ice," "snow," "freeze," and "snake" (Swadesh 1955:124), which by no means occur in all languages.

One further problem with glottochronology is that "the initial hypothesis of a constant retention rate" of supposedly culture-free vocabulary "has not been substantiated" (Bynon 1977:270). Most linguists today are of the opinion that such mass comparison of data as is involved in glottochronology "can in no way serve as a substitute for reconstruction." The view is that the fact of linguistic relationship is of little interest when what is really at issue is the "internal history of the languages concerned, *how* they are related, what was the structure of their common ancestor, etc." (Bynon 1977:272). Still, for the anthropologist interested in culture history where there are no written documents, the glottochronological effort does provide evidence that languages (such as those of the Bantu family) "which now cover a wide geographical area" (or those of North America) which "are separated by a considerable distance in space once had a common origin" (Bynon 1977:272). As was noted earlier, common language origin does imply that the speakers may also have a common political, social, and cultural history.

3.3.2 Areal Classification/Language and Culture Spread

Areal and genealogical classifications of languages and cultures are not rival approaches but exist for different purposes. When trying to show that two languages share a common ancestor, much effort is devoted to being sure that their common words are cognate rather than the result of borrowing the thing and the label that represents it when the groups were in contact. The idea of culture-free vocabulary was intended as a way to be sure that compared items were basic to the language and not loan words. For areal classifications, the main evidence is exactly that excluded in genealogical groupings, namely, **borrowing**.

Areal groupings of languages are historical. They are similar to *culture-area* classifications used by anthropologists to classify cultures (Greenberg 1968:123). Speech communities, like cultural communities, interact with their neighbors. Things are transferred back and forth from community to community from time to time. Just as material goods are mutually exchanged, so too are patterns of behavior. The process is known as **diffusion**. When cross-cultural diffusion occurs, the names for the objects or patterns of behavior that have gone from one group to another are likewise spread about, producing **linguistic diffusion** (or as we mentioned above, **language spread**).

In linguistics and anthropology are the concepts **language area** and **culture area** respectively. With regard to language area, Boas noticed in North America that "... notwithstanding fundamental differences in structure and vocabulary [that is, genealogical differences], similarities in particular grammatical features [are] distributed in such a way that neighboring languages show striking similarities. ... It seems ... almost impossible to explain this phenomenon without assuming the diffusion of grammatical processes over contiguous areas" (Boas 1929:6).

It is important to understand that the diffusion of common linguistic (or cultural) features may be found wherever languages (and cultures) come in contact. In fact, culture areas and areal groupings of languages may coincide whereas there is no *a priori* reason to assume overlap between areal groupings of cultures and the distribution of genealogically related languages.

To illustrate this point (and the possibility of confusion), note that the anthropologist Melville Herskovits commonly made reference to the culture areas of Africa, with each area an aggregation of certain **traits**. In Africa, Herskovits identified the following areas: Khoisan (Bushman and Hottentot); Southwestern Cattle Area; East African Cattle Area; Congo Area; East Horn; Eastern Sudan; Western Guinea Coast; Desert Area; and Egypt. The scheme was based on sets of common culture traits in those geographical regions. Similarly, Northwest Coast North American Indians were seen to occupy different areas such as Puget Sound and the Lower Columbia River region, depending on whether for example the people had basket hats, wore tattoos, wore skin or fiber clothing, and so forth.

Scholars seeking to discover genealogical relationships among languages have occasionally used labels such as Khoisan, Western Sudanic, Lower Columbia, or Puget Sound to refer to groups of languages related in terms of sound and meaning (cognate) correspondences. Western Sudanic, in reference to a group of languages, refers only to a set of languages genealogically linked as members of a language family; the Western Sudanic culture area is a part of Africa inhabited by people who speak a number of languages both genealogically close and distinct, yet inhabit the same ecological space and thus will have similar materials to use (and talk about) in their daily lives. As speakers of the different genealogically related languages interact more and more in a particular area they may begin to borrow words and things from each other yet continue to exist as ethnically (genealogically) distinct though culturally (areally) mixed. In Chapter 5 we will discuss the way in which sociolinguists are beginning to study the process of language and culture mixing in such contact situations.

A by-product of the language-area/culture-area concept was the idea of the **age-area** principle, a method of inferring the relative age of traits (be they types of consonants or types of baskets) from their geographical distribution. The idea is that where certain traits are prevalent, it is likely that they originated there and later tended to diffuse in all directions from their center of origin (consider Wissler's "law of diffusion"; 1926:182).

When linguists look at areal features of languages, just as anthropologists do (for cultures), they look for common traits rather than cognates. For example, the number and type of consonants in a language is often thought to be an areal feature; there are clicks in South Africa; labiovelar consonants $[k^w, q^w, g^w, x^w]$ on the Northwest Coast. Perhaps the most commonly recognized areal linguistic features are lexical items associated with particular geographical dialects. People who live east of the Connecticut River in Massachusetts drink *frappes* and *tonic* whereas to the west they sip *milkshakes* and *soda* or *pop* or *soft drinks*. It is generally thought these days that the distribution of language and culture distinctions (traits) like these is less a matter of geography or area but more a function of social (and economic) factors. The belief is that:

> In any community some speakers at least will be capable of varying their speech according to circumstances, using perhaps the local dialect when talking among themselves but a more widely acceptable variety of the language when talking to strangers or for official purposes. (Bynon 1977:197)

The social study of languages in contact falls generally within the purview of sociolinguistics; the use of two varieties of a language whereby a "high" form is used in official circumstances and a "low" form more casually is referred to as **diglossia** (Ferguson 1959). For some languages, such as Arabic, diglossia is manifest for example in a colloquial versus a classical form of the language. In other cases diglossia is less structured and people may switch their style of speaking from "street talk" to "school talk." The study of how people use their repertory of languages, language varieties, or styles will be discussed in detail in Chapter 5 under the headings of *language mixing, codeswitching, bi-* and *multilingualism*.

We will see that languages have both a social and a linguistic structure and the *social stratification* of language use involves language change within a particular geographic area. Bostonians, for example, may—for reasons of perceptions of greater social prestige—say "milkshake" and also pronounce "car" as [kar] or continue with "frappe" and [kæəh]. That is, sociolinguists are interested in the way features of language (and culture) are borrowed (diffused) across socioeconomic lines, while comparative/historical scholars look at diffusion with regard to what it tells about language and culture history. More about social stratification of language and the sociolinguistics of language change will be discussed in Chapter 5.

It remains in this section to characterize what may be the epitome of language and culture diffusion—an epitome, ironically, resulting in a new sociolinguistic unit. Where isolated areas are seen to preserve early traits, urban areas give rise to new entities. **Pidgins** are languages spoken by people who have no first language in common—generally formed via adult speakers' attempts to communicate in the other person's language as simply as possible. Generally, most scholars feel, the **target** language is a well-known (often European) language. That is, one speaker will attempt to learn another speaker's language when the second speaker speaks a European language. The "target" then is the language whose grammatical structure will be simplified and end up as the pidgin's structure. The **pidginization** process involves the simplification of complex grammatical aspects that the target language may have had; inflection, case marking, noun class, prefixes, and the like. The effect of pidginization is that in the process of borrowing the structure of one language, the resulting grammar is simpler than the grammar of either the borrower or lender. Eventually the grammar and lexicon of a pidgin will expand as the new communication form is used. Interestingly, the resulting **creole** may develop a structure not traceable to the full form of either donor language. It should be clear from what we have said here that a pidgin is nobody's first language as such. If a person's first language would have been a pidgin, say if two pidgin speakers had a child and proceeded to speak only pidgin to that child, then as that child acquires language his or her language will be acquired as a creole.

Bynon provides an interesting example of pidginization/creolization in the context of diffusion in her discussion of Neo-Melanesian as spoken in South East Asia. There is a form /fɛlə/ which, though donated by English "fellow," has a totally different distribution in its creolized form. The form is a plural marker for first and second person plural pronouns: *mi* "I"; *mifelə* "we"; and *ju* "you"; *jufelə* "you" plural. Beyond this, the form is used to link adjectives, numerals, and demonstratives to their nouns;

"a good man"	*gudfelə mæn*
"one boy"	*wənfelə məŋki*
"this boy"	*disfelə məŋki*

This is the kind of thing that makes English speakers suppose they understand a language like Neo-Melanesian because it sounds like English. But because "the syntactic distribution follows altogether 'un-English principles'" (Bynon 1977:259), it is in many respects a different language altogether. Scholars have set up what is referred to as **post-creole continua**: at one end is a creole "totally unintelligible to speakers of the target language" (Bynon 1977:259), and at the other end the creole sounds like a local version of the target language. It depends upon a person's social position whether that person's creole will be more or less like the target language. In Jamaica, for example, official Jamaican Creole is mutually intelligible with English but in more remote areas and in the streets it is not (see DeCamp 1971). As Bynon notes, "the situation is in every way parallel to that of social or geographical variation or of the situation known as diglossia (Ferguson 1959) in traditional societies" (1977:259).

3.3.3 Language Typology

In addition to being compared for genealogical or areal purposes, languages and cultures are also commonly classified according to common features of their structure. The result of such analyses of similarities and differences in structure (rather than of historical relationships or proximity) is classes or typological groups referred to by phrases such as "tone languages," "SVO languages," and so forth. As we saw earlier, regarding interpretations that have been made of culture history (as opposed to what has been done in historical linguistics), there are cases where the analogy of language and culture has had some unpleasant ramifications, especially in the study of culture. The area of typology provides another example. Cultures have been grouped together on the basis of common features of social organization and the way those features function. In anthropology the scholars most associated with the approach are called **structural-functionalists**. Radcliffe-Brown may be seen to exemplify this approach in *African Systems of Kinship and Marriage* (Radcliffe-Brown and Forde 1950). Such studies have been interpreted as presenting the structural aspects of tribal societies as static, with a resulting use to perpetuate colonial policies where it is likely that the purpose of describing and grouping different forms of social structure was, indeed, otherwise. Langness (1987:94) cautions:

> . . . there is a great difference between motives and functions. Even if it can be clearly demonstrated that the consequence (function) of twenty-five years of functionalism was to help perpetuate an unchanging colonial situation, it still does not follow that the functionalists' intention (motive) was that their approach would have that consequence.

One of the problems with typology is that any criteria may be employed. An early example of the use of typology in anthropology was in the nineteenth-century work of J. C. Nott and G. R. Glidden, *Types of Mankind* (1854), in which the people of the world were grouped according to race. Nott and Glidden then argued that all races were created separately and that each race has both moral and physical features unique to that race and perpetuated through time. Such an approach presupposes some validity to the concept "race" for classification purposes, just as Radcliffe-Brown's work implies the same for kinship and marriage structure. Throughout this book so far we have seen that the theory and method of the researcher is largely responsible for the analytical units employed—to impose them, once "discovered," on the people in the society said to make use of such structural features represents a logical leap of some magnitude.

Since any criteria will do to set up a typology, then, it is useful to choose criteria that may be assumed to have significance. Roman Jakobson as a structuralist linguist (see also Chapter 2 above) saw utility in typology (that is, in a structuralist-functionalist approach to language) as long as the basis for grouping languages was the system of language (*langue*):

> . . . a linguistic typology based on arbitrarily selected traits cannot yield satisfactory results any more than the classification of the animal kingdom which instead of the productive division into vertebrates and non-vertebrates, mammals and birds, etc., would use, for instance, the criterion of skin color and on this basis group together, e.g., white people and light pigs. (1958:20)

Linguists have found it useful, for example, to see which languages have case systems and which ones do not and to compare case in languages where it exists to see how it functions. For example, within the Indo-European language family French seems to be moving from the class of languages that has case systems to the class that lacks them.

Of course, to group languages according to whether they have case systems or not assumes that there is some significance to the answer. Over the years a number of different criteria have held sway in linguistic typology. In the nineteenth century, languages were classified as belonging to one of four categories depending upon the way morphemes were arranged in the language—that is, did they stand alone or combine? If they combined, did they do so in clumps or pairs? The resultant typology had it that there are **isolating** languages exemplified by Chinese with only free morphemes (that is, with no prefixes, infixes, suffixes); in contrast are **agglutinative** languages, like Turkish for example, with single-word sentences composed of roots that combine with various affixes in various orders. Between these two extremes are languages like English, which makes semantic and syntactic distinctions using prefixes and suffixes and also makes use of free forms. Such languages are **polysynthetic** (or **analytical**). Languages like French and Latin (that is, with case systems) are referred to as **inflectional**, using productive suffixes to make a number of semantic distinctions.

The years since 1975 have seen a resurgence of interest in linguistic typology, particularly according to syntactic criteria. Linguists are interested in the order in which "the basic constituents, subject (S), verb (V), and object (O), occur in simple declarative sentences" (Greenberg 1966, cited in Bynon 1977:263). This typology assumes that concepts of subject, verb, and object are valid cross-linguistically. Assuming that they are, scholars propose that there are three main language types: SVO, VSO, and SOV. It is thought that if the basic word-order type of a language is known then other facts of the language follow:

> . . . it would appear that if a language (such as Japanese) has basic OV order it can be predicted that it will also have postpositions and that its adjectival, genitival and relative clause modifiers will precede the noun. Typical VO languages (such as Thai), on the other hand, are said to place their possessives, adjectives, genitives, and other modifiers after the noun and to have prepositions. (Bynon 1977:263)

Linguists find this form of classification interesting because of the implication it has with regard to understanding language change. If Japanese were to go from OV to VO word order the position of modifiers with respect to the noun would also change and the language would lose postpositions and gain prepositions. Indeed, such a change may explain why some French adjectives (*grand* "big," *vieux* "old") come before the noun and all other modifiers follow the noun; that is, "big" and "old" are "relics" of an earlier OV order (Lehmann 1973).

Other approaches to linguistic typology include grouping languages according to whether or not their utterances conform to a *subject/predicate* or to a *topic/comment* analysis. For example, Charles Li and Sandra Thompson have suggested that Mandarin Chinese is a topic-prominent language while English is subject-prominent. To illustrate, consider the following sentence (from Li and Thompson 1978:226) of Mandarin:

> Neikuai tian women zhong daozi
> that   field we   grow rice
> "That field (topic), we grow rice (on it)."

In this sentence, "that field" is the topic of the comment "we grow rice," yet does not stand in any *subject* grammatical relationship to it. Indeed, the comment "we grow rice" is in and of itself a structure with a subject/predicate relation. In languages like Mandarin, it is difficult (if not impossible) to determine whether it makes any typological sense to attempt to characterize sentences as SOV or OSV at all.

Recently Talmy Givón has suggested that languages be classified according to whether they manifest a **pragmatic** or **syntactic** communicative mode. Languages that make use of the pragmatic mode show topic/comment utterance structure and make use of no grammatical morphology. Old information is communicated before new information in pragmatically oriented languages, whereas word order in languages seen to be characterized by a syntactic communicative mode usually signals what Givón sees as **semantic** case functions.

Givón's approach is that languages can be typologically classified according to how they work as communication systems rather than being based on purely syntactic or morphological criteria. Indeed, Givón makes the point that in preindustrial societies the pragmatic communicative mode predominates whereas the industrial world has "syntacticized," arguing that the context of language use interacts with the resulting structure. When we are preliterate and existing in "societies of intimates" (Givón 1979:307) the features of pragmatic communication are paramount. People tend to share more information and discuss it—rooting what they say in the context where it is said—hence they precede new information with old, using known topics and following them by comments. They are able to use culturally shared gestures and lexical items needing relatively uncomplicated grammatical patterns to manipulate them. On the other hand, strangers converse outside of any shared context and require more complicated grammatical structures to convey the information otherwise handled by context (that is, by pragmatics). The idea that language-use structure varies with the context of use will also be seen in the next chapter as it has figured in attempts to relate language and world view. There we will see that people may use either an **elaborated** or a **restricted** code depending, some say, on the social class to which they belong; similarly, the way people think (their conceptual style) will be seen by some as "discoverable" from language-use data. The question in all this has to do with whether there is anything inherently linguistic about such typologies. At this point, before going on, I would like to point out that Givón's ideas, controversial as they are, nevertheless are not inconsistent with the idea of a common universal linguistic ability. Givón's position is that this ability interacts with the world one way when the world is simple (nonindustrial, preliterate) or new (to the child or people who share no first language yet and need to communicate), or familiar (when communicators share values, information, settings and so forth). When the world is complex and what we talk about may not be in sight (literally or from the perspective of prior shared values and information), the structure of language adjusts to fit those literate, industrial, unfamiliar communicative needs.

Still, it remains controversial whether or not linguistic typology is a useful undertaking. There needs to be an empirical basis for both the typological criteria and for claims that languages change type over time. Givón (1979) feels that languages have evolved in exactly the same way a child acquires language. That is, Givón is a strict adherent of the idea that "Ontogeny recapitulates phylogeny." Children first acquire a pragmatic form of communication in their first language and then later learn the full grammar *if* their first language is a syntacticized language. Otherwise the language-acquisition process stops once the child has acquired the features of his/her language as a pragmatic form of communication. Further, Givón feels that the process whereby pidgins become creoles (and repidginize) manifests the way in which the pragmatic mode is replaced by the syntactic mode of communication (and back again) (Givón 1979:223-226). Indeed, the idea is that both pidginization and child language acquisition are the very same processes as linguistic evolution!

In recent years, linguists have begun to devote much more attention to the study of pidgin and creole languages. One area of inquiry suggests that "children can learn language only because they already know one" (Romaine 1988, discussing Bickerton 1981)—that is, they are hard-wired from the start with what Derek Bickerton calls a **bioprogram**. This consists partly of "species-specific structures of cognition and partly of processes inherent in the linear expansion of language. It ensures that people will have a particular type of grammar in much the same way as a 'physical bioprogram' ensures that they will have a particular skeletal structure" (Romaine 1988:257). To Bickerton, a creole "is the realization of the instructions of the bioprogram with minimal cultural admixture." Thus a creole-like language unfolds in every child but, as the child grows it is "quickly overlaid by the local cultural language." The bioprogram hypothesis of Bickerton shares some points in common with Chomsky's ideas about universal grammar and language acquisition.

In contrast to the situation giving rise to a creole, a pidgin may arise when adults who know distinct languages (which have masked their bioprogram features) come into contact. The processes of pidginization and creolization, according to this line of reasoning, are distinct. Creolization is similar to first-language acquisition (see J. H. Schumann 1978). The study of pidgins and creoles is often within the purview of *sociolinguistics* rather than of *comparative* and *historical* studies since it commonly involves attention to what happens in situations of modern language contact, as we will see in the remaining chapters of this book. Still, as Romaine (1988:309) has observed, the changes "which occur in both pidginization and creolization are just like other cases of historical change" regardless of any bioprogram or universal grammar. So "more work needs to be done on language change in general" (Romaine 1988) in order to test ideas such as those of Givón, Bickerton, and others regarding the structural features of language as they develop in the individual and through time. The study of pidgins and creoles as a matter of comparative and historical linguistics as well as of sociolinguistics has ramifications for an overall theory of language as cognition and universal grammar. The interested reader is directed to Suzanne Romaine's *Pidgin and Creole Languages* (1988) for an overview of the field up to this time.

3.4 Summary

The entire subject matter of this chapter has been the concern of the well-known linguistic anthropologist Joseph H. Greenberg. In an article looking back on his career so far, Greenberg describes a common thread linking the various comparative and historical approaches to language and language groupings. Throughout all such work is the recognition of the importance of historical factors in attempts to come up with language universals and the idea that facts of language history may be found using typological, genetic, and areal criteria. Greenberg, as was noted above, is continuing to work on setting up genealogical classifications of the world's languages, taking into consideration typological universals and areal features. He urges that the task of language classification be completed in order to provide "a tool of immense importance for human cultural and biological history" (Greenberg 1986:19), a tool which "will help to shed light on the nature of communication systems in general" (1986:23).

In the pages preceding, we have seen that some linguists are concerned with how closely specific languages are related to each other in order to find out how many language *families* there are in the world. Others are interested in studying the process by which languages borrow from and mutually influence each other. Still others seek to discover the range of variability in linguistic structure throughout the world. People classify languages according to word order, syllable structure, word-formation processes, and communicative mode.

As we have seen with regard to the various approaches to linguistic analysis as such (as discussed in Chapters 1 and 2), analogous efforts to look at culture also exist when it comes to matters of history and comparison. Anthropologists seek to classify cultures just as linguists seek to classify languages. They are interested in comparing cultures and describing cultural change through time. How societies and cultures are related ethnically, with regard to the sharing of material goods (through exchange or borrowing) and in the way they structure their social institutions (for example, via different types of kinship, kingship, economic, or religious systems), are areas of interest to the ethnohistorian and the cross-cultural analyst.

What the linguistic record reveals by means of comparative and historical investigation has been shown to have attracted the attention of archaeologists and historians as well. *Cognate sets* and *loan words* respectively provide information regarding what people and aspects of material culture (food, clothing, crops) were in a particular place at a particular time in the past. The comparative method carried both linguistics and anthropology into the twentieth century. Nineteenth-century anthropological scientists were adherents to an evolutionary framework, seeking to show the development of cultures from the simple to the complex by comparing "primitive" to "civilized" societies. The discovery that good descriptions of cultural traits were lacking led to a general abandonment of comparison in favor of description, on the basis that such descriptions would facilitate eventual comparison of data. This descriptive era was described in Chapter 1. Twentieth-century historical linguists use linguistic reconstruction to demonstrate that languages which appear (in their unreconstructed form) unrelated or dissimilar actually are closely related. Modern ethnohistorians make use of the findings of historical linguists as well as of other data, including the traditions of the culture bearers themselves, in order to provide particular culture histories.

Chapter 4 **Language and Culture**

4.0 Introduction

In the preceding three chapters, most attention was directed to parallel and analogous developments in linguistics and anthropology—to descriptive methods in both fields, to structuralist approaches used by linguists and anthropologists, to the generativist view in linguistics and its relevance to the study of Culture as well as of Language. At various points in the discussion so far, mention was made of certain outgrowths of the approaches discussed that would be the subject of this and the following chapter. In this chapter the focus will be on efforts to ascertain the relationship between language and culture, with culture defined generally as a system of meaningful symbols.

We will begin the discussion here, examining efforts to link language, thought, and reality in the context of what has come to be known as **world view**. We will see that psychologically oriented scholars, especially social/experimental psychologists and cognitive anthropologists (particularly interested in correlating linguistic and nonlinguistic behaviors such as color labels and color perception) study what they see as the relationship of language and thought. Next we will look at recent efforts by anthropological linguists to study **discourse**, that is, chunks of language larger than the sentence, including conversations and written text as well as the "talk" of an individual. Researchers are suggesting that discourse is the area where language and culture interact in a way that can be fruitfully investigated. Approaches to the study of language in context come under such labels as *pragmatics* and *semiotics* (also *semeiotic*)[1]. Essentially the term **pragmatics** refers to the study of the connotative (inner) and denotative (outer) meanings of "expressions when used in a conversation or a written work" (Paul 1987b:4). That is, pragmatics is the study of the meaning of *discourse*. **Semiotics** is the study of **signs** and their meaning and as such encompasses communicative behavior on a far broader basis than language. Further, the emphasis in pragmatics and discourse

---

[1] The various rendering of semiotics as semeiotic in these pages reflects a growing awareness of the fact that the work is derived from the Greek word for "sign" not from the Latin *semi*—"half." Similarly it is more properly singular (Val Daniel, personal communication).

analysis is on empirical research while semiotics rests on a symbolic and interpretive basis (see Chapter 2 above). The tension we have observed between approaches—rational and empirical, interpretive and behaviorist—continues when attention is paid to the study of meaning and world view.

We will conclude the chapter with a discussion of the study of meaning in terms of language-culture overlap—specifically with regard to efforts by linguists to characterize the **lexicon** and the way in which linguistic knowledge is tied to cognitive ability. We will see what generative linguists propose as the semantic component of a theory of Language.

Essentially the linking content of this chapter will be whether and how language and culture are connected to thought. This focus distinguishes what is of concern here from Sociolinguistics, which will be discussed in Chapter 5. Sociolinguistic studies share a common concern with the patterned ways in which language use and social behavior go together. Sociolinguistics has an empirical basis and seeks practical applications. Nonetheless, some of the research done straddles both interests—for instance, the study of the way in which people use different languages in a single conversation (codeswitching) may be analyzed with regard to both its discourse and world-view aspects as well as from the perspective of what the switches reveal about the relative status of speakers and about the social structure of the context in which switching takes place. Discourse analysis will be examined with regard to the language-culture link while codeswitching will be seen more as an aspect of sociolinguistics.

As we have seen in previous chapters, linguists to date have had the least success in semantic analysis or semantic theory. Meaning continues to be elusive. Sapir saw language as a mixture of forms and concepts and suggested a "psychological reality" for the phoneme. Other -emes were suggested as being equally real in the heads of speakers though the demonstration of such psychologically real elements of language was fraught with problems. Bloomfield, in response, abandoned such "mentalist" notions in favor of refining methods for describing directly observable data.

Saussure's notion of langue as the system underlying speech (parole) marked the structuralist's attempt to get at inner language, again bolstered by efforts of anthropologists as well to find the system underlying cultural behavior. With Chomsky's notion of competence the mentalist approach has become full-blown in linguistics. However, the nature of the human cognitive (mental) ability to acquire language, so far, is best understood with regard to the nature of acquiring the phonological and syntactic rules for languages. The rules or associations guiding the way concepts are imbued with semantic content and regarding how such content is interpreted by speakers and hearers are still a mystery.

It appears ever more likely that attempts to understand linguistic content may have to take account of context and experience in the outer as well as the inner worlds. The subject matter of this chapter has to do with such attempts.

4.1 World View

As was pointed out in the first two chapters, the history of American linguistics may be seen to follow a chain; Boas taught Sapir, Sapir taught Zellig Harris, Zellig Harris taught Chomsky. Another chain, however, is that leading from Boas to Sapir to Benjamin Lee Whorf and onward, focusing on the question of the ways in which language, thought, and reality interrelate. Whorf also was a student of Sapir, particularly interested in extending Sapir's view that "The 'real world' is to a large extent unconsciously built up on the language habits of the group" [1951(1929):160 in Kay and Kempton 1984:66)]. Whorf took one step further this notion that the reality of a speech community is constructed through language, by asserting that "an intellectual system embodied in each language shapes the thoughts of its speakers in a quite general way" (Kay and Kempton 1984:66). These ideas together constitute what has come to be known as the Sapir-Whorf Hypothesis: that one's language determines how one segments the world.

This idea stems from a number of papers by both Sapir and Whorf, including Sapir's "Conceptual Categories in Primitive Languages" (1931) and Whorf's "A Linguistic Consideration of Thinking in Primitive Communities" [1936 in Carroll (ed.) 1956]. This view counters any universalistic idea that reality is the same for all people.

The views of Sapir and Whorf have been taken to mean that people who speak different languages segment their world differently: thus, the French language structures French reality by constraining what French speakers pay attention to, Swahili does the same for the Swahili "world"—if there's a word for "it" in the language we see "it," if not we don't. This idea goes beyond vocabulary to include grammar. Thus, in languages where the choice of a verb has to do with the shape of its object, shape is a more distinctive cultural category than it is in languages where verbs do not change in response to their objects. To illustrate this idea, consider the Hopi language in which exactly this situation obtains: that is, transitive verbs require shape of objects of verbs to be encoded. Hopi speakers use one form of "hit" if a round object is hit, another "hit" if what gets hit is square, and so forth. In English, no such distinction is involved in saying "Mary hit the baseball with the bat" and "Mary hit the window with a rock," or the like. Hence one might say that English speakers somehow see balls and windows as the same (both being hittable) whereas Hopi speakers would use different verbs and accordingly would see balls and windows as requiring different actions. Another way to refer to the Sapir-Whorf Hypothesis has been to see it as a theory of **linguistic determinism**. Whatever the label, this question of the relationship of language and thought to reality or of language to thought and reality or of thought to language and reality has given rise to a great deal of research and has generated much controversy since the 1940s. In some ways the entire question may be seen simply as the World View Problem.

What is interesting about the issues raised here is that people are always intrigued and at a gut level seem to know from the outset whether they are proponents or opponents of the idea that language determines the way we see the world. Recently there has been a great deal of attention in the anthropological linguistic literature to rereading the ideas of Whorf in an effort to demonstrate that his position is not as extremely deterministic as many have interpreted it to be.

Joshua Fishman (1980) saw the World View Problem as a question of whether or not cultural behaviors are shaped by different language structures through which they are expressed. We need to find out if different verb-plus-object relations, for example, correlate with different cultural behaviors. Do differently structured languages lead their speakers to different views and experiences of reality (of nature, of life)?

Opponents of this idea criticize proponents for looking simply at the surface differences between languages. Indeed, with regard to the Hopi example just given, advocates of universal grammar (generativist linguists) would say that both Hopi and English speakers "see" a window and a baseball as hit in the same way and can express what they mean regardless of the way their respective grammars put morphemes together. That is, they would see no justification in saying different language structures relate in any way to reality (or value) structures.

Critics of the idea that one's language constructs one's world often cite multilingual communities. If a first language constructs an individual's reality then how can intercommunication (or pidgins, creoles, bilingualism) come about? Still other critics argue that thought is prior to language. Indeed, the Chomsky idea of a universal innate linguistic ability that once "in play" takes on the characteristics of language use in a particular speech community exemplifies this critical position. In many ways (recall our discussion of Edward Sapir's ideas of psychological reality, leading in a sense directly to the views of Chomsky, in Chapter 2), Sapir himself would see language and thought as interrelated but not as in any way determining that people who speak different languages inhabit different worlds.

Sapir viewed the relationship of language to culture as somewhat different from the way he viewed language in relation to thought. This difference is often overlooked when we think of him in terms of the Sapir-Whorf Hypothesis. For example, in his book *Language* (1921), Sapir insists that language and culture are mutually independent and that there is no causal connection between the two. Culture is *what* society thinks and does and language is *how* people think (1921:218). Language is related to thought in that "language is primarily a pre-rational function. It humbly works up to the thought that is latent in, that may eventually be read into, its classification and its forms; it is not, as is generally but naively assumed, the final label put upon the finished thought" (1921:15).

Whorf, however, believed that the idea of language influencing culture would enable researchers to find out how the peoples of various cultures think. This discovery would be made by investigating the grammar and lexicon of different people's languages. Since Whorf's time the field of ethnoscience (cognitive anthropology) has developed largely in response to Whorf (which we will see below). In addition, the question of the way language and thought interact has been tackled by a number of social and experimental psychologists.

Kay and Kempton (1984:66) point out that "[U]ntil a technique is developed for assessing the world view of a people independently of the language they speak" there is no way to test the idea that the structure of our first language "strongly influences or fully determines the world view" (Roger Brown 1976:128) we acquire as we learn the language. Nonetheless, it is possible to conduct research to find out: (a) how structural differences across languages parallel nonlinguistic cognitive differences in first-language speakers of the different languages; (b) whether "the semantic systems of different languages vary without constraint" (Kay and Kempton 1984:86).

4.1.1 Color Terms and Color Perception

Perhaps the most common nonlinguistic cognitive ability tested in relation to language is that coded in the semantic domain *color*. Studies of color terms as correlated with cross-cultural perception prior to 1969 have tended to support the idea that languages come with a fixed color lexicon. The Wolof language (spoken in Senegal) does not have a monolexemic label for *blue*. It uses a single term for what in English is labeled *red* and *orange*. Wolof does have a word for *yellow* but it is rarely used (it has **low codability**). Thus one would expect that Wolof children in an experiment with French children would behave differently with respect to colored objects.

Bruner, Greenfield, and Olver (1966) conducted an experiment with Wolof-speaking and French-speaking children in Senegal, showing them pictures of people carrying out certain functions using differently colored objects. In both French and Wolof the functions pictured were deemed equally expressible with color being the variable at issue. The first-language speakers of each language plus a group of children bilingual in French and Wolof were given pictures in sets of three (triads) and asked to choose the two pictures out of each set that were most alike and to state why they made their choice. The expectation was that Wolof-speaking children would group the pictures based on function, since in Wolof there are fewer color distinctions than in French. Bilingual children would show more color groupings than would monolingual Wolof speakers, but fewer such groupings than monolingual French speakers. That is, it was expected that this experiment would validate the Whorfian hypothesis (show a *Whorfian effect*). However, the results went directly against expectations. Monolingual Wolof children used only color to form their groupings! The bilingual and French-speaking children grouped less by color and more by shape and function. Further, the tendency for these nonmonolingual Wolof speakers to group by shape and function rather than by color increased with age. Clearly the fact that the Wolof language does not have certain specific color words which French has does not inhibit the Wolof speaker's perception category of color.

Another experiment was designed to test whether the lack of color words in Wolof affects color discrimination. In this case subjects administered the triads test were asked to group pictures overtly on the basis of color. Each set of three pictures contained two sharing a predominant color such as orange. Perception errors were noted, that is, groupings of orange with red, for example, rather than orange with orange. It was found that monolingual Wolof speakers made the most such errors, bilinguals somewhat fewer, and French-speaking children the fewest. From this distribution the researchers concluded that the fact of a language having a color label (i.e. there is a **name strategy** available to the speaker) does influence color discrimination to some extent. Here too, with older subjects, the errors declined regardless of language.

From such studies, despite apparent contradictions as in the first Wolof experiment above, came the idea that linguistic labeling (or coding) affects cognitive operations. It remained to figure out how such Whorfian effects come about and why, as in the Wolof children grouping color even when their language lacks the color labels, the effects appear to work inconsistently.

Perceptual representations came to be thought of as consisting of a *schema* (linguistic label) and a *correction* (visual image) (after McNeil 1965). The schema aspect is less important, vague, and not useful when the cognitive task has to do with the entire perception (both its label and its image) as in the first experiment. When the task is overtly geared to schema only, then there seems to be a language-perception link in the Whorfian sense (Greenfield and Bruner 1966). The next step in research along these lines involves efforts to find out about the nature of cognitive organization both from the perspective of how schemata (labels) are organized (in terms of formal semantics) and how corrections (visual images) operate in relation to schema.

In 1967 two anthropologists, Brent Berlin and Paul Kay, published research on the lexical coding of color in 80 different languages representing unrelated language families, designed to test the then prevailing idea that languages segment color space in a totally arbitrary manner. Most of the studies of color terms stemmed from research in experimental psychology. Berlin and Kay brought to their research a background in cross-cultural research specifically from a cognitive anthropological perspective (see below). Their methodology stresses the importance of gathering data in the language of the culture bearers and dealing with each language and culture in its own (emic) terms. They questioned the idea that variation in the color lexicon from language to language (as between, say, French and Wolof) implicitly argues against the existence of semantic universals (Berlin and Kay 1967:2) and sought to determine whether differences in color coding correlate with differences in world view. Their thesis was that "color words translate rather too easily among various pairs of unrelated languages" and that it is untrue that each language "segments the three-dimensional color continuum arbitrarily and independently of each other language" (2,3).

Using speakers from 20 languages and grammars of 60 others, Berlin and Kay determined the basic color words in each language. Only single lexical items referring to color were counted as basic. This monolexemic restriction ruled out phrases such as *light blue* or *dusty rose* and also, generally, words that referred not only to color but had other reference in a language. For example, in Swahili the word for green is *majani* but *majani* means "leaves," hence cannot be counted as a basic color term. The native-speaker subjects from whom color vocabulary was elicited supplied the words that fit in a frame; for example, " ___ is a color term in my language." Then each was asked to indicate the **focal point** and **outer boundary** of each term by selecting from a set of color chips which chip represents the purest *blue* and where among the chips or on a color chart *blue* stops being *blue* and becomes another color.

The study revealed that speakers of all languages center the foci of their labels for color at nearly the same location. Some languages have more color terms than others, but the focus for each term in a language is the same as the focus for the corresponding term in other languages. In sum, despite different labels, people perceive color the same way. This finding goes against much of the earlier work on color that had been seen to support the Whorfian hypothesis to the effect that language forces its speakers to divide the spectrum in a certain way, with each language making "its own distinctions, which need have little to do with the distinctions made by other languages" (Burling 1970:46).

This challenge to the idea of linguistic determinism led further to the idea that "there exists a total inventory of about eleven basic color categories from which the eleven or fewer basic color categories of any given language are always drawn" (Berlin and Kay 1967:2). Indeed, Berlin and Kay predict the order of acquisition of color terms in language; if a language has two colors lexically coded, the labels will refer to "black" and "white"; if three, they will refer to "black," "white," and "red." The fourth term lexically coded refers to "green" or "blue" (then seen as *grue*, which will be discussed in more detail below). The fifth added is whichever was not fourth of the "grue" pair.

A number of analogies come to mind here: linguists have proposed universal distinctive features in phonology, such that languages differ in the features selected

as distinctive in their sound systems according to what features they select from
the universal set (see Chapter 2). In the evolutionary aspect of the Berlin and Kay
findings, where the number of color terms lexically coded in a particular language
correlates with the degree of industrialization in the society where the language is
spoken (many terms occur in highly industrial societies, fewer in traditional ones),
we see a language-context link in line with the work of pragmatically oriented
scholars (compare Givón's idea of the pragmatic versus syntactic communicative
mode mentioned at the end of Chapter 3).

   The psychologist Roger Brown interprets such results that counter the idea of
linguistic determinism as supporting instead the idea of *linguistic relativity*. Perceptual categories that are frequently used receive labels, while unused categories
may be seen as universal, "sitting there, waiting for a label" (Burling 1970:48).
Roger Brown's idea is that a perceptual category used by people more often than
others is a category which is more "available" than ones less frequently used. To
illustrate his point, Brown uses an example that has become "folklorized" over the
years (see Martin 1986). Brown cites Whorf to the effect that the Eskimo lexicon
has three words for snow while English does not have three single-word equivalents
and interprets Whorf to mean that Eskimo people and English speakers see snow
differently. Brown's view, instead, is that some people have more words for things
like snow because they *need* more than one label. People in industrial societies
need to discriminate more colors as colors than do people in more traditional
societies where there is a common understanding, for instance, of what "leaves"
are colorwise so the Swahili word *majani* can have the two referents. To counter
what Brown sees Whorf's snow example to be about, he cites English speakers
who ski or make snowballs. Such people, as do speakers of Eskimo languages,
have more than one word for snow. Therefore, Brown argues, world view is not
determined by language but, instead, we categorize our world (that is, we attach
labels to what's out there) by using our language to do what we need it to do:

> . . . linguistic relativity holds that where there are differences of language there will
> also be differences of thought, that language and thought covary. Determinism goes
> beyond this to require that the prior existence of some language pattern is either
> necessary or sufficient to produce some thought pattern. (Roger Brown 1958:260)

   The research of Berlin and Kay (1967) and that of Kay and Kempton (1987), as
we will see below, supports this idea of **linguistic relativity**. As Laura Martin
(1987) has pointed out, however, the particular way in which Brown argues his
relativity (versus determinism) point and the fact that the "Eskimo words for snow"
example has come to be seen as the classic proof of the Whorf hypothesis needs to
be seen in context. Eskimo languages are generally agglutinative (see Chapter 3
above) and form words by attaching various affixes to roots in such a way that the

same word for something is unlikely to recur "because the particular combination of suffixes used with a 'snow' root, or any other, varies by speaker and situations as well as by syntactic role" (Sadock 1980, in Martin 1987:419). Indeed, Eskimo has an "incalculable" number of "snow" or any other kind of words; research on the lexical elaboration of semantic domains in any language needs to be cognizant of the fact that the cross-cultural salience of items from one language to another must be sensitive to facts of linguistic typology (see Chapter 3). One language's "word" may be another language's "sentence." Martin's point is that this one "snow" example and its proliferation in the literature (including texts like this) does a disservice to Whorf and his insights with regard to language and culture: "the complexity of the interrelations of linguistic structure, cultural behavior, and human cognition" cannot and should not be reduced to "Eskimo words for snow" (1987:419). The grammars available to Whorf, whether describing Eskimo or Hopi or other languages, written in a descriptivist, or earlier, framework (and often by nonlinguists) would frequently contain lists from languages of items labeled as words which were really translation equivalents corresponding to the language of the researcher, missionary, traveler, or whomever. This fact also compounds the problem with cross-linguistic comparison. Berlin and Kay got around this difficulty to a great extent by working with native speakers where possible. By way of illustration, it is possible to look up the words for most colors in an English speaker's vocabulary in a Swahili dictionary. To know if what one finds there is a word for the color in Swahili one needs to know Swahili to be sure that the dictionary entry is not, for instance, a sentential explanation of what "green" means (or as we have seen the actual case to be) a word for something else (such as "leaves").

Still, it appears to be the case that world view is a matter more of linguistic relativity than linguistic determinism. Expanding on the idea of relativity, Roger Brown (1958:235–236), cognizant of Zipf's Law (or the Principle of Least Effort), observed (in English) that "the length of a word is negatively correlated with its frequency of usage": for example, *automobile* → *car*; *bicycle* → *bike*; *television* → *TV* or *tube*; *videocassette recorder* → *VCR*, and so forth.[2]

If a language has a proliferation of such (usually) short single words or abbreviations for items within a single domain (such as color, forms of transportation, kinds of entertainment), one would say of this domain that it represents an *available* perceptual category. The items within the domain representing its contents have *codability*. Some languages have more color words than others,

---

[2]   It appears to be the case that the process of lexical elaboration with regard to culturally salient items (in English at least) is one of going first from the long word, then to an acronym or abbreviation such as TV or VCR, and then to the short word which will often bear no phonetic resemblance to the long (input) form; hence television to tube through TV, and the like.

some more mode-of-transportation words than others, some more form-of-entertainment words. When labeled items within a domain are compared across languages, care must be taken to be sure the words themselves are in fact comparable. Do Eskimo languages actually have a vast number of separate words for "snow" or is there perhaps a particular root morpheme referring to "snow" which, in combination with various affixes, accounts for many different meanings? In English, one may discuss "powder snow" or "good snowball-making snow" by using other words to modify the noun in a larger noun phrase. Attention needs to be paid to what "counts" as a word from one language to another. The same problems we saw (in Chapter 3) as inherent in efforts to compare basic vocabulary across languages in the interest of lexicostatistics need to be addressed in research involved in cross-cultural comparisons of lexical organization even though the goals of the research are so different—language and culture history on the one hand and the relationship of cognitive organization (as evidenced by linguistic labels) to world view on the other.

In this section it remains to discuss one more pair of experiments focusing on the color lexicon and the Whorfian question.

Paul Kay and Willett Kempton (1987), in light of much of the research on color and world view and the growing support of the idea of linguistic relativity, sought to explain the persistence of Whorfian effects in the kinds of experiments being done. Working with speakers of English and Tarahumara (an Uto-Aztecan language of northern Mexico), they performed two experiments using eight color chips (representing two levels of brightness but all in the greenish blue/bluish green or "grue" perceptual range). Where English has the two terms "blue" and "green," Tarahumara makes no such lexical distinction but uses the single term *siyoname* for "green or blue" ("grue"). The researchers wanted to find out if the linguistic difference would produce a difference in what speakers of each language perceived to be the distance between colors. The Whorf Hypothesis predicts that color chips representing color near the green/blue boundary would be seen as "subjectively pushed apart" by English speakers while Tarahumara speakers "lacking this lexical distinction will show no comparable distortion" (1984:69). And this prediction is exactly what Kay and Kempton found to be the case. That is, English speakers exaggerated the difference in colors close to the boundary, saying that a color quite close to green is definitely blue and vice versa.[5]

However, Tarahumara speakers, though not labeling the colors as different, did judge two chips from the separate boundary areas labeled in English as more distant than two colors within, for example, the English blue zone. From this observation Kay and Kempton conclude that the categories labeled in English are covertly present in Tarahumara (and other languages). Covert categories are "out there," available yet of low codability. If the category is needed it will become highly codable and the language will come up with a "word" (or the equivalent) for it. In the case of color, universal available categories correspond to "the six categories of fundamental neural response" (see Kay and McDaniel 1978; De Valois and others 1966).

> Most languages that have a word "grue" and no separate words for "blue" and "green" nevertheless contain fixed or semifixed expressions such as "grue like the sky"/"grue like the leaves" that demonstrate that the concepts of "blue" and "green" are present even if not named at the level of basic color terms. (Kay and Kempton 1984:71)

The second experiment performed by Kay and Kempton was designed to block the use of what they refer to as a **name strategy** from influencing the way English-speaking subjects sorted the blue/green chips. In both experiments (the one with Tarahumara and English speakers, the other with English speakers only), subjects were to pick out "the most different chip from the three presented." In the second experiment subjects were asked to tell the researcher "which is bigger: the difference in greenness between the two chips on the left or the difference in blueness between the two chips on the right" (1984:73). The point of this wording was to ensure that subjects not ask themselves whether a particular chip "is called *green* or *blue*." In effect each subject has already assigned a label to each color by agreeing to compare one in *greenness* to another; another in *blueness*. By blocking the naming strategy in this way, Kay and Kempton were able to get at the actual perception of the colors (without linguistic interference). The results of this version of the two experiments were that the Whorfian effect of the first experiment disappeared. From this disappearance Kay and Kempton proposed name strategy as an explanation for the persistence of Whorfian effects in color-term research.

Essentially what the name strategy does is support the idea of linguistic relativity while not supporting the deterministic stance that language structure "imposes its categories as the only categories in which we can experience the world." By showing that the distortions in the judgments of English speakers found in the first experiment can be made to disappear if the name strategy is blocked, Kay and Kempton feel they have proven that "we are not at the mercy of our language" (1984:75). At the same time they feel they have vindicated a "kind of modest Whorfianism." That is, English and Tarahumara speakers do have a difference in nonlinguistic cognition (manifest in judgments of similarity and difference in color chips) correlated with differences in linguistic structure (Tarahumara speakers don't distinguish blue/green; English speakers do). Semantic differences and universal cognitive processes are not mutually exclusive.

4.1.2 Cognitive Anthropology

In the previous sections of this chapter we have discussed the idea that perceptions involve both linguistic labels and associated visual images and that which visual images are labeled in any one culture differ from culture to culture. Within the study of language and culture, interest in cognition ranges from what is most generally referred to as **cognitive science** or specifically **cognitive anthropology** to the study of language and the brain within the broader area of **psycholinguistics**. Cognitive anthropologists focus on the organization of aspects of language use as a reflection of how humans organize the way they think about the world. Indeed, as was noted above, the work of Paul Kay, Brent Berlin, and Willett Kempton represents cognitive anthropology as applied to questions of experimental psychological interest. In this section we will look at the field of cognitive anthropology in general as it has grown from an interest in the analysis of semantic domains such as color or kinship to encompass studies of thought processes.

The field of cognitive anthropology is a direct outgrowth of issues raised by the Whorf hypothesis. Early cognitive anthropology may be seen to fall into the general analytic approach known as **ethnoscience**. Ethnoscience shared a common goal with descriptive linguistics—the observationally adequate description of actual behavior. The subject matter, however, represented quite a departure from that of descriptive linguistics. Ethnoscience (also referred to as **ethnographic semantics** or **ethnosemantics**) was "the systematic study of the meanings of words and the role of these meanings in cognitive systems" (Kay 1969:2). Ethnoscientists developed methods they felt allowed them to get at the meanings of words and to determine how the meanings were tied together within *semantic domains* representing conceptual systems in particular languages.

The major technique of ethnoscience is **componential analysis** (or **formal semantic analysis**). The technique is applied to *semantic domains* or classes of objects "all of which share at least one feature in common which differentiates those objects from other *domains*" (Tyler 1969:8). A domain is commonly labeled by a term encompassing all the objects in it ("color," for example, is a domain label in English). To discover what objects make up a domain, the ethnoscientist attempts to elicit words that fill a blank as in "_____ is a kind of *color*" (or whatever domain label at issue). Above, we saw this as the data gathering procedure used in Berlin and Kay's (1967:69) study of basic color terms. Labeled objects in a domain are called **lexemes** (see Chapter 1); that is, they are minimal units of referential meaning in language. In the section below, where we talk about **semiotics** as an approach to the study of meaning, it will be seen that *lexeme* and *sign* are essentially the same concept; that is, a lexeme is both word (signifier) and a thing (what is signified). Words and things are unified by linguistic labels— lexemes. The way this is expressed in semiotic terms is that meaning is a tripartite relation among signs, signifiers, and what is signified.

A lexeme may be distinguished from a word in that the term *lexeme* encompasses the word and also its paradigm set (the usual other forms of the word such as its plural, its possessive, and so forth) (Greenberg 1968:58). For example, *mouse* is a lexeme encompassing the words *mouse, mice, mice's*. What is of interest to the ethnoscientist is the relationship lexemes have to each other within a domain (in the case of *mouse*, for example, a domain of interest to semantic analysis would be RODENT. Other members of this domain would be *bat*, *rat*, and the like).

Interestingly, ethnoscience essentially is a technique for analyzing relationships among objects and attributes ("things") lexically encoded in language. As such it tacitly assumes that meaning in language is a function of nouns (and adjectives) rather than of verbs. As a method, it has contributed little to the study of meaning outside of that which is overtly referential.

Ethnoscience is an outgrowth of descriptive linguistics in the interest of describing the next level of language above the sentence: **meaning**. The idea is that by comparing lexical items in a domain to each other it is possible to find out what the domain as a whole means. The meaning of a domain is the meaning of the total range of objects within it. Thus, "color" encompasses all the colors labeled in English, "rodent" refers to all the things we call by that term and by their own name. As we saw above, more recent work in cognitive anthropology includes not only labeled terms as constituting the meaning of a domain but also **covert categories** out there waiting for a label (such as "blue" and "green" in Tarahumara). That it is possible to think of a "rodent" for which we may not have a name—for example a 300-pound rat—indicates where there is a hole in the domain for a new label and its distinctive feature. Suppose bigger than usual rats did become common in our culture (and therefore salient), we would need a more efficient label than "giant rat" and would eventually assign it its own lexeme—perhaps "grat." The feature of [size] would distinguish it from all other objects in the domain, while the other features of *ratness* would group it with rats and separate it from bats and mice and their likes. As is indicated above, the more salient something is, the more likely it will be monolexemically encoded; other objects/attributes associated with a domain may require a phrase. This is the case with respect to nonbasic terms such as "light blue," "dusty rose," "giant rat," and other combinations of noun and modifier.

It was hoped that ethnoscientific analysis would allow semantic universals to emerge from the analyzed domains. The features of meaning discovered in the terminological sets (all the lexemes in a domain exclusive of the domain label) subjected to componential analysis were seen as steps toward an empirically based description of an assumed psychic unity of humankind.

Great care was taken to urge researchers to gather data in the language of the culture bearers whose semantic domains were at issue. The idea was that culturally significant cognitive features, as subsets of an assumed universal set of cognitive features, are coded in particular languages. To find out which ones are used in a particular culture, it is necessary to find the basis upon which people classify objects within domains. Translation into the language of the investigator would obscure distinctions salient in the other culture. In Chapter 3 we saw this observation with regard to body parts. The word in Swahili for "hand" is *mkono* and the word for "arm" is *mkono*. English has two words where Swahili has one—this fact would be missed if the data were translated into English, leading to an analysis indicating that Swahili either has no word for "hand" or no word for "arm"!

One ever-present problem in data gathering for ethnoscientific purposes is that of knowing whether or not a particular domain has been exhausted. That is, how does a researcher know that *all* the terms in a domain have been elicited? In general it is sufficient to be aware that there may be possible labeled entities out there, just as it is possible to be aware that there are covert categories waiting for a label, so long as common sense has been used to ascertain that data were gathered from representative members of the community reasonably familiar with the domain at issue. This caution is responsible for the color researchers we have discussed above being sure that the people they worked with were, as they put it, "color-normal" (Kay and Kempton 1984).

The focus of ethnoscience was on the internal structure of semantic domains. Domains may be analyzed in terms of the hierarchical arrangement of lexemes within them. The data (lexemes) are displayed on a *taxonomy* showing that at successively lower levels in the hierarchy lexemes are included in the meaning of lexemes at the higher levels. **Taxonomies** are hierarchical arrangements constructed by means of features of contrast and inclusion. The domain label is the uppermost category in a taxonomy for it includes all members. The hierarchy then successively sections the domain by means of contrast and inclusion into its members (objects, lexemes). In taxonomies, "categories at the same level contrast with one another while categories at lower levels are included in categories at higher levels. Categories at the same level differ from one another, but when included in the same higher level category are somehow like one another" (Tyler 1969:26).

Taxonomies may be represented either by branching diagrams or by matrices, as illustrated by Figure 3, an example of a partial taxonomy of the domain LIQUIDS (suggested by a figure in Rinnert 1979:286). The domain label LIQUIDS is opposed to that of SOLIDS, a subset of the larger domain food.

Figure 3. Branching Diagram, Partial Taxonomy

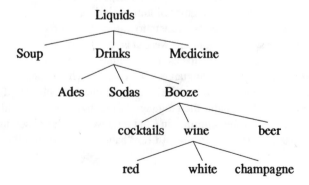

Table 5. Matrix

Liquids (Domain Label)

Soup	Drinks						Medicines
	Ades	Sodas	Booze				
			cocktails	wine		beer	
				red	white	cham- pagne		

Taxonomies are less powerful and less interesting for ethnoscientific data than other forms of data arrangement and analysis. In fact, the taxonomy of LIQUIDS is simply an arrangement of data and does not say anything about the basis for class inclusion other than the demonstrated subset/superset relations. We can tell from this what "liquids" are but not much about what "liquids" means.

At the outset of interest in cognitive anthropology, ethnoscientists seeking a form of semantic analysis to reveal more than contrast/inclusion relations among lexemes suggested that a better way might be to look as well at the features that intersect within a domain. The issue now was to consider, within the domain LIQUIDS, what features intersect at the spot where the lexeme "champagne" fits on the branching tree diagram. The intersecting features allow for the discovery of a description of the principles of organization of a domain.

In order to analyze a semantic domain in terms of intersecting features of opposition as well as contrast and inclusion, the data need to be arranged so that each node of a branching tree diagram represents one and only one lexeme. Such an arrangement is referred to as a *paradigm*. The lexemes at the nodes of the tree are seen as having their meaning in the intersection of features that come together— intersecting features are *semantic components*. Proponents of componential analysis see the results as indicative of how people think, perceiving the semantic features that emerge during analysis as "psychologically real."

The following branching tree diagram of the partial paradigm of liquids has each node (other than the uppermost of first node indicating the "root" of the domain) labeled by the feature that intersects at that node. That is, each node "represents a selection of a single feature from some particular dimension" and "each node corresponds to a lexeme" (Kay 1966:22). Such a labeled paradigm is called a *key* and as such represents the semantic structure of the domain. That is, we know from our componential analysis that the word "beer" in English has the following semantic components [+liquid], [+alcoholic]. We also know that "beer" is

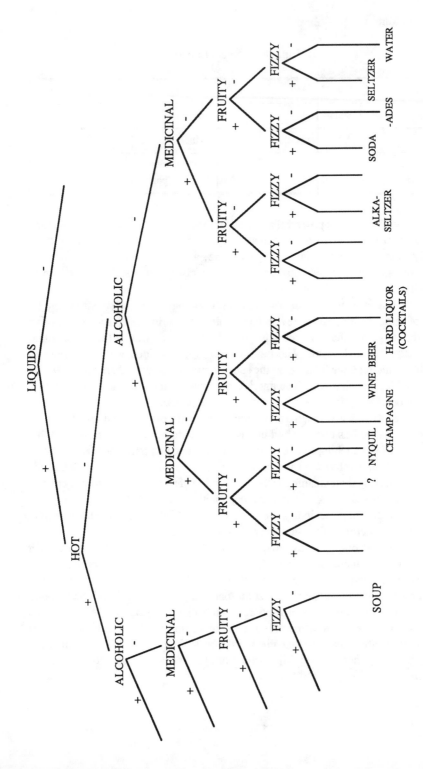

Figure 4. Partial Paradigm of Liquids

[−medicinal], [+fizzy] (it can "go flat"), and does not involve fruit. The fact that features such as [hot], [medicinal], [fizzy] (or [carbonated]), [fruity], and [alcoholic] emerge from the data indicates that these aspects of meaning are involved in the way English speakers see their world of drinkables. Yet where there is no label for a bundle of features such as [−hot], [+alcoholic], [+medicinal], [−fruity], and [+fizzy], one can imagine the likelihood of an Alka-Seltzer-type product on the market with alcohol added. Indeed, a likely label for such a liquid exists: "cold toddy" (on analogy with "hot toddy"). Such a bundle of features out there waiting for a label is an example of a covert category, as was discussed earlier.

Note that to distinguish "red" from "white" wine an additional feature [color] would be needed on a more complete paradigm, which would also distinguish "milk" from "water" and the like. Observe, too, that Americans these days commonly separate hard liquor (and "cocktails") from beer and wine. This partial paradigm does not allow for this distinction because there is no feature [hard] versus [soft] that is otherwise distinctive for potable liquids in this culture. Also, if [grape] were a feature, it would be significant on all nodes marked [+fruit] but meaningless on all others. Clearly, then, neither [grape] nor [hard] versus [soft] are distinctive in a LIQUID domain while [color] would be.

Recent work in cognitive anthropology has begun to pay attention to the fact that the features of meaning discovered through componential analysis or the inferences drawn on the basis of class inclusion may not necessarily be the basis upon which all speakers of a language make their distinctions. This is especially the case where it appears that class inclusion may be based on other relations. Rinnert observed that in English, at least, there are many kinds of "kinds of": "orange juice" is both a kind of "frozen food" and a kind of "canned food"; "juice" is a kind of "drink" within a larger encompassing "food" domain. Furthermore, *orange product* and *concentrate* are classifications for *orange juice* both otherwise not related to each other. People have different classification criteria for different aspects of a domain. Again using the "orange juice" example, Rinnert notes that there are aspects of production and selling that have meaning: we can get it in concentrate form, fresh, freshly squeezed, canned, or even mixed with other fruit ("cranorange"?). There are also aspects of packaging such as whether the liquid is in a bottle, a can, a cardboard container, or a cup that make differences in meaning. Notice that the feature of [±canned] is important when the classificatory criteria are mode of production, packaging, and selling (see Rinnert 1979:290). As D'Andrade (1976:167) has stated, "it seems likely that other kinds of relations manifest themselves as subset/superset relations" than those that result from formal semantic analysis.

Rinnert feels that these other relations need to be incorporated into the study of semantic organization along with the components that emerge in a componential analysis. She sees components as "values for dimensions that constitute some of these relations." Thus the component of [hot] versus [cold] separating "soup" from the general and medicinal drinks in the LIQUIDS domain above is in a dimension of what might be seen as a *feel* relation; the components [fruity] and [fizzy] and separating "champagne" and "wine" from "beer" are dimensions of what might be seen as an *ingredient* relation. Rinnert suggests that these relations might "in some way constitute the structure of the lexicon" (1979:294), urging that before their significance can be understood more research needs to be done to find out how they are used.

Cognitive anthropology, whether through componential analysis or taxonomies or the search for semantic relations, seeks to attain an emic goal for cultural description. The classification of terminological systems and the relations that exist among the components of meaning that structure a semantic domain are seen as means of investigating cognition. Critics of early ethnoscientific methodology faulted some of the early work for being preoccupied with discovery procedures and with assigning cognitive status to the resultant analyses. They were skeptical that semantic components extracted from a terminological set reveal distinctions in the mind of the native speaker. More recent efforts showing that components may answer just such questions show a sensitivity to these concerns. Cognitive anthropologists during the past fifteen years have turned somewhat from their belief that they are "discovering the cognitive systems of the people" to a more tempered interest in "showing how terms in language are applied to objects in the world." Their goal is neither to discover "psychological reality," (that is, to find what Burling has referred to as God's Truth) nor is it to come up with a set of procedures and rules that account for the data (Burling's idea of Hocus Pocus). Neither God's Truth nor Hocus Pocus are pursuits as worthy as that of showing how "terms in language are applied to objects in the world" (Burling, 1964:27).

This approach to cognitive anthropology has led in a number of directions. For example, D'Andrade (1976) studied American beliefs about illness. Using other methods of analysis, in a previous study (1972), he found that features found to define particular illnesses were *not* necessarily salient features to the people for whose culture the illnesses were a part. D'Andrade found that "consequences and preconditions of the illnesses rather than the features which were used to *define* them" (1976:161) formed the core of American beliefs. In order to understand this, he analyzed the "subset-superset relations" in the data on American beliefs "because other kinds of relations [as we saw just above] often manifest themselves as subset-superset relations." Such relations are determined from "a two-by-two table by the presence of one or more zero (or near zero) cells" (p. 162). Consider the example "Sign of Old Age/Catching."

For the 30 diseases D'Andrade was asking about none is both a "sign of old age" and "catching." This example represents what D'Andrade refers to as the relation of **contrast** "which is formally identical to the subset-superset relation in which

Sign of Old Age

		yes	no
Catching	yes	0	17
	no	7	6

diseases that have the property of being a 'sign of old age' are a subset of the diseases that do not have the property of being 'catching' " (p. 164). Among the diseases that are not contagious but are associated with aging are bronchitis and cancer; those that are not contagious and not associated with older people include appendicitis and malaria; the longest list encompasses the contagious diseases of young people, including syphilis, gonorrhea, and mononucleosis as well as whooping cough, chicken pox, and the other traditionally children's diseases. From knowing the relations that emerge through analysis, it is possible to "generate . . . large numbers of propositions about diseases" (p. 172). These propositions can be found in networks of subset relations that cluster around certain concepts. For example, "the subset relations between potentially 'catching' diseases, diseases which one can catch only 'once,' and the 'children's' diseases can be derived from a causal network that involves notions about how contagious infections can cause the production of various kinds of 'antibodies' which 'cure' the disease and result in more or less permanent 'immunity'" (p. 174).

The study by D'Andrade exemplifies the cognitive anthropological move away from reliance on the analysis of distinctive features (that is, on componential analysis) to include the study of **connotative features**, seen as attributes which are found in association with the members of a class, but which are not criteria for the definition of a class

> . . . what people know about cancer is not what defines a cell as cancerous, but rather that having cancer is often fatal and painful. If tomorrow a biologist discovers a serum that cures all cancers the defining features of cancer will not change. Such a discovery, however, would certainly change the way cancer is thought of, and that is what is culturally and socially, as well as psychologically, important. (D'Andrade 1976:177-178)

The shift in focus from distinctive to connotative features in the context of an emphasis on relations adds to cognitive anthropology a processual dimension that was not highlighted in early ethnoscience. As D'Andrade points out, however, some of the earlier work did investigate various types of relations.

The work of Spradley (1970) may be seen as looking into *part-whole* relations.

The object of his study was to determine the relationship between a group of men Spradley referred to as "urban nomads" and institutions of law enforcement and also to provide outsiders with an understanding of how these men see themselves (as part) in relation to the rest of culture (to whole). Spradley's method was to ask members of this population to name other kinds of *tramps* once the term *tramp* had emerged as the cover term for labels the men used for themselves. The data were arranged on a taxonomy and then the tramps were asked to choose which in sets of three items (the *triad* test again as discussed with reference to color terms above) was "the odd man out" in order to show what criterial attributes distinguish the different kinds of tramps. From these data he came up with a **componential definition** of *tramp* such that *mobility, mode of travel, home base,* and *livelihood* are the dimensions of contrast used by members of this particular subculture in relation to the larger society and to law-enforcement people in particular.

In a later section of this chapter, when we discuss the study of language and social identity, we will see that such approaches, which began in cognitive anthropology, have received much attention. This new processual or generative approach to the study of cognition in culture may also be seen in research that comes under the label of **planning** or **schemata** analysis. Agar (1986) points out that the terms *goal, frame, plan,* and *schema* are all in vogue at once to refer to attempts to understand how knowledge changes (p. 27). The idea is that when something goes wrong, an alternate plan or schema comes into effect to bring about resolution.

As cognitive anthropology, ethnoscience has evolved into the study of how people everywhere express their innermost thoughts, feelings, and states of mind. As such it is really the emic analysis of folk conceptual systems or folk models, where a folk model "is a cognitive schema which is intersubjectively shared by a social group" (D'Andrade 1983).

The ideas discussed in this section owe a debt to the work of Roger Schank and Robert Abelson. Their *Scripts, Plans, Goals, and Understanding* (1977) is a pioneering work from the perspective of seeing situational information as well as lexical/semantic information as cognitively processed. From their work and that of D'Andrade and others, a distinction may be made between scripts and schemata. A *schema* (pl. *schemata*) is a system of interrelated concepts which represent a mental model of something or a plan for it. Schemata are adaptive and processual, whereas *scripts* are prescriptive invariant forms of linguistic and cultural behavior. Efforts to deal with the cognitive process by which language adapts to situations come within the interests of research by cognitive psychologists interested in what they call **parallel distributive processing** (PDP). That is, the researchers want to know how both semantic and situational information are cognitively processed. Research into planning or schemata is an effort to answer that question.

Schemata are linked together by *inferences*—the "glue of coherence" that links pieces of knowledge together and to the world (Agar 1986:33). For the cognitive anthropologist, an interest in planning is seen as a way to find out how inferences are formed in the process of resolving breakdowns in ways of behaving.

> Thinking involves inferences, and an effective structure for making inferences requires at least the use of relations. Relations when applied to appropriate objects become decisions. Inferences occur when a decision is made about the truth of a proposition based upon what is believed about the truth or falsity of other propositions. (D'Andrade 1976:179)

D'Andrade looks forward to the possibility one day of a universal typology of relations (1976:179). The work of Robert Randall will provide a useful example of this mode of cognitive anthropological research.

Randall's hypothesis is that "daily activities are integrated into and controlled by more abstract and complex long range plans" (Randall 1987:39). Building on ideas that have liberated cognitive anthropology from the mechanical analysis of reference to a focus on relations, Randall's work and that of others as well has shown that routine sequences of "hundreds of activities and activity alternatives" (p. 40) are part of the thoughts and beliefs (system of cultural knowledge) of members of different cultures. Once it became clear that componential analysis cannot account for situational elements that figure in labeling, interest shifted from the "attributes of meaning" (of an address term, for instance) to "plans for selecting an address term" (see Geohegan 1966; 1971).

This new research moved cognitive anthropological approaches to formal semantic analysis beyond the usual delimitable domains such as color and kinship, firewood or disease terms, to an interest in the *actions* lexemes are involved in—particularly in the rules or inferences that guide routine activities. Routine actions that people do (such as fishing in fishing communities, making coffee every morning in the United States) are determined both by the way people understand the meaning of lexemes involved and by aspects of the situation in which the lexemes (as bundles of semantic features) are manipulated.

The logic here, the reader may have noticed, is similar to that which gave rise to early forms of generative grammar, especially Phrase Structure Grammar. In Chapter 2 we saw how anthropologists applied the idea of an underlying set of rules generating a number of grammatical sentences to an account of acceptable forms of household composition (Burling 1969). From the perspective of planning research, this same general approach may be seen in the concept of the *routine plan* or *routine action plan*. Certain conditions are stated that determine the selection of a particular alternative.

Initially, this type of research was applied primarily to residence selection (see Geohegan 1969, 1971a) and address-term selection (see Ervin-Tripp 1972) gradually branching out to encompass a wider range of tasks in areas such as agricultural decision making (see Gladwin 1976). Proponents of action-plan analysis claim 90-percent accuracy of their predictions of alternatives in a routine. A routine plan is made up of sequences of categories or goals—". . . a large hierarchical structure which partitions a very long sequence of motor activities into shorter sequences of more abstract categories" (Randall 1987:43). Associated with each goal is a "routine for selecting among activities which could realize the goal" (Randall 1987:43).

Routines not only follow a fixed sequence of actions but also are sensitive to situational variables. Indeed, in response to situational variables, fixed sequences may have certain of their elements rearranged, deleted, or replaced by substitutes and new variables may be added to a sequence. That is, exceptions to routine activity bring about *transformations* in the interest of being sure that the goal is attained. Another notion which plays a part in planning research is that of *markedness*. We saw earlier that *unmarked* terms are the usual or more commonplace in a pair. Geohegan (1973) saw that marking is not only a linguistic process but also a cognitive process that likewise figures in plans—we "mark" or notice the unusual and take steps to transform the unusual to the usual. As Randall reports,

> Philippine fishermen, for example, usually head for Sapan Shoal *unless* "word strikes" that "the scad are really biting at the Little Island"; and they usually buy number 24 hooks *unless* they "happen to hear" there are number 25 hooks in stock. (1987:48)

Interestingly, it appears, gossip has a marking function in language; it renders the unnoticed noticed. Again, as generative linguists have proposed for language, plans are seen as composed of obligatory, optional, and preference rules. As planning research has begun to reveal the interactive linguistic and cognitive processes that enter into tasks such as "nail hammering, chess playing, address terminology, or restaurant eating," the need for incorporating the "full hierarchy of goals people actually use" (Randall 1987:57) has become increasingly apparent. The question is one of integrating increasingly larger hunks of linguistic knowledge and cultural knowledge (see Keesing 1980) into plans so each sequence of behavior fits into the "full hierarchical structure" of behavior in the culture.

To illustrate what a routine action plan might involve, an example suggested by Eugene Hunn (personal communication) seems appropriate. Americans routinely (habitually) make coffee every morning and if asked what they did might find it difficult to say exactly. Yet it may well be that Americans share a schema for morning coffee making that well exemplifies the interaction of linguistic and cultural (contextual) factors. The "usual" sequence of activity may be to get out the coffee pot (type of coffee maker represents one set of choices made right at the outset from the semantic domain COFFEE POT in English). Choice of pot type determines the next step in the routine (indeed pot and coffee type need to be correlated for most Americans). If the pot of choice is "Mr. Coffee," for example, then filters are required as well as a fine grind of coffee and the whole business needs to be in the vicinity of both a water supply and an electricity outlet. Some exacting coffee drinkers may also need to grind their own beans, doing which would then set a whole subroutine into motion. If, during the night, an electrical storm happened to interrupt the electricity usually available, it may not even be until the brewing stage that this has been noticed at which point some behavior needs to be substituted for the usual. The lack of electricity is a marked feature (the usual mode is [+electricity]) and other alternatives need to be substituted for the goal to be attained. Alternatives available are many and far ranging—going to work without coffee, finding the old nonelectric coffee maker and starting over, getting coffee at McDonald's, and so forth. Had all gone well and the electricity remained unmarked (that is, "on" not "off"), the entire coffeemaking procedure (like toothbrushing and other such routines) would have been accomplished without a hitch—automatically. The analysis of the patterned ways in which linguistic and cultural knowledge are manifest in behavior are seen by cognitive anthropologists as a way of understanding how goals (intentions) as an aspect of cognition are organized and conceptualized (Randall 1987:71).

4.1.3 Language and the Brain

As we saw in Chapter 2, generative linguistics has taken off in a philosophical direction seeing language as just one cognitive ability manifest by the mind. In this section we will take a brief look at efforts to see how language relates directly to the brain and at efforts on the part of linguists to discover the structure of the lexicon as part of the semantic component of the theory of Language.

In the previous section, the research discussed on planning and on schema theory by cognitive anthropologists is similar to the kind of research psycholinguists do. That is, cognitive anthropologists look at language and culture, psycholinguists look solely at language, but both are concerned with developing processing models. In fact, in this book, no separate section is devoted to psycholinguistics as such since much of the kind of research done overlaps that in cognitive anthropology. Indeed, in both cognitive anthropology and psycholinguistics much interest is also taken in the acquisition of language and culture—specifically in the development of language or speech and plans in children. In our discussion earlier of color-term research we saw that some of the differences in observed behavior surrounding certain tasks appeared to be a function of age. Both psycholinguistics and cognitive anthropology are concerned ultimately with arriving at a theory of performance, that is, of how linguistic and cultural knowledge is processed and understood as well as acquired—"encoded . . . decoded, produced, and understood" (De Vito 1971:4).

Above, in our discussion of schema, we saw that cognitive processing is increasingly of interest to language and culture research. We also saw that one of the best ways to find out how a routine unites linguistic and cultural knowledge is to notice what happens when the routine goes wrong. Similarly, much of what is known about language and the brain comes from studies of **aphasia**, the general term used to refer to problems manifest in people's ability to communicate with language. The relationship of speech and language deficits to brain damage is of concern to scholars in the field of **neurolinguistics**. Neurolinguists are interested in where language is in the brain, how speech and language are encoded and decoded by the nervous system, and whether or not the components of language (phonology, syntax, semantics) are separate in the brain (Akmajian, Demers, and Harnish 1985:494).

As Fromkin noted, aphasia data provide support "for the components, structure, units, and rules posited by linguists." The interest of linguists in aphasia is not so much in where impairments show language components to be (in Broca's or Wernicke's area of the brain, or the like) but in the idea that

> . . . if, in the abnormal brain, we find differential impairments to different parts of language or components of the grammar, then such independent parts must exist in the normal intact brain and grammar. (Fromkin 1987:5)

The finding of correlations between the brain and language would move us in the direction of understanding the biological basis of the theory of Language. It is Fromkin's view that there is evidence from available data on aphasia which contributes to an understanding of the structure of the lexicon as a component of grammar. As we saw in Chapter 2, the lexicon is increasingly being seen as a necessary component of a grammar in the most recent versions of generative grammar (lexical-functional grammar, LFG; generalized phrase-structure grammar, GPSG; and government binding models for example). From the outset, cognitive anthropology has seen the lexicon as of prime importance (through formal semantic analysis of lexemes). Nonetheless "large gaps remain in our understanding of the lexicon that is accessed in speech production and comprehension" (Fromkin 1987:7). By working with people with *acquired dyslexia* (that is, people whose reading and writing ability was affected following a brain injury while their speech and comprehension remained intact), Fromkin was able to show that "for normals, each sublexicon is connected to the others" while for persons with various forms of acquired dyslexia certain parts of the lexicon have suffered pathway disruption.

A literate person who is not brain injured, hearing the word *cape*, can say what it means, write it, pronounce it from its spelling, or tell someone what it means without pronouncing it. A performance model of the lexicon, then, may be seen as a process model such that there is a set of grapheme-to-phoneme rules (where we get from spelling to pronunciation), and three sublexicons: orthographic, phonological, and semantic. Each sublexicon is connected to the other and has access to the grapheme-to-phoneme rule component as well unless there has been brain injury. By blocking various pathways, Fromkin is able to account for various forms of acquired dyslexia that lend support for "the modularity concept within the grammar and within the mind." That is, it appears to be the case, at least with regard to the lexicon, that the structure of grammar (as a theory of Language) is in accord with the structure of the mind.

What Fromkin found was that in the case of **deep dyslexia**, "there is no pathway between the orthographic and the phonological lexicons" (p. 19) nor is there access to the grapheme-to-phoneme rules. Deep dyslexics make semantic substitution errors. That is, they will read *bun* as *cake, oz.* as *pound* instead of *ounce*, *XII* (the Roman numeral for 12) as *B.C.* (Before Christ), or *etc.* as *and sons limited* (p. 9). Interestingly, the substitutions are semantically related to what is read—what is manifest is a kind of "right church, wrong pew" phenomenon. The deep dyslexics know what they've read but they can't get the spelling related to the sound.

Phonological dyslexia patients can get pronunciation from spelling but do not get the meaning. There is no pathway to the semantic sublexicon nor is there access to grapheme-to-phoneme rules. Neither deep nor phonological dyslexic patients can read nonwords. Phonological dyslexia results in being able to read but not to know what any of the reading matter means.

Fromkin's model also accounts for **surface dyslexia**, in which one is unable to pronounce a word from its spelling and uses a different set of grapheme-to-phoneme rules. Surface-dyslexia patients pronounce every letter they read and can get the meaning of a word only from its pronunciation. Thus, if a word does not sound the way it is spelled, it will be missed by such a person. Thus *begin* may be read /bɛgɪn/ "beggin" and understood as "That's collecting money" (1987:14).

The central nervous system involves both the brain and spinal cord and is thought to be hierarchically organized with the highest level, the cerebral hemispheres, "responsible for voluntary activity" (Akmajian, Demers, and Harnish 1985:498). These two hemispheres have areas which serve specific functions yet can communicate with each other across the *corpus callosum*. This need to communicate from hemisphere to hemisphere derives from the fact that if, for example, an object is held in one's left hand, it is recognized in the right hemisphere but can be verbalized only in the left hemisphere. The left hand tells the right hemisphere what it is and the right hemisphere tells the left hemisphere how to say it. Indeed, the left brain is seen as the locus of language.

Most of what is known about the different areas of the brain stems from what has been learned from classifications of the various forms of aphasia. For example, Broca's aphasia is at the frontal or anterior part of the left hemisphere and affects the fluency of speech—function words like *the, but*, and grammatical morphemes may be missing. There are questions regarding whether the syntactic as well as phonological component of grammar is involved here (Akmajian, Demers, and Harnish 1985:510). Wernicke's aphasia affects the back or posterior part of the left hemisphere and people who have it cannot understand language though they can pronounce well. It is thought that Wernicke's aphasia affects the semantic and syntactic components of grammar.

It is not our purpose here to go into much detail about language and the brain beyond indicating that the suggestions of cognitive processual models to account for language and culture are seen as directly related to efforts to study the way the brain works. Efforts to relate anatomical differences and differences in "human ideation and behavior" are increasing (Sanches 1978-1979:35).

For such efforts to make sense they need to hold cross-culturally.[3] Sanches has found evidence that culture (defined as "meaning systems") (p. 37) has an effect on which hemisphere handles the same processing input. That is, different cultural traditions accord the same information different interpretations "which will then be handled by that hemisphere which is best suited to that kind of information processing" (pp. 37-38). One's first language influences which hemisphere processes what particular information. What Sanches did was look at a number of studies that seem to indicate that the Japanese brain is lateralized differently for language, leading to statements such as "Consonants and steady-state vowel sounds, shown by experiment to be processed in the right hemisphere for English speakers, are, for Japanese speakers, mainly processed in the dominant (that is, the left) hemisphere (Tsunoda 1971, 1972, and 1973)" (Sanches 1978-1979:38).

Instead of concluding that the Japanese and English brains are different, Sanches hypothesized instead that Japanese speakers process both linguistic and nonlinguistic information in the left hemisphere as communicative or meaningful information. English speakers, in contrast, distinguish linguistic from nonlinguistic communicative information. That is, English speakers, unlike Japanese, do not perceive "insect cries, traditional Japanese music, vowel formants, humming, snoring, animal sounds, etc. . . . as having anything to do with their communication-act meanings" (pp. 41-42). Sanches studied five children learning Japanese as a first language and found that the first syntactic-semantic relation acquired is of the structure [ideophone] + [signaller] rather than the [agent + action/object] or similar structure acquired by English children. That is, Japanese children's first "two-word" utterances are of the form "bow-wow/goes" rather than of the "doggie/food" variety. Further, she found that the earliest "words" of Japanese children are

---

[3]   Sanches (1978-1979) feels, too, that anatomical associations with information-processing functions need to be seen as "analogous to similar functioning in other mammals, especially the primates" (p. 37) as well. The question of animal communication as related to the study of language and culture is generally outside the scope of this work but will be addressed in brief in the last section of this chapter.

onomatopoeic sound/symbolic representations, including "encodings of the sounds of insects and animal cries, as well as those of inanimate things like bells, trains, radio static, horns, and noises of things breaking" (p. 44). Furthermore, Sanches found that Japanese children early on also acquire a "quotive" grammatical form allowing them to report on communication events that have taken place for which there is no English equivalent. Finally, she reports that Japanese parental "baby talk" encourages the encoding and reporting (quoting) of "idiophonic and onomatopoeic representations of the environment." These findings lead her to suggest that since English- and European-language speakers do not incorporate "animal cries and insect sounds" as communication acts, they do not lateralize them in their language-dominant hemisphere whereas Japanese speakers do p. 46).

Clearly the area of language (and culture) and the brain is in the midst of exciting new discoveries that will benefit from linguistic and anthropological input as well as from the continuing research in neuro- and psycholinguistics.

4.2 Language, Thought, and Reality

It remains in this chapter to look at other ways scholars of language and culture envision the relationship between language and thought in context. The study of language, thought, and context (reality) will be seen to be of concern in the fields of *pragmatics, semiotics*, and the study of *social identity*. We will also take a brief look at the relationship between language and nonverbal communication, distinguishing language as a human attribute tied to both thought and reality (the environment constructed socially and culturally) from forms of animal communication. Our discussion will center on American Sign Language as human language in contrast to animal communication as representing nonhuman aspects of intelligence. Humans and animals will be seen as sharing the ability to communicate nonverbally but not the ability to "language" either verbally or nonverbally; this difference may account for why humans have culture and animals do not, though both interact communicatively with their environment.

4.2.1 Discourse, Pragmatics, and Sem(e)iotic(s)

When linguists talk about meaning, they do so generally from the perspective of the sentence or proposition. They look at how the structures of language (*langue*) are imbued with sense and reference by the mind through semantics. Essentially the linguistic view of meaning is that it is that part of linguistic knowledge or competence through which interpretation of structure is accomplished. Meaning in this linguistic sense represents

> those moments of an utterance which *can be repeated* and yet *remain identical to themselves*. Meaning actually signifies nothing except for the potentiality, the possibility of meaning within a concrete theme [discourse]. (Bakhtin, cited in Todorov

1981:168 and in Farris 1988:25)

For the study of language and culture, what is of interest instead is the kind of meaning that is "inherent in discourse" (Farris 1988:25), which "arises from the interaction of meaning with the equally unique context of the speech-act" (Todorov 1981:168). As Ricoeur (1979:75) has stated it, "whereas the signs in language only refer to other signs within the same system . . . discourse is always about something. . . . It is in discourse that the symbolic function of language is actualized."

> No member of the verbal community will ever discover any words in language which are totally neutral, devoid of another's aspirations and evaluations, or free of another's voice. . . . A word reaches one context in terms of another context, penetrated by the intentions of another; its own intentionality encounters a word which is already inhabited. (Bakhtin in Todorov 1981:170)

In this section, we will see how ideas from both linguistics and symbolic anthropology (as discussed in Chapter 2) combine in the study of meaning in context—an especially vibrant area of interest in recent work on language and culture. In general the unit of analysis is **discourse**, the approach is a *pragmatic* one, and the understanding arrived at is *sem(e)iotic*.

Sherzer (1987) proposed what he calls "A Discourse-Centered Approach to Language and Culture." Sherzer's view is that discourse is the pre-eminent expression of the way in which language and culture interrelate. "It is discourse that creates, recreates, focuses, modifies, and transmits both culture and language and their intersection" (p. 295). The ways in which discourse creates a particular language and culture are many, ranging from poetry to politics. Discourse uses both grammar and cultural symbols as the tools for setting up a language-culture link within a society.

To Sherzer, culture is "patterned organizations of, perceptions of, and beliefs about the world in symbolic terms." As such, culture can be manifest in individuals though it is generally shared within groups, that is, within society. Society, then, "is the organization of individuals into groups of various kinds, . . . that share rules for the production and interpretation of cultural behavior." Language both represents one's "symbolic organization of the world" and reflects/expresses "group memberships and relationships" (p. 296).

By seeing discourse (utterances constituting a spoken monologue, a conversation, or a written text) as the unit of analysis, Sherzer is able to make the point that the issue surrounding the Whorf hypothesis is not one of whether language determines/reflects thought or thought determines/reflects language in any way. What is at issue, instead, is the analysis of discourse as "the embodiment of the essence of culture and as constitutive of what the language-culture-society relationship is all about" (p. 297).

To make his point, Sherzer argues for example that the grammatical category of *position* in Kuna (the language of the Kuna Indians of Panama) serves as a resource or "potential" that the language may call upon to conceive of and perceive the world. As a grammatical category, *position* in Kuna expresses body position in relation to ongoing action: there are verbal suffixes for (1) standing, in a vertical position; (2) lying, in a horizontal position; (3) sitting; or (4) perching in a hanging position. When a verb is used with one of these four positional suffixes the verb is marked for position. For example, Sherzer notes, if someone falls asleep in public on a bench this might be remarked upon using the usual verb for "sleep" with the "sitting" positional suffix added to it to convey the idea that the way in which the person is sleeping is particularly noticeable. In Kuna, positional suffixes become particularly salient in magical formulas and in politics. In a speech during the inauguration of a new chief, the chief is spoken of in such a way that all of the positional categories are used as metonyms (substitutes) extending the meaning of the verb "sit" to characterize him above and beyond the ordinary people for whom the unmarked form of the verb will do.

> Chiefs are *-nai* (hanging) because they are perched in their hammocks in the center of the gathering house when they chant myths in public performances, or *-mai* (lying) because they rest or even sleep in these same hammocks while other chiefs are chanting or at various times during the day. Chiefs' spokesmen are *-kwici* (standing) because they stand when making speeches in the gathering house or *-sii* (sitting) because they sit on special benches surrounding the chiefs. And ordinary villagers are *-sii* because they sit on ordinary benches behind both chiefs and spokesmen. (Sherzer 1987:299)

The positional suffixes provided by Kuna grammar take on social significance when they are manipulated symbolically in culturally significant contexts. This same category is manipulated in a Kuna snake-raising chant where there is a shift from *-mai* (lying) to *-nai* (perched) during the climactic lines. The suffixes are semantically ordered with respect to one another such that *-nai* is stronger than *-mai* in this case and with regard to the inaugural speech perching ranks over lying, which has higher status than standing and anyone and everyone "sits."

In the Bhojpuri language of northern India there is a grammatical form referred to as the *echo word construction*, in which lexical items are reduplicated to express an extended meaning of ". . . and the like." For example the word *dudh* is "milk" so *dudh-udh* is "dairy products." What is interesting is why "milk" is selected as the word to be reduplicated so as to refer to the entire semantic field of "dairy products" instead of perhaps the word for "butter" or "cream" or "buttermilk" or "curd." It turns out that lexical items in a semantic field (domain) are hierarchically ordered and that the ordering affects which is chosen for reduplication (echoing) to typify the set. The ordered rank depends upon socioeconomic factors involving speaker and addressee.

> If the addressee is of the lower income class, it is appropriate to select *maTha-o Tha* (buttermilk and the like), since buttermilk is used by those who cannot afford other dairy products. On the other hand, forms such as *dudh-udh* (milk and the like) or *dehi-ohi* (curd and the like) are appropriate for individuals of means, who can afford these items. (Sherzer 1987:300, citing Tiwari 1968)

This example, according to Sherzer, is a clear indication "that language does not reflect culture but that language use in discourse, creates, recreates and modifies culture" (p. 300). In social situations such as at the market there ensues a bargaining not only of price but also with regard to status and role. To buy milk, both buyer and seller negotiate their respective roles using language (what each respectively calls "dairy products") as well as price. A buyer wanting to pay a low price will call dairy products by the "buttermilk and the like" term rather than the "milk and the like" form. In the following section we will see how discourse situations such as bargaining, market encounters, and ordinary conversations in various settings are used specifically in the interest of establishing social identity.

To Sherzer, *discourse structuring* is "the locus of the language-culture relationship." Grammar provides potentials that are "actualized in discourse" to realize a particular group's *cultural logic* (pp. 305–306).

To see how discourse operates, the tool of *pragmatics* is seen by many to be useful. Pragmatics is concerned with how discourse is constructed and how prior and subsequent discourse is built in. Scholars look at **speech acts**, choice of *topics*, rules for *turn-taking* and the like (Schieffelin and Ochs 1986a:168). Michael Silverstein proposed a pragmatic analysis of speech behavior as a way to describe "the real linkage of language to culture, and perhaps the most important aspect of the 'meaning' of speech" (1976:12).

We saw just above that meaning is thought to derive from discourse and that discourse, for many scholars of language and culture, has become the unit of analysis of meaning. Meaning is located in what scholars refer to as *speech acts*. Speech acts are the things we do with utterances such as promise, bargain, inaugurate chiefs, warn, curse. Whether or not a particular chunk of speech is interpreted as a promise, an attempt to bargain, a curse, a warning, or whatever depends on how the context of the utterance influences it. As Fromkin and Rodman have stated it, "the general study of how context influences the way we interpret sentences" is called *pragmatics*. To Silverstein (1976:20), pragmatics is "the study of the meaning of linguistic signs relative to their communicative functions. The theory of speech acts is part of pragmatics and pragmatics itself is part of . . .

performance." Pragmatics "includes how language users apply knowledge of the world to interpret utterances" (Fromkin and Rodman 1983:189).

Here we will briefly discuss the way scholars are beginning to incorporate the world into the study of discourse through pragmatics. To illustrate what is meant by pragmatics, it is useful to consider ways in which people make assumptions about language use based on context. For example, language users make use of certain **presuppositions** when they participate in discourse. In the question "Would you like another beer?" (Fromkin and Rodman 1983:190), the questioner is implying that you've already had at least one beer. The word *another* has this presuppositional pragmatic information as part of its meaning. In addition to such presuppositions embodied in language use, there are also cases of reference or **deixis** with built-in presuppositions. In English there are **deictics** of person, time and place which, when used, embody implications about the world. For a hearer to know who is being talked about it is necessary to know what referential connection "he," "she," and "it" have in the real world when those pronouns are heard in conversation. Similarly, the words "now" and "then" presuppose that the hearer knows when the utterances that the words are in were said. If you read the phrase "this big city" it doesn't mean anything unless you are reading "its" newspaper or the author has mentioned the setting earlier.

Scholars interested in the study of discourse feel that pragmatic knowledge needs to be understood just as much as linguistic competence does if we are ever to understand the way language and culture intersect. In order to do this Silverstein suggests that we distinguish **referential** from **nonreferential** signs. Recall that a linguistic sign is a lexical unit consisting of a **signifier** and what it **signifies** (Saussure 1916, 1966). Pragmatic analysis is based on the assumption that knowledge of the world rests on the triadic (three-way) relationship of sign, signifier, and signified.

In the example above concerning the way positional suffixes in Kuna mean in a cultural context, each suffix is simultaneously a sign as it exists formally (*-mai*), a signifier as it means grammatically and referentially ("lying"), and also what is signified—that is, it also means what it conveys culturally (less than *-nai* but more than *-sii*, or the like). Pragmatic analysis seeks to describe the total meaning of linguistic signs, not just the sign/signifier relations that have occupied most forms of linguistic analysis. To get at what is signified, attention needs to be paid to the nonreferential aspects of a sign's meaning, that is, to its function.

Furthermore, there are certain forms in language whose meaning is both referential and nonreferential. That is, what these **signs** refer to in the real world, what they **index** or point to, **shifts**. What such a duplex sign means depends on pragmatic information. For example, the grammatical category "tense" is a shifter in English; in Kuna, "positionals" are shifters—their meaning derives from what we know about the situation and the particular verb to which they are attached.

Similarly, terms with built-in presuppositions—such as the deictics discussed above and words like "another"—are shifters. In order to understand discourse, rules of use for shifters are necessary just as rules of grammar are necessary if we are to understand just their **semantico-referential** meaning.

In addition to signs that have traditional semantico-referential meaning and signs with indexes that shift, languages also make use of signs that have nonreferential indexes. That is, what the signs refer to is purely an aspect of the speech context (Silverstein 1976:30). In the Koasati language (a Muskogean language of southeastern United States), for example, a verb suffix -*s* marked every utterance spoken by "a socially female individual" unless the speaker was quoting someone else. That is, the suffix has no other meaning in the language than to mark the sex-role of the speaker. Accordingly, men playing women would need to use it to mean the same thing they would mean speaking as men. The suffix conveys the pragmatic information that for purposes of the social situation the speaker is female (Silverstein 1976:30, citing Haas 1944).

Pragmatically, referential indexes, nonreferential indexes, and shifters work together in language constituting discourse *creatively* or *performatively* (Silverstein 1976:34). In English, personal pronouns demarcate the participants in a speech event. In languages with "extra" pronouns such as familiar versus formal second-person pronouns (like French *tu* vs. *vous*) the boundaries between participants are even more complex.

> Social indexes such as deference vocabularies and constructions . . . are examples of maximally creative or performative devices, which, by their very use, make the social parameters of speaker and hearer explicit. Adherence to the norms specified by rules of use reinforces the perceived social relations of speaker and hearer; violations constitute a powerful rebuff or insult or go into the creation of irony and humor. (1976:34–35)

In Chapter 2 above, when we discussed the work of Grice and the idea of presuppositions or implicature figuring into conversation, the kind of performance violations resulting in insults, irony, and humor that Silverstein is talking about here were seen. Whereas Grice is concerned with the *flouting* of conversational maxims from the perspective of discourse strategy, Silverstein is interested in the way in which discourse is created via the language/culture interface.

Indeed, Silverstein sees a continuum of discourse creativity ranging from the extreme presuppositionality of deixis to the more openly creative use of "subtle social indexes." It is his view that the indexical mode of meaningfulness is what links language "to the wider system of social life" (53). His pragmatic perspective on language and culture derives from the approach to meaning known as *semiotics* (*semeiotic*) as developed by Charles Peirce.

Where structuralism (see Chapter 2) looked at the world in terms of binary oppositions and their relationships ([tense] vs. [lax]; [male] vs. [female]) semiotics (from the word *seme* meaning "meaning"; compare "semantics") is an approach to the world based on tertiary relations. We've been talking about the sign, the signifier, and the signified. These three modes of the sign fit into a larger triad—the **icon,** the **index,** and the **symbol** as "modes of meaningfulness" versus modes of reference. Silverstein's pragmatic approach suggests that the language/culture link is an indexical matter. To Silverstein, what linguists have hitherto not known about language is culture, and culture is pragmatic. By plugging culture into language, knowledge of the combined "iconic and indexical modes of meaning" may be arrived at, leading ultimately to an understanding of language's unique symbolic mode and to **cultural description** "as a massive multiply pragmatic description of how the social categories of groups of people are constituted in a criss-crossing, frequently contradictory, ambiguous, and confusing set of pragmatic meanings of many kinds of behavior" (p. 54).

In the sense of the term as it is used by the pragmatically, semiotically, discourse-oriented scholars discussed in this section, culture is a system of knowledge, not a system of behavior. Culture in this sense is also necessary if language is to be used. Keesing (1979) cites the case of Kwaio speakers, for whom an understanding of the Kwaio universe is necessary before those speakers can use that language's semantic system. The Kwaio live in the interior of Malaita Island in the Solomon Islands and their world is so organized that humans live in the **phenomenal** or physical world while ancestors are in the **noumenal** or spiritual realm. It makes a difference in the language whether the agent/actor in an utterance is human or ancestor. A verb will have one meaning if its subject is human, another if its subject is an ancestor. Similarly, Keesing found magical/nonmagical actions plus a number of oppositions among terms paralleling the ancestor/human division.

Keesing agrees with Silverstein that the "indexical (situational context-dependent) aspects of meaning" need to be considered in studies of language and culture—what native speakers "take for granted" when they use language needs to be heeded. Keesing feels that "ethnographies of cultural knowledge and linguistic grammars" need to be seen as complementary aspects of a single enterprise. To understand what a Kwaio verb means to Kwaio people, one needs an understanding of their symbolic structures and religious premises. Where lexical representations handle what a word refers to, critical evocations are missing. To bring the point closer to home for English speakers, Keesing notes that

> It may be true that the word "marshmallow" conjures up to some . . . childhood memories of campfires and roasting charred, melting objects on sticks. But such evocations, and whether for particular speakers they happen to be associated with falling in love or a tyrannical Cub Scoutmaster, are irrelevant to the analysis of English. (1979:18)

Such evocations, however, are not irrelevant to the analysis of the language and culture of English speakers.

4.2.2 Language, Nonverbal Communication, and Culture

In the preceding sections of this chapter we have been talking about the various ways language and culture are linked. In particular, we have examined issues of world view and discourse. In this final section we will briefly address questions that may have come to mind as you have read this far. One question has to do with whether or not animals other than *H. sapiens* have language and the consequences of the answer. The other issue is that of nonverbal communication, particularly *sign language*. People who do not have the sense of hearing are able to communicate using various forms of sign language; animals are also reported to be able to use forms of sign language. Does this ability mean that both humans and animals have *linguistic competence*? And, as follows from this, does it mean that animal and human intelligence are somehow the same? We will discuss animal communication first and then nonverbal communication in general, taking up American Sign Language, the issue of its linguistic status, and the question of animal versus human *intelligence*.

The line of argument in the previous chapters suggesting that for humans, language and culture are inextricably bound together (at least from the research perspectives addressed by anthropological linguists and by language and culture scholars) would lead us to conclude that if animals have language, then they also have culture.

4.2.2.1 Animal Communication

It is beyond the scope of this present work to go into much detail with regard to the various arguments and research efforts that attempt to prove/disprove whether animals have language. That they can and in fact do communicate seems now to have become a matter of some agreement. The behavior is clear to anyone who has a pet dog or cat. Such pets communicate with us and we with them. It is also clear that animals do not talk like humans do—anatomy and physiology have quite a bit to do with that. A number of researchers, however, have shown that despite the fact that birds, monkeys, gorillas, or bees do not have the human vocal apparatus they do get messages across to each other. Chimpanzees, gorillas, dolphins, and monkeys of various types not only communicate with each other but use various systems of nonverbal communication to talk to their human teachers (see for example, Rose 1984).

In the previous pages we have been discussing language as *speech*, as *structure* underlying speech in speech communities, as *cognitive ability*, and, in combination with culture, as *discourse*. So far we have not looked at it as a form of communication. If language is defined solely as a system of communication then obviously many species communicate. Indeed, humans use language as just one mode of communication. Like animals, humans use cries, grunts, and the like for certain purposes. Humans also gesture, smell, make faces, and use various sensory modalities for specific purposes.

The question, many scholars think, comes down to "whether other creatures share with humans the ability to learn and use languages creatively" (Fromkin and Rodman 1983:348). Do animals "string together *discrete units* to form an *infinite* set of 'well formed' novel sentences?" Also, if animals have language, why do they have to be taught to use it? One further question, asked less often, is: If animals have language why don't they use it with each other instead of waiting until humans teach them to manifest this ability?

When we define language as a *system of communication* we admit the possibility of other than linguistic *signs* as units of communicative behavior. Such a view broadens the scope of the signaling (or *semeiotic*) system being examined. Just as we saw the admission of context as a variable in the study of language and culture to broaden the scope of *semeiotic* (or) signaling analysis to include discourse, the admission of the range of communicative modes changes the nature of language as an object of study in another direction.

In the 1960s and 1970s a number of studies produced evidence that chimpanzees are able to communicate using a system that has a number of the features hitherto thought to be ascribed to *human* language only. Roger Fouts, among others, building on earlier work by Beatrice and Alan Gardner with the chimp Washoe, claims that the way the chimpanzees manipulate gestural signs of American Sign Language (Ameslan) indicates that they can use abstract notions (the signs and their referents are dissimilar) and use signs for specialized purposes (for example, to get food). What remained unclear for a long time was whether animals (specifically primates using Ameslan or manipulating a synthetic language of tokens using a computer keyboard) communicate interchangeably. That is, do they intercommunicate so that what one is conveying to another is conveyed and responded to? Also, do animals communicate in such a way that what is communicated is culturally transmitted? That is, do chimps who know a gesture (that the others don't know) teach the others to use it appropriately? Do mother chimps, for example, teach their infants Ameslan? (Eastman 1978:174; see also Linden 1974).

If Roger Fouts's chimpanzees fail to teach Ameslan to their offspring, would this mean they have no language or that Ameslan is not salient for chimpanzee cultural transmission?

Other features of human language that animals would need to show if their communication system is to be seen as language include: creating new signs for never-before-seen objects; using signs to communicate about events in the past or future in places other than the immediate environment. Humans with language use it to recall the past and speculate about the future. Animals are generally thought of as being able only to respond instantly to stimuli; they do not initiate conversations. As Fromkin and Rodman (1983:360) put it, animal communication is **stimulus bound** while human language is creative.

Disagreeing with this view is the research of Francine Patterson based on her work with the gorilla Koko, who has been taught Ameslan. Patterson feels she has demonstrated that Koko can hear differences in words such as "ear"/"dear" or "funny"/"money"/"bunny." Koko is said to respond to learning tests at the level of a 4-year-old human child. Washoe, now 22 years old in 1990, is said to have "overheard remarks made by researchers and later inquired about them using sign language" (Ricks 1987:A10). The idea being expressed is that chimps and humans begin to acquire communicative skills at about the same time (age 4–5 months); the difference is that humans acquire adult language while the primates and other animals remain childlike communicators. The question as to whether animals are just imitating rather than communicating continues to bother some skeptics.

It is a fact that the animals' brains and those of humans are different. As Fouts has stated, "the cerebral cortex of chimpanzees is silent" (Ricks 1987). Jeffrey Laitman of the Mount Sinai School of Medicine in New York, however, has data that suggest ". . . if we were to reconstruct the vocal tracts in . . . early forms [of humans], we would probably find that they were not much more advanced than today's living chimps" (Ricks 1987). Whether or not the shape of the brain, the presence of a vocal apparatus, or the ability to gesture has to do with language is also a matter of debate. Researchers such as Fouts and Patterson claim primates communicate to themselves in sign and communicate emotively (Koko has been insulted, expressed sadness, and responds comparably); others remain totally unconvinced. E. Sue Savage-Rumbaugh of the Yerkes Primate Center at Emory University and Georgia State Language Research Center reports that Kanzi, a 4-year-old pygmy chimpanzee, acquired the ability to communicate using geometric symbols spontaneously along with the ability to comprehend spoken English. Kanzi did not have to undergo the long sessions of training that Ameslan-using primates are usually subject to and is claimed to be "the first ape to show, in rigorous scientific tests, an extensive understanding of spoken English words" (*Seattle Post Intelligencer*, June 25, 1985:C2).

Taking a different approach from the experimental one of the Gardners, Fouts, Patterson, the Rumbaughs and others, David Premack (1976, as reported in 1981) decided that the question worth asking is not "Do animals communicate?" but "Do animals have intelligence?" Working with the chimpanzee Sarah using an artificial language of plastic chips (for instance, a blue plastic triangle means "apple," an orange rectangle represents the concept "same"), Premack would ask Sarah to put the appropriate symbol on the language board and expect a reward or ask her to respond to sequences of symbols in order to produce her own reward. Since Sarah could respond to sequences of chips such as "Sarah insert apple dish" or "Sarah insert pear pail," Premack asserted that she understood the relationship between "insert" and nouns such as "apple," "pear," "dish," and "pail."

Premack feels chimps can comprehend statements about "things that are not there" since they are able to store representations of items and use words to retrieve the stored information. That they are also able to respond to questions of the type "Is the red chip on the green chip?" provides added evidence of this representational capacity.

From these observations Premack (1976, 1981) concludes that there are different *representational systems* and that language is just one variant. The representational system of chimps is another variant. Chimps use their system to discriminate between conditions exemplifying "same" and "different," "all" and "none," "red" and "black," and the like. They can process "if-then" conditionals such as "If you touch that, you'll get burned." They can, Premack argues, also make causal inferences. This line of argumentation leads to Premack's point that chimpanzees have intelligence, can reason, and can process abstract information. Their representational system manifests both an abstracting ability and an interpretive ability. The language board that Sarah uses, as were the communicative systems Fouts uses with the chimps he has and that Patterson uses with Koko, has been used to assist children who are unable to use language. For example, children may be taught to manipulate geometric symbols, to push buttons on a computer, and to make certain gestural signs in order to achieve the same ends the animals can achieve, where without such aids children with impaired brain function would not be able to talk. When children with brain damage use such communicative systems, however, they (like the animals) do not achieve the level of communicative skill (involving complex reasoning and creativity) that adult-language users achieve. This difference is clear when what is learned is Ameslan—neither chimps nor retarded children use it as people for whom ASL is a first language or as adult signers do.

In summary, Premack suggests that (1) all species have intention, (2) all primates attribute intention to others, (3) all (adult) humans attribute the attribution of intention. That is, the birds and the bees and the chimps and the humans communicate purposively. Chimpanzees and humans know that we (and the birds and the bees) communicate purposively. But *only* humans think that humans and chimpanzees, birds and bees have intentions. That is, they [the animals] don't know that we know that they know! What is being investigated now is if and how chimps take into account the order of actions as well as the rules that guide their system of communicative representation—*how* do they think the way they think? This same question is what is guiding the research of the generative linguists we talked about in Chapter 2. Where linguists feel that how humans think may be discerned via a theory of Language, primatologists such as Premack feel that the nature of animal intelligence may be discerned via a theory of communication and the range of representational systems of communication used by animals and humans.

Evidence of various forms of animal intelligence comes from facts. For example, dolphins learn the vocabulary of artificial languages and can grasp certain principles of grammar and syntax. Pigeons can comprehend general concepts such as "people" and "tree" (they know which to drop droppings on and which to land in). Bats can locate objects from their echoes. Vervet monkeys can use a number of alarm calls to convey specific information about different kinds of threats. There is even evidence that bees have dialects. The waggle dance of honey bees is such that to an Egyptian bee a waggle means five yards but means fifty yards to an Austrian bee.

Studies of animal communication looking at various forms of communication indicate that "Every animal living in the world today is smartest for the ecological niche in which it finds itself. If it weren't it would not be here" (Abrahamson 1983:13). Thus, every animal to its own system of language and culture.

4.2.2.2 American Sign Language

As is clear from the previous section, there is doubt as to whether Washoe and other research subjects actually communicate in a human language. Does the fact that chimps are seen using signs recognizable as signs in Ameslan (ASL) mean they know it as a language? Some scholars feel that there are problems with the way data from such learning/teaching experiments with chimpanzees have been interpreted (Akmajian, Demers, and Harnish 1984:485). Herbert Terrace, in the process of setting out to demonstrate that chimpanzees do actually acquire ASL and to quiet critics, actually came up with results indicating that gesture combinations by chimps may not be legitimate sentences. Terrace's work was with the chimpanzee Nim Chimpsky, so named (the story goes) because the study was expected to "make a chimp out of Chomsky"—discredit those who doubt that animals have language. Nim was taught ASL for four years by more than 60 teachers with the result that he "learned to express 125 signs during his first forty-four months" (Akmajian, Demers, and Harnish 1984:486). What Terrace noticed was that the length of Nim's utterances never increased despite the increase in vocabulary. Further, most meaning was conveyed by two-sign utterances, with three-sign combinations adding only redundancy. For example, Nim would sign "play me" and "play me Nim" with the addition of "Nim" adding only emphasis (Terrace 1979:213). One of the most startling findings of the Nim project was that only 10 percent of the videotaped utterances were spontaneous and 40 percent were variations of what the teacher had signed, while others were purely imitative. Terrace compared Nim's acquisition of ASL to what happens in child language acquisition and found that "Nim's utterances were less spontaneous and less original than those of a child and . . . his utterances did not become longer, both as he learned new signs and as he acquired more experience in using sign language . . . [suggesting] that much of the structure and meaning of his combinations was determined, or at least suggested by the utterances of his teachers" (Terrace 1979:221).

To understand the difference between human language and animal communication, it is useful to look at the process of child language acquisition on the part of first-language signers of Ameslan (ASL). As was noted above, the idea that speech is a necessary aspect of language has faded into history. Clearly, deaf children who do not hear spoken language do not acquire it the way hearing children do. This difference is certainly no indication that they do not have language. In fact, "deaf children of deaf parents who are exposed to sign language from birth parallel the stages and development of language acquisition by hearing children learning oral languages" (Fromkin and Rodman 1983:337). The sign languages acquired as a first language use hand and body gestures rather than sounds to represent morphemes and to convey an infinite number of new sentences and to express meaning. The fact that sign languages develop among people who are born without the ability to hear seems to be good evidence for the idea that all people (regardless of speaking/hearing ability) are indeed born with linguistic competence (that is, the ability to acquire language). It seems that what nonhearing people do is use their innate linguistic ability to gesture rather than to speak. The gestures have all the structure and function that sounds have in spoken language.

In the United States, the "major language used by the deaf . . . is American Sign Language" (Fromkin and Rodman 1983:337), the same language taught to primates in some of the experiments discussed in the previous section.[4]

Whereas linguists have analyzed speech as made up of minimal units of sound structure called *phonemes* (see Chapter 1 above), the minimal units of gestural form in ASL were called **cheremes**. It is more common these days to refer to these gestural units as **primes**. Primes combine into meaningful units (akin to *morphemes* in spoken language) by means of (1) hand **configuration**, (2) hand(s) **motion** toward or away from the body, (3) **place of articulation** (that is, where the sign movement is located.) For example, the sign meaning "arm" is a flat hand moving to touch the upper arm. Its three primes are: (1) configuration—flat; (2) motion—toward; (3) place of articulation—upper arm. Sign language has minimal pairs just as spoken language does, such that one prime can be the only difference between two gestures that are distinct. For example, the signs for "summer" and "ugly" are exactly the same except that where the sign is made makes a difference. If the sign is made at eye level, it means "summer"; in front of the nose and mouth it means "ugly." This same sign below the chin means "dry." Also, as is the case

---

4   "ASL is an independent, fully developed language that historically is an outgrowth of the sign languages used in France and brought to the United States by the great deaf educator Gallaudet, after whom Gallaudet College for the Deaf in Washington, D. C. is named" (Fromkin and Rodman 1983:337).

with spoken languages, sign languages have ungrammatical sequences and sequences of primes that cannot go together. As Fromkin and Rodman state it (1983:338), "A permissible sign in a Chinese sign language may not be a permissible sign in ASL, and vice versa."[5]

Native signers, like native users of any language, begin with single signs and then begin to combine them. Grammatical and functional signs are acquired by signers at about the same time child speakers begin to use corresponding sounds in their speech and the differences between child signing and adult signing are similar to those between child speech and adult speech. Interestingly, children acquire their first signs somewhat before children not hearing impaired acquire their first words. Fromkin and Rodman (1983:341) report research indicating that this earlier proficiency may be due to the fact that children are able to control hand muscles earlier than they can control their vocal apparatus. Research on sign languages indicates that as acquired by humans they have all the features and creative aspects of language. Sign languages use conventional and arbitrary (rather than imitative) signs; these represent a different mode of performance or expression of the human cognitive ability to acquire language (competence). The human language ability may be expressed via speech or via sign language. It is not clear what ability it is that animals are expressing when they use certain signs in limited combinations that they have seen used by humans. It does seem, from the research that has been done so far, that the human cognitive ability expressed as language (whether spoken or signed) is qualitatively different from the kind of intelligent communicative behavior enacted by animals interacting with each other or with humans. It is also clear that if we are to understand the nature of cognitive ability and its relationship to cultural behavior, research on both animals and people interacting with each other in the "real world" needs to continue.

4.3 Summary

This chapter has centered on the relationship of language to culture and to thought. Much of what was discussed here stemmed from interest in the Whorfian hypothesis of linguistic determinism and in the idea that language structure may structure reality. Studies of color perception cross-linguistically indicate that

---

5   ASL is not the only sign language in the United States. The other, Signed English or Siglish, is quite different from ASL in that it replaces spoken English forms with signs and uses the syntax and semantics of ordinary English. Fromkin and Rodman characterize Siglish as unnatural in the sense that "speaking English but translating every English word or morpheme into its French counterpart" is unnatural (1983:338-339). With Siglish, if there is no sign for something, signers employ *finger spelling,* using visual symbols of the English alphabet to indicate what the word is in English. (See Fromkin and Rodman 1983:339 ff., and also Klima and Bellugi 1979).

reality is actually the same for all people, but how different societies segment and label that reality is culture-specific. Such linguistic relativity holds that one's language adapts to the situation in which it is used: if we need a word for something, our language will provide one. The field of cognitive anthropology is concerned with how different societies categorize elements within various semantic *domains*. The hierarchical relationships that obtain among elements in a domain reveal how we think about objects relative to each other (cocktails and champagne, for example, are alcoholic beverages within a domain of drinkable liquids, but only champagne is also wine). Other societies may not elaborate the category of alcoholic beverages as extensively as middle-class American society does but may elaborate another category further (for instance, American Indian groups on the Northwest Coast will have a large number of terms for "salmon"). Cognitive anthropologists are also interested in the features of meaning or components that define lexical items in a semantic domain. We saw that certain drinkable liquids may be distinguished according to temperature, carbonation, medicinal quality, or even color. Language use also reveals how people in a particular society enact culture-specific routines. Such studies indicate that the way language and thought and culture relate is a matter of the interaction of common human thought in the context of a particular culture. Language use is the expression of thought in context.

The concept of *markedness*, as discussed in Chapter 2, was seen as especially relevant here. Things that are culturally salient are unmarked (expressed by a single lexical item), whereas what is new or, at least relatively unfamiliar, will be expressed by a whole phrase.

Brief mention was made of research on language in relation to the structure of the brain insofar as there is interest in seeing whether the models that cognitive anthropologists and linguists have of semantic organization may relate to the way the brain functions, the way it organizes information.

Whereas linguists tend to focus their concern with meaning in language on attempting to formulate a model of the structure of the lexicon and semantic component of a generative grammar, anthropologists are interested in how meaning is socially constructed. Language and culture are seen to meet in *discourse*—in conversation, for one example. The meaning that occurs at this juncture may be discerned by analyzing *speech acts*. Various approaches are taken to such analysis, known variously as *pragmatics* and *semiotics*. Anthropological approaches to meaning in context are an extension of structuralist approaches to meaning as discussed in Chapter 2. Where the structuralist looked at language as a system in and of itself and at meaning as derived from a series of binary oppositions interrelating within that system, discourse-oriented scholars see meaning as a matter of understanding how the item itself refers to something, is something in and of itself, and receives an interpretation in context. Such a triadic approach to meaning sees meaning as a matter of *both* language and culture.

If the language-culture distinction blurs when it comes to understanding how social reality is constructed and how meaning is communicatively accomplished, one is led to ask what, if anything, distinguishes communication in general from language as such? We looked at research on animal "languages" to see if, in fact, there is any difference between what chimpanzees, gorillas, and the like do when they communicate and what humans do when they use language. Could it be that there is both a communicative system that humans and animals both have and a linguistic system peculiar to humans?

Chapter 5 Language and Society

5.0 Introduction

As was mentioned in Chapter 3, some scholars look at linguistic variability as related to social, cultural, and economic factors giving rise to the study of subcultures and to the way they are constituted by means of language use. A social dialect is seen as the expression of the world view of a subculture, after Spradley's definition of a subculture as "the symbolic system of knowledge people use to order their behavior as members of a group" (1970:263). In this regard the study of language use and social identity that has developed as an aspect of the study of language and culture will be discussed. Further, we will survey the two flourishing fields of sociolinguistics and applied sociolinguistics. Whereas Chapter 4 looked at language and culture and centered on a concern with the relationship of language and culture (as systems of symbols and meanings) to each other from the perspective of cognition (meaning), the exploration of sociolinguistics in Chapter 5 looks outward to examine the social context within which linguistic and cultural activity occurs. Sociolinguistics is concerned with the interaction of language and setting. In addition to studying language use in relation to class, status, sex role, and ethnicity, sociolinguists investigate the way two or more languages or language varieties are used in the same or different social contexts. Such studies fall into categories such as bilingualism, multilingualism, or codeswitching (mixing).

5.1 Language and Social Identity

Schieffelin and Ochs (1986a, 1986b) refer to the way people use language in particular social settings as **language socialization**. People's talk reveals their ethnicity, sex role, social class, and status. The way we acquire these places in society is thought by many to be a process of **negotiation** as we learn to behave appropriately with others in groups. The idea that we negotiate our positions in society using language is a relatively new view, alongside the traditional view that we are each born into a certain group, with a particular language, and with gender defining each individual's sex role. In the section below on language and status we will discuss the ideas that our place in society and the way we think are matters of social class and cognitive style. It will be seen that these ideas are being challenged from the perspective of language socialization.

Research suggesting that social identity is negotiated is often based on the analysis of conversational data (as we saw much of Discourse Analysis to be in the previous chapter). Indeed, conversation analysts have come up with a number of conventions designed to transcribe the very speech forms that are suspected to reveal social differences in language use. These symbols are intended to be used along with conventional International Phonetic Alphabet symbols in the transcription of speech style. For example, Farris (1988) has determined that voice quality (labialization and nasality) is an aspect of sex role in Chinese. Children use these features in their speech and they are retained in the speech of adult women while not used in the speech of adult men. The resulting speech style characterizing women and children is called *sajiao*—a kind of "petulance" which is also visually

Table 6. Sample Symbols for Prosodic Notation

/	minor, nonfinal phrase boundary marker
//	major, final phrase boundary marker
`	low fall tone
`	high fall tone
/	low rise tone
/	high rise tone
v	fall rise tone
^	rise fall tone
–	sustained tone
ı	low secondary stress
ı	high secondary stress
⌐	pitch register shift, upwards
∟	pitch register shift, lowered
acc	accelerated tempo
dec	decelerated tempo
ı	lenis enuciation
stacc	staccato enunciation
[	conversation overlap
..	speech pause
...	long speech pause
( )	unintelligible word

[from Gumperz 1982b:xi]

perceptible as speakers extend the lower lip and curl it downward. Farris's transcriptions of *sajiao* speech indicate the labialized and nasalized consonants and accompanied pouting. Gumperz (1982a:xi) provides a list of some of the forms of prosodic notation that are useful to researchers looking for social aspects of language use, as seen in Table 6 above.

Note that pauses, pitch, tempo, and overlapping (indicative of interruptions) are common aspects of different speech styles. Men and women differ with respect to such features as do members of different ethnic groups, subcultures, and social classes. For example, as we will see in the section below on language and social class, Bernstein (1964) found that working-class teen-age schoolboys in London used speech which was more rapid and had fewer pauses than that of middle-class teen-age schoolboys.

What seems to be of particular importance in the way speech and social identity interact are features of **paralanguage**, that is, forms of modulating the voice to convey effect. For example, in English affection is usually conveyed in a soft voice, "whereas aggressive arguments are conducted in a loud voice with extreme shifts of pitch" (Crane, Yeager, and Whitman 1981:22).

The cartoon of Sam and Silo pivots on the kind of social message that paralinguistic features are capable of carrying. Commands are expected to be given in a deep voice. Here the idea of singing an order at all, and in addition the issuing of the command in a soprano voice (female), is what makes this cartoon funny. Sexism is involved here as well—since the implication is that it is tenor (male) to give orders. Both gender and voice quality are off if Sam and Silo really expect the crook to come out!

SAM & SILO

Reprinted with special permission of King Features Syndicate, Inc.

It is also the case that vocabulary and topics reveal much about where a person is with regard to membership in or out of a group. In my own work in southeast Alaska, I found that language use as an aspect of social identity involves culturally specific vocabulary, context-sensitive topics, and shared attitudes. That is, as people become members of a social group, they learn to share in that group's collective identity largely by acquiring **group talk**. In the section below on sociolinguistic theory and method we will see that the process of acquiring group talk involves aspects of two approaches—the *ethnography of communication* and *accommodation theory*. Essentially people are participant observers in their own society, becoming full members only once they have mastered the ethnography of it—that is, figured out what behavior is appropriate for them to perform. In the southeast Alaska village "Haidaville," in order to be "of Haidaville" at the time of the study, one needed: (1) to be able to use the local system of nicknaming, know a special vocabulary of points of reference, have the appropriate attitudes about certain topics such as what will happen once "the road" connects the town to another on the island; (2) to participate frequently in certain social activities such as those at the Alaska Native Brotherhood Hall; (3) to be ambivalent about the recent history of the cannery; (4) to be suspicious of television; (5) to be familiar with the practice of returning from "away" for access to local medicine; (6) to value fishing "down inside" and berry picking; (7) to speculate about the "running" of the fish; and (8) to be aware of the cultural significance of the Fourth of July as a summer festival and of Thanksgiving as the town's "birthday" (a form of winter ceremonial).

Inappropriate language use marked persons whose social identities were not entirely constituted by being "of Haidaville." For example, one woman expressed optimism about the road coming in and felt that tourism might be developed profitably in town once it had arrived (that is, was built). In Scotton's (1983) terms, this constituted making a **marked** code choice. When this inappropriate view was expressed, talk stopped. Indeed, talk stoppage is a frequent indicator of inappropriate language use and would occur if it became clear that someone did not understand a nickname reference or expressed a wrong value.

It appears that people acquire social identity as members of a group by acquiring its vocabulary, topics, and attitudes as well as the structural forms of its language. Our social identities are many, ranging from that of our entire community and including the way we use language in our work, play, religion, and other forms of social interaction. In fact, understanding the larger-than-language language-use aspects of social identity is often critical in figuring out problems that people encounter as members of a group. Swigart (1984) observed that people who work in restaurants may use their individual social identities when conversing with one another (though constrained by such factors as sex roles as we will see below) but in the role of waitperson addressing a cook or beverage person the way they must use language is fixed. Cooks and bartenders may refuse to fill an order not given in the correct sequence and a waitperson who fails to respect such a "linguistic hierarchy" is likely to discover the need for a career change!

Focus on vocabulary, topics, and attitudes conveyed by members of a group to which one aspires to belong may be seen as complementary to Scotton's (1983) "set of maxims governing the negotiation of identities in conversation." Scotton sees the social purpose of conversation to be the negotiation by participants in sets of rights and obligations (RO sets). Each participant in a conversation projects a social identity to the other from which appropriate rights and obligations may be derived. A newcomer to a speech community not yet fluent in its (unmarked) code necessarily uses another (marked) code. Likewise, the person a newcomer addresses cannot follow or reciprocate the usual (unmarked) code, that is, the newcomer's "way of speaking" (Hymes 1972). As Scotton describes it, speech-community members think of newcomers as using "foreigner talk." As long as they think thus, members of the community who want to talk to the new people will "suspend the rules" (Eastman 1985:3 citing Scotton 1983) of conversation and assume that no shared rights and obligations exist. The process of acquiring group talk legitimizes people as group members and "unmarks" their language use. As I have noted elsewhere:

> People who have established and share group social identities are able to engage in mutually intelligible group talk and are, thus, in a position to negotiate successful conversations (i.e., to share RO sets). (Eastman 1985:3)

In the following subsections we will discuss studies of language and social identity from the perspective of language use and social class, sex roles, and ethnicity.

5.1.1 Language and Social Class

Perhaps the most well-known view of language and social class derives from a controversial study by British sociolinguist Basil Bernstein. Bernstein published a study in 1964 in which he investigated conversations of groups of English teen-age schoolboys in London. He found that schoolboys from working-class homes use what he calls a **restricted code** while those from middle-class homes use an **elaborated code** and also have access to a restricted code. This distinction in form of language use has been used to imply that social structure determines the type of linguistic code available to members of differing segments of society. Furthermore, this study gave rise to the idea that a person's linguistic code affects the ability to learn. Certain programs to enhance a child's ability to learn (such as Head Start in the United States) were based on ideas such as those of Bernstein. Thus:

> . . . if we want to provide all children with equal opportunities we will have to catch them very early so that we can give them enough enriched verbal experience to let

them rise above the restricted code to which their own family and social class background would condemn them. (Burling 1970:166)

Indeed this view has given rise to enrichment programs of various kinds all over the world. However, it may be that what Bernstein found was more "the *effect* of educational deficiencies rather than the cause" (Burling 1970:167). The working-class schoolboys in his study manifested their restricted code in a number of ways, including using the active voice more than the passive voice, using simple short sentences, avoiding complex utterances, using very few adjectives, and peppering their speech with phrases such as "wouldn't it?" or "you see" (Burling 1970:164).

What appears to be the case is that a restricted code is a casual, informal style of speech used to reinforce group membership. It is also very closely tied to the context of its use and it is characterized by a kind of glibness. Middle-class boys could use such a code but also were conversant in an elaborated code making use of longer complex sentences, a wider range of vocabulary, ideas abstracted from the context of the conversation, and typified by thoughtful pauses. The anthropologist Rosalie Cohen (1969), looking not at language and social class but at what she calls **conceptual styles**, noted that a number of these same characteristics distinguish what she terms *relational* thinkers from *analytical* thinkers.

Cohen's view is that people do not all have the same conceptual style—they may have different "rule-sets for the selection and organization of sense data" (1969:828). Like people with an elaborated code, *analytical* thinkers are able to abstract salient information from a situation in a formal way. On the other hand, *relational* thinkers, like those with a restricted code, see meaning as tied to its context. Such people tie ". . . actors to actions, causes to results, means to ends" (849). The speech of a person with an analytical way of organizing reality involves complex grammar, sentences of varied length, many adjectives and adverbs, and pauses for verbal planning. The relational individual is highly fluent, speaks in short sentences, and uses few adjectives. Thus, Cohen and Bernstein see the same forms of language use as due respectively to cognitive style and social class.

What is clear from both views is that the expectations of the school are generally in conflict with what is manifested by either a *restricted* code or a *relational* conceptual style, whether or not the cause of either is deprivation, class difference, or cognitive organization. The case is that the social knowledge and forms of language use that children acquire at home and bring to school do not always match those "valued in formal schooling activities" (Schieffelin and Ochs 1986a:164). In fact, the educational process children embark upon is one of substituting the language and culture of the school for that of the home. The *restricted* code and *relational* style of Bernstein and Cohen may be more an aspect of the language and culture difference between home and school that the child confronts than reflections of social class and cognitive organization. Bernstein's middle-class boys were able to *codeswitch* (see more about *codeswitching* below), that is, to use the language of the school in school situations and to use the language of the street in street situations. In fact, the child who is able to use only an *elaborated* code may have difficulty in peer interactions yet do well with adults (of the teacher type).

As we will see below in the discussion of codeswitching, people need to have control of a variety of forms of language use in order to interact in the different social groups to which they belong. Though there are class differences and perhaps different modes of "reality organization," it may not be the case that, in the absence of physical abnormalities, human beings are condemned by their "family and social-class background" to remain in the one language and culture group they first encountered as children.

The approach to language and social status under the rubric of **language socialization** (Schieffelin and Ochs 1986a, 1986b) has a more interactional thrust and seeks to link "analyses of children's discourse to more general ethnographic accounts of cultural beliefs and practices of the families, social groups, or communities into which children are socialized" (1986a:168). Peters and Boggs (1986:81) suggest the term *interactional routines* to refer to the structured situations of socialization via language: "An *interactional routine* is a *sequence of exchanges* in which one speaker's utterance, accompanied by appropriate nonverbal behavior, calls forth one of a limited set of responses by one or more other participants." Interactional routines occur within *participant structures* specifying who can say what to whom: "In learning an interactional routine a child thus develops an understanding of social role appropriate to age and sex." Generally a child learns "new and more flexible routines" over time, expressing values embedded in his/her culture and social structure as a *mode of speaking*.

Cohen's *relational conceptual style* and Bernstein's *restricted-code* users may have acquired *modes of speaking* associated with only certain segments of society. It is not that they are "condemned" to their way of thinking or their social class, but instead that the various *modes of speaking* available in their society and culture's **speech economy** need to be made available to them. The concept of *speech economy* as "the distribution of specific routines and modes of speaking over the various relationships and situations in a society" (Hymes 1974:94) suggests that what is needed is not to "enrich" the child in the language and culture of the school to the detriment of the child's own language and culture but rather to have the schools be responsive to the full range of a society's speech economy.

The range of variation in how children learn to talk needs to be examined both cross-culturally and within subcultures (such as British working-class and middle-class families). Demuth (1986) and Peters and Boggs (1986) looked at interactional routines used to teach children forms of language use in southern Africa and in the Solomon Islands among other places. In the process children are socialized as well as taught language. In my own research on coastal Kenya I found that the songs

Swahili children sing often contain the values espoused by adult society and that the learning of these songs and their content amounts to a form of education (Eastman 1985). The distinction made in the West between education and play with regard to the socialization function is of no importance. Similarly, much of what Basotho parents (for example) do when they teach their children to speak is a matter more of socialization than prescriptive grammar. The Basotho people, like the Kwara'ae of the Solomon Islands (Watson-Gegeo and Gegeo 1986), use interactional routines consisting of **prompts** to indicate what language use is appropriate in a particular context (somewhat as parents do in English when they urge a child with "Say 'thank you'" or "Say 'bye-bye'").

> Prompts are . . . used in everyday conversational situations where young children are told how to request, how to give instructions to others, and how to participate in daily interactions that are not necessarily culturally defined. . . . These prompts are found in indirect form. Thus, when Hlobohang (26.6 months) was having trouble tying his shoes, his grandmother finally told him to ask his older cousin for help: *Ere abuti Mololo a u roese* "Say (that) brother Mololo should put (them) on for you." (Demuth 1986:72)

The *prompt* "Ere" ("Say") indicates that what follows represents information about appropriate interaction. Studies of language socialization increasingly confirm that "education" comes in a number of guises, only one of which is sanctioned by many forms of schooling in the West. Other linguistic forms of socialization such as question/answer sequences and turn-taking routines in conversation likewise have this function in society.

One function to which education in the West pays attention is not an aspect of education in more traditional societies, namely, *literacy*. Indeed, literacy is generally realized in the form of language use characteristic of an analytic conceptual style or elaborated code. Schools in Western societies function to inculcate literacy skills as much as to socialize students. It should be clear from our discussion here that the kind of language socialization in working-class homes (like that in Basotho homes) "does not facilitate . . . success in traditional Western classrooms" (*ibid.*). Schieffelin and Ochs (1986a:182) observe that "It is only when a bridge is built in classrooms between traditional speech events and participant structure that children can successfully participate in literacy activities." Recognition that speaking and reading/writing are different activities and an examination of their interrelationships might also be useful in bridging the education/socialization gap separating social classes in the West and the schooled from the unschooled in traditional societies.

5.1.2 Language and Sex Roles

Maltz and Borker (1982), in reviewing much of the recent research on language and sex, express concern with explanations of differences in men's and women's speech in English as being due to psychological factors or male dominance. Fishman (1978) argues that "norms of appropriate behavior for women and men serve to give power and interactional control to men while keeping it from women" (Maltz and Borker 1982:199). Lakoff (1975) feels that women have been taught to act like "ladies" and in the process become "as unassertive and insecure as they have been made to sound" (Maltz and Borker 1982:199). An interesting other view, however, is derived from an understanding of the way in which men and women in the United States have learned how to engage in conversation in the English language. The idea is that, despite what many people think, American men and women represent different subcultures—from the perspective of conversation.

Maltz and Borker note that differing women's features and men's features are evident in conversation. For example, women ask more questions, make more effort to keep conversation flowing, and encourage *positive* **minimal responses** during a conversation. That is, women give and expect to get "mm hmm" all during a conversation. On the other had, men interrupt more, challenge what the other has said, and usually offer *minimal responses* not during a conversation but at the end (*delayed minimal response*).

A number of prior researchers have discussed sex roles in societies where sexual segregation is common, particularly in Muslim countries and in southern Europe. In those societies there is both spatial and interactional segregation whereas, we assume, there is neither in the United States. In my research in Kenya I described two distinct adult subcultures in Swahili coastal society (1984), such that *wanawake* (women) have a form of expressive culture (set of songs, rituals, distinct oral literature) distinct from that of *waungwana* (gentlemen). The domain of male activity is the *baraza*, where political discussion abounds, and aboard fishing boats and in the mosque. The men have a culture with a literate tradition resting heavily on epic poetry, religious chants, and the like, whereas Swahili women dance, continue traditions originating in African forms of spirit possession, and engage in creative and spontaneous versification. Thus one of the major aspects of subcultural differentiation in Swahili male versus female society is sociolinguistic—exemplified by different systems of expressive culture, perhaps ultimately representing different ethnic origins (Arabic males/Bantu females). Harding (1975) similarly argues for separate sociolinguistic subcultures in rural Spain. Because men and women have "different experiences and operate in different social contexts, they tend to develop different genres of speech and different skills for doing things with words" (Maltz and Borker 1982:200). As I found in Kenya, Harding found that men's sociolinguistic skills were honed in the public political arena whereas those of women grew in the home via such activities as gossip, social analysis, second guessing, and verbal prying.

Maltz and Borker (1982) were interested not so much in the idea of separate subcultures but rather in what happens when the two interact. The literature on interethnic miscommunication indicates that problems arise due to people "wrongly interpreting cues according to their own rules." By looking solely at the "mm hmm" *positive* minimal response characteristic of conversations in English, Maltz and Borker came up with an analysis that does much to account for certain stereotypes that men and women have of each other in American culture.

In American society, men complain that women always agree with them so it is impossible to know what they "really" think. Conversely, women think that men don't listen. What Maltz and Borker have found is that the respective subcultures of men and women in the United States have different rules for the use and interpretation of "mm hmm" as a minimal response. They point out that school-age children learn the rules for carrying on friendly conversations from each other rather than from adults and that little boys and little girls consider members of the same sex their peers but not the opposite sex: "A major feature of most middle-childhood peer groups is homogeneity; they are either all-boy or all-girl" (Brooks-Gunn and Matthews 1979, cited in Maltz and Borker 1982:203). It turns out that women use the positive minimal response to mean something like "I'm listening to you; please continue," while men use it to mean "I agree with you" or "I follow your argument so far." Thus what men stereotype as women "always agreeing" with them is a misunderstanding on their part; what women interpret as men "not listening" to them is a misunderstanding on their part. Maltz and Borker go on further to indicate that what men and women mean by asking questions also is different: men want information, women intend to keep the conversation going. In sum, the same linguistic forms may function differently in different subcultures and cause misunderstandings when the subcultures interact. This confusion will also be seen below when we discuss language and ethnicity. In fact, Tannen has found that conversational style is learned through communicative experience and that family and group habits become a part of the way we converse. Consequently, with respect to male-female conversation, there will be further differences when the couples talking are from another ethnic background. Tannen found that the gulf in direct style between American men and women in conversation appears not to exist when Greek men and women talk (1982:225).

Silberstein (1988) studied the way male and female members of a couple narrate their courtship story. She looked at couples from different ethnic backgrounds spanning three generations and found that the narrative strategies used "constitute conventionalized representations of gendered cultural positions" and "reproduce dominant meanings and values about courtship and gender." Silberstein found that women's stories change across generations to accommodate changed perspectives in American society with regard to the role of women. Interestingly, the ideology shift is seen only in the women's versions whereas the male "vocabulary of motive" (in particular the reason for marrying, but also rationales for choices in general) remains the same—reflecting the fact that indeed women's role (not men's) is what has undergone a transformation in recent years.

Discourse, however, is not the only area in which language and sex roles interact. The lexicon itself provides interesting insights regarding the different places men and women occupy in American society. As Fromkin and Rodman (1983:270) point out, "Language cannot be sexist itself, just as it can't be 'dirty,'" but it can reflect sexist attitudes just as it can reflect attitudes as to what is and is not considered taboo. To illustrate, a few examples will suffice. In English, the interpretation of the sentence "My cousin is a physicist" is most often that the cousin is male while "My cousin is a prostitute" generally evokes the idea that the cousin is female. More difficult to understand is why "My neighbor is a blond" similarly connotes that the neighbor is female (Fromkin and Rodman 1983:270, citing Saporta 1974). Fromkin and Rodman speculate that these connotations may be linked to female physical features being marked in American society in relation to the fact that "women are constantly exploited as sex objects." This idea is supported by the fact that the language has a number of words for women "with abusive or sexual overtones," such as "dish, tomato, piece, piece of ass, chick, piece of tail, bunny, pussy, pussycat, bitch, doll, slut, cow, to name just a few" (271) and that there are far fewer such words for men.

The fact of gender differences in paralanguage, lexicon, and other aspects of language indicates the way society views men and women. If men and women in a particular society were equal such asymmetries as those Fromkin and Rodman (272) describe here would disappear. The social place of members of minority groups and the handicapped is also discernible in linguistic asymmetries. In the following section we will discuss language-use aspects of ethnic interaction. It is relevant to point out here, however, how the process of putting people in their social place via language extends beyond putting women down. Consider for example what is conveyed by phrases such as "wheelchair bound" or "confined to a wheelchair." The imagery of punishment does not enhance the equality of the individuals being referred to by distinction from the rest of society.

Rudes and Healy (1979) studied the way the pronoun "she" is used by members of the male Gay community in Buffalo, New York, and found that the asymmetries of the larger society are perpetuated in the Gay world. The pronoun "she" is associated with the stereotypical aspects of maleness and femaleness and these aspects are common in both Gay and non-Gay society. Rudes and Healy suggest that this association may result from the concepts of maleness and femaleness being acquired by children at an early age and becoming "solidified and removed from consciousness long before the effects of the Gay Liberation or the Women's Liberation Movements [were] felt" (1979:54). Just as we saw with regard to the linguistics of male/female conversational rules, pronominal reference appears to be fixed to the extent that it remains "impervious to the changes induced in the

conscious image of males and females brought about by . . . liberation movements."
Some examples will make this point clear (each sentence refers to a male):

1. "Oh, *she's* so cute—sexy too."
2. "*She* was the most gorgeous thing I've seen here all night."
3. "Who does *she* think *she* is?"
4. "Get *her* in that dress."

Female referential pronouns are used by Gay men when what is meant to be conveyed is youth, glamor, artificiality, contrivedness, lack of control, preoccupation, frivolity, excess, outlandishness, promiscuity, verbosity, bitchiness, and the like—the stereotypical (derogatory and abusive) notions of the social meaning of what it is to be female.

5.1.3 Language and Ethnicity

Language and ethnicity are also linked from the perspective of individual self-identification. People grow up with a sense of their sex roles and social standing and also with an idea of who they are as members of a particular group of people in contrast to members of other groups. The way we use language to symbolize our view of ourselves and ascribe ethnicity to ourselves as distinct from others is known as an **ethnic speech style**. We saw above that this view comes through in the way we tell stories as men and women of a particular ethnic background. It also comes through in a number of other ways. Giles, Bourhis, and Taylor (1977:327) exemplify this by observing that Jews all over the world have a distinct accent in whatever language they speak, using words and phrases peculiar to the culture and experiences they have brought with them to the host language and culture. Also, Irish and Scots hang onto their brogue and burr.

Members of different ethnic groups may speak entirely different languages that go along with their ethnic background. Although Italians may speak Italian, French may speak French, and so forth, it is equally possible to be ethnically Italian or French and not know how to speak those languages. Instead, for purposes of ethnicity, one may have an **associated** language (Eastman and Reese 1981) that one invokes for *emblematic* or *symbolic* purposes. When we hear people talk about their family history such purposes often become apparent in remarks such as, for instance, "My grandmother *always* spoke to me in Danish" or "My mother still counts in Italian." In fact, one area wherein ethnicity enters language is what Silberstein (1988) has called **competence markers**, where we legitimize ourselves as speakers representing a particular group by providing the necessary demographic facts that make what we say real. To speak as an Irish person it is necessary to use certain idioms and phrases that mark the speaker as ethnically authentic. These idioms and phrases constitute what I see to be **culture-loaded** vocabulary—referring to items from another language for which there is usually no equivalent term in the host language. For example, as I have observed elsewhere (Eastman 1983:48):

> . . . the Northwest Coast Haida Indians have words for the moieties (social divisions) and clans (kinship divisions) that mark their social structure (Eagle, Raven, Bear, and so on); a word for the bentwood box used traditionally to store food; and many separate words for different kinds of salmon that outsiders perceive as just salmon or even just fish!

To study language use as it covaries with ethnic differences, it is necessary to consider the power relationships among groups in a particular place (Parkin 1974). Language may be used either to delimit ethnic boundaries or to cross them. In areas where language and culture contact are sporadic or where there are efficiently functioning subcultures, the expression of ethnic differences is not required. When a group uses its own language, rather than a second language (including pidgin, creole, or *lingua franca* to be discussed in more detail below) it expresses, by implication, a socially integrated world view, cultural homogeneity, and economic well-being.

However, intact urban groups with a sense of group loyalty may impose their language onto other groups with whom they are in contact and in so doing begin a move from ethnicity to something bigger—in some cases nationality. When we talk (below) about language change as studied from a sociolinguistic perspective we will see that the tendency of a group to shift from one language to another is influenced by that group's power in relation to the power of other groups with which it is in contact. Power is often accompanied by prestige (another major factor of language change); groups with power are able to maintain their language to some degree because it is imbued with positive values. In some ways it is possible to understand why few American Indian languages have survived in the United States once we understand the social facts of the contact situation. Language shift is likely to occur when the group that ultimately shifts has less than equal power in relation to the other, if the shifting group is colonized rather than incorporated by the other, if it has fewer people, or/and if it has limited social mobility. Indeed, such power differential factors do much to explain why language shift has been the prevailing strategy among most immigrant groups to the United States. What is unusual with regard to the American Indian situation is that one factor commonly aiding language maintenance is residence in an area for a long time. Even this aboriginality was compromised by moving American Indians to reservations while their numerical strength was being sapped by disease and warfare.

Fishman (1977) sees both social and psychological intergroup factors as related to language. His view is that primordial ethnicity prevails before groups come into contact. **Primordial ethnicity** is the sense individuals have concerning to whom they belong. The idea is that everyone carries "attachments" through life "derived from place of birth, kinship relationships, religion, language and social practices" that are "natural," " 'spiritual' in character," and that form a framework for "an easy 'affinity' " with others sharing that background (Brass 1979:1). When groups come into contact and remain in contact, a new sense of common origin needs to develop. "No longer can we think that *we* are the people with a right to exist, and *they* are not" (Eastman 1983:167). Language will be altered to reflect how the many groups in a new polity interrelate. In the process of alteration people may assume that they share a common language (as we saw above in the case of male-female friendly conversations) while the actuality is systematic miscommunication.

Hansell and Ajirotutu (1982) documented communication problems between white and Afro-American long-time residents of a common urban area. They were able to locate paralinguistic (for example, in stress placement and intonation) and formulaic expression differences that occurred in conversations where speakers assumed they were speaking and understanding each other's English. In conversations involving a white professor and a research assistant and two Black teenagers, Black variables were used both as ethnic identity markers and also for specific communicative ends (accounting for the miscommunication). Examples of what researchers consider to be Black variables consist of using [æ] for [ɪ] in "thing," saying "you" for "your," and using third-person verb forms with second-person pronouns ("was you?" instead of the Standard "were you?"). Hansell and Ajirotutu (1982) noted that such devices were used alternatively with Standard forms in conversations as **metaphorical codeswitches**. That is, the choice of Black English rather than Standard English is made "in relation to particular kinds of topics or subject matters rather than to change in social situation" (Blom and Gumperz 1972:425). The use of Black English forms in conversations with whites, Hansell and Ajirotutu found, included using "tense voice quality, with a repeated marked intonation pattern and tone group boundaries after each word" (1982:89) to indicate a non-Black foreign form was being used. Such paralinguistic features convey the sense of "as you [white] people say . . . ." One instance of this occurred when one of the Black speakers used the phrase "military service life," implying "you may call it this, but to us it's something else!" Such switching back and forth within a speech situation (metaphorical switching) is a part of the process of *negotiating an interpretive frame*. By alternating phonological forms, marking foreign forms, and other devices such as variously joking and being serious, members of one ethnic group may keep control of a conversation from others. The non-Black participants in a conversation with Blacks will be confused as to whether they are being put on or not—that is, they will wonder which pronunciation is normal ([ɪ] or [æ] in "thing") for the speakers, be confused about the marking of "military service life," and not perceive jokes. Blacks may switch into a preaching "call and response" style as well. Even though Black and white speakers in conversation may share a language they may variously use discourse features in conversation for purposes of ethnic identity and control. Such control is subtle, since white participants will think that what is happening is a matter of style difference and not realize that their own participation in the discourse is being manipulated. Below we will discuss various kinds of **codeswitching** and the effect language mixing has on intergroup interpretation in many instances—including situations where status, gender, and ethnic-identity factors are at issue, as we have been discussing here.

5.2 Sociolinguistics

Since the 1960s and 1970s **sociolinguistics** "has become a recognized and established perspective on the study of language and language use" (Baugh and Sherzer 1984:1). One of the early definitions asserts that sociolinguistics examines the "patterned covariation of language and society" seeking rules to account for instances of covariation in such matters as social dialects and stylistic differences (as seen in the previous section). Sociolinguistics, according to Joshua Fishman (1968:5-13), is the only discipline concerned with language in its behavioral context. According to John Gumperz and Dell Hymes, the central notion of sociolinguistics is "the appropriateness of verbal messages in context or their acceptability in the broader sense." What sociolinguistics examines is **communicative competence** defined as "what a speaker needs to know to communicate effectively in culturally significant settings" (Gumperz and Hymes 1972:vii).

In Chapter 4 we talked about discourse analysis as an approach linked to the study of language and culture. Discourse analysis, in its linkage of language and culture, is akin to sociolinguistics in its inclusion of the real world as an aspect of study. One way to distinguish discourse from the subject matter of sociolinguistics as it will be discussed here is that discourse focuses on how messages in text "are expressed through prosody and the syntactic and lexical choices" people make (Gumperz, Aulakh, and Kaltman 1982:29). Discourse analysis reveals what is implied by language use (which is often a reflection of sociobehavioral factors): "To explain any indirect communication we must understand where and to what extent speakers rely on obligatory convention and where and to what extent they have expressive flexibility" (Gumperz, Aulakh, and Kaltman 1982:29). Sociolinguistics, on the other hand, begins (as it were) with the result of discourse analysis to find out how what is said conventionally or flexibly goes along with differences in the structure of society.

Essentially there are three branches of sociolinguistics: the **ethnography of communication (ethnography of speaking)**; the study of **linguistic variability**; and the field known as **language planning**. Language planning is a form of *applied* *sociolinguistics.* In any applied field there is the danger of "simple (and irrelevant) direct application of theory to any available problems; this stage may perhaps be characterized by the example of the small child, given a hammer, who is looking for things to hit" (Spolsky 1986:452). In what follows we will discuss the ethnography of communication and linguistic variability, and then survey the kinds of things done as applied sociolinguistics keeping this caveat in mind. In the process we will see, as Spolsky also observed, that applied fields also enter "a more sophisticated stage," seeking "independent principled solutions to current problems."

> . . . the various areas of pure and hyphenated linguistics can—in combination with findings from psychology, education, sociology, anthropology, political science, economics, and other fields contribute to the development of principled approaches to second language learning and teaching. (Spolsky 1986)

5.2.1 The Ethnography of Communication (Speaking)

The **ethnography of communication**, as we saw the field of cognitive anthropology to be in Chapter 4, is an outgrowth of descriptive linguistics (see Chapter 1). Much emphasis is placed on procedures for eliciting data and on a necessary interdependence between linguistic data and the procedures that elicited the data. According to John J. Gumperz and Dell Hymes, "The basic elicitation method can be regarded as an extension of the linguist's practice of studying the same linguistic forms in different linguistic environments" (1972:24). The constant factor is the basic message and the varied factor is the social context. The ethnography of communication provides criteria for defining the various aspects of context that are involved in differing interpretations of language use. The basic unit of analysis is the **speech community** and not a given language (or dialect). Indeed, particular languages may crosscut speech communities. Any given language may be only a part of the resources of a speech community. Its members may use different languages and social dialects, with various degrees of fluency and acceptability, in different contexts. This covariation in a speech community is the object of sociolinguistic study embraced by ethnographers of communication.

Dell Hymes outlined a descriptive method intended as an explicit model for researchers to use for describing language use in a speech community. His descriptive method is called the "ethnography of speaking" (Hymes 1967:8-28) and aims to make explicit a set of notions or components that must be included in an adequate description of communicatively competent language use. That is, his method is seen as enabling scholars to describe what people know that allows them to behave appropriately using language in the various settings (situations, events) encountered in a speech community. Hymes believed that a specific and explicit descriptive model "can guarantee the maintenance and success of the current interest in sociolinguistics" (1972:52) since:

> It was the development of a specific mode of description that insured the success of linguistics as an autonomous discipline in the United States in the twentieth century, and the lack of it that led to the until recently peripheral status of folklore, although both had started from a similar base, the converging interest of anthropologists, and English scholars, in language and in verbal tradition. (1972:52)

The components of a descriptive ethnography of speaking are (paraphrased from Hymes 1972:52–70):

Speech Community: The basic unit of sociolinguistic analysis. It is a community in which rules for the conduct and interpretation of at least one linguistic variety (language) *must* be shared.

Speech Situation: The context or environment in which speech events occur.

Speech Event: The activity in which rules or norms for speech use operate.

Speech Act: The minimal unit of a *speech event* which implicates both social norms and linguistic form. The *speech act* mediates between aspects of grammar and a speech event or situation.

Speech Style: The quality, expression, and intensity of speech including co-occurrences and contrastive choices people make among such aspects of speech.

Ways of Speaking: The totality of rule-governed behavior in a diversified *speech community* as compared to the *way of speaking* in another *speech community*.

Components of Speech: The features of *speech acts* (which themselves are the minimal units of *speech events*). Hymes, using a linguistic analogy, expresses the aim of arriving at a universal set of speech features from which all communities choose bundles to comprise *speech acts*. Just as certain distinctive features of sound, grammar, or meaning combine to form words, sentences, and texts in one language and a different set is chosen in another language, Hymes feels that different *speech communities* use different combinations of *speech components* in their *speech acts* (within *events* in *situations* specific to a particular *speech community*).

The components of *speech acts* conform to a mnemonic, SPEAKING:

Setting and scene
Participants
Ends: goals and outcomes

Act sequence: the order of message form and message content

Key: tone, manner, spirit (for instance, mocking or serious, light or heavy)

Instrumentalities: channels and forms of speech (written, spoken, mutually intelligible, pig latin, and others)

Norms of interaction: for instance: Are certain things taboo? May interruptions occur? Can only women speak?

Genres: Is the speech a poem, myth, letter, advertisement, conversation, or other?

Rules of Speaking: The structured relations that exist among the components of *speech acts*. The idea is that rules may be formulated to account for shifts in the components SPEAKING, as "from normal tone of voice to whisper, from formal English to slang, correction, praise, embarrassment, withdrawal, and other evaluative responses to speech which may indicate the violation or accomplishment of a rule."

Thus, a descriptive sociolinguistics may be seen as a description of *speech events* (which have been defined to take place in *speech situations*) of a *speech community* in terms of *speech acts* which are made up of *speech components*. The rules of speech proposed by Hymes describe the presence or absence and types of components of individual events.

The idea, much as is the idea behind descriptive linguistics, is that a person reading an observationally adequate account of language use in a *speech community* would be able to participate in that community as a member. That is, the descriptive ethnography of communication seeks to describe the *communicative competence* of a speech community. It details the aspects of language use beyond grammar that account for people's ability to behave appropriately using language in the various speech situations they encounter. Indeed, the descriptive ethnography of speaking shares the goal of **observational adequacy** with both descriptive linguistics and ethnoscience, as we have discussed in earlier chapters. Sherzer and Darnell (1972) have observed that adequate descriptive ethnographies of speaking provide the kind of data necessary for understanding *language attitudes* (the attitude of members of a *speech community* toward speech use) and also lead to an understanding of *communicative competence*.

The extension of sociolinguistics to a concern with attitude moves it beyond description toward an understanding of thought (as attitude), just as ethnoscience proposed to understand thought (as cognition). It may be that sociolinguistics, as Burling suggested for ethnoscience, ought to be content with the more modest goal of observational adequacy (see Chapter 2) in analyzing speech events in the absence of any demonstrable psychological reality that can be ascribed to such analysis. Nevertheless, a theory of communication is needed for describing what people acquire by way of knowledge that allows them to use language appropriately. A theory of language (Chomsky 1965:4) is likewise needed for describing what the cognitive ability that underlies language acquisition is. The *communicative*

competence the sociolinguist seeks to describe is in some sense a type of performance (see the *competence* vs. *performance* distinction as discussed in Chapter 2);
that is, it is concerned with how language is used (or performed) in context. One
aim of descriptive sociolinguistics is to describe the various aspects or components
of speech events as they occur (or are performed) in context. Another is to describe
the acquisition of the ability or knowledge (competence) to communicate. Communication involves more than knowing a language—this more is what descriptive
sociolinguistics hopes to account for. Hymes's ethnography of speaking is essentially a proposal for a general methodology to apply to the integration of language
and society. In Section 5.2.2 we will look at the way William Labov proposes to
study language and society by focusing on the linguistic variables that correlate
with social differences. Hymes's approach seeks to present the context of language
use in as full a form as possible whereas Labov's correlates specific phonological,
syntactic, or lexical choices with social features such as class, status, gender, and
the like.

An example of the kind of study conducted in an *ethnography of speaking/com-
munication* framework is Judith Irvine's study of formality and informality among
Wolof speakers in Senegal. She found that four kinds of formality may occur in
social situations:

1. *Increased code structuring*: Extra conventions are added to make
   behavior in a particular situation "special"; for example, the Wolof
   practice praise singing and have insult sessions in which intonation-
   al patterns are used that are not used in ordinary conversation. For
   praise singing, pitch is more structured than in talk; in insulting,
   meter is strictly regulated; in conversation, both pitch and meter are
   relatively loose.

2. *Code consistency*: In formal situations people use the talk associated with their social status. Among the Wolof, Irvine reports
   that "high pitch, high volume, and high speed all suggest low social
   rank while low pitch, low volume, and laconic slowness suggest
   high social rank." (1984:215)

3. *Invoking positional identities*: The more formal an occasion, the
   more likely a person will use a position or public identity (say, as
   doctor, lawyer, or the like) rather than a personal identity (say, as
   parent, school chum, or classmate).

4. *Emergence of a central situational focus*: The more formal an occasion, the more likely a central focus will emerge, thus:

This focusing process can be seen at work in the organization of events at a Wolof naming-day ceremony. Much of the ceremony involves decentralized participation: the guests sit in small groups, chatting and eating. At various points, however, a *griot* (praise-singer) may start shouting bits of praise-poems in an effort to capture the attention of the crowd and establish a focus of attention for his performance. If he succeeds, the situation changes character, altering the patterns of movement and talk for all participants, and bringing caste identities (rather than more personal relations) into the foreground. (1984:217)

Irvine looked at political speech events across cultures by examining cases among Wolof, and also among Mursi (southern Ethiopia) and Ilongot (northern Philippines) speech communities. She found that in all instances the more formal events are more structured from both spatial and discourse perspectives, involve more consistency in choices of alternative forms of behavior, and have a more central focus. Within such diverse communities, despite the way formality is manifest, other-than-*key* (such as formal vs. informal) components of speech acts will vary. For example, participants and ends will vary greatly despite the commonality that the events are "political." By using an ethnography of communication "lens," Irvine has been able to show that from a cross-cultural perspective *formality* has two aspects: As an aspect of the *key* component of a speech act it is also an aspect of the way a communicative event is organized. She has demonstrated that "there is too great a risk of mistaking one kind of formality for another or assuming that kinds of formality are really the same. That an ordinary English word has multiple meanings . . . does not make those meanings essentially homogeneous, nor should we unwittingly elevate this word's polysemy to a social theory" (1984:226).

As Saville-Troike (1982:148-149) has noted, the components of speech events are interrelated. It is important to discover how genre and topic influence each other. How do genre, setting, and topic or purpose interrelate? How does message form affect topic?

Responding to Hymes's call for a descriptive ethnography of communication, scholars have also attempted to come up with the rules that guide communicatively competent behavior in speech communities. *Rules* to the sociolinguist, in contrast to those of the generative linguist, are "prescriptive statements of behavior, of how people 'should' act" (Saville-Troike 1982:147). They are formulated after observations indicate to the researcher what language use is appropriate in specific contexts.

How, and the degree to which this "ideal" is indeed "real," is part of the information to be collected and analyzed, along with positive and negative sanctions which are applied to their observance or violation. (Saville-Troike 1982:147)

Perhaps one of the best ways to discover a sociolinguistic rule is to observe mistakes happening. One example from English is the case of turn taking in conversation. When a person gives another a compliment, the person complimented is expected to respond. Generally the response is "Thank you" or something self-effacing such as "It's nothing." No response at all is considered inappropriate by the person giving the compliment, who will be unlikely to give another one soon. But some people do not live by this rule. As Philips (1976) reports, speakers who live on the Warm Springs Indian reservation "would not require any response, or the response might be given at a later time" (Saville-Troike 1982:147).

Clearly, one of the benefits of sociolinguistic analysis in the ethnography-of-communication framework is to point up just such information that may account for problems in social interaction. Even though people from Warm Springs may share a knowledge of English with other speakers, their rules of communicative competence may differ and thereby lead to misunderstandings.

That is, underlying all studies that may be construed to involve sociolinguistic data is the idea that speakers of a common language may have differing rule systems. One of the consequences of differing sociolinguistic rule systems, both within and among communities, may be that speakers "misread each others' intentions" (Ervin-Tripp 1972:214). In social interaction, such misreading of intentions may cause serious problems, especially in urban areas, in schools, and in interaction between minority groups and society at large.

Susan Ervin-Tripp has suggested two types of rules for sociolinguistics: **alternation rules** and **co-occurrence rules**. *Alternation rules* set out the sociolinguistic choices an individual has prior to speaking. For example, a person may either respond or not when complimented. The choice depends upon whether one is in the Warm Springs speech community or in a broader American context. Alternation rules also function in the decision-making process involved when we decide what to call another person. They outline the basis for the choices we make to call or not to call a specific person *Dr., Ms, Miss, Margaret*, or *mom*. The effect of the operation of alternation rules may be seen in this excerpt from a report of an incident involving a Black psychiatrist and a police officer who did not know (or care?) who the person was to whom he was talking (Poussaint 1967:53, reported in Ervin-Tripp 1972:218):

> "What's your name, boy?" the policeman asked . . .
> "Dr. Poussaint. I'm a physician . . ."
> "What's your first name, boy? . . ."
> "Alvin."

This exchange represents an insult by the police officer. Its impact comes from the sociolinguistic alternation rules the two speakers share. Both the police officer and the physician "were familiar with an address system which contained a [social] selector available to both blacks and whites for insult, condescension, or deference as needed."

The decision sequence used by a speaker to choose which form of address to use or which way to interpret a form used is envisioned by Ervin-Tripp as one able to be formalized on a flow-chart diagram. Each path leads to an alternative through a series of conditions of choice. These conditions of choice are called *social selectors* and lead to the most appropriate term for use given the conditions at hand. For example, in English, in deciding what to call a person whose name is known, it is also necessary to know if the setting is marked for status, if the person is older or younger than the speaker, if the person is kin or not, and so forth. These social selectors account for why a particular child might address her mother as *Mrs. Smith* (in a classroom) and as *mom* (at home) if the mother is also a teacher. As the Poussaint exchange above illustrates, a shared language does not necessarily imply a shared set of alternatives. The police officer can call the physician "boy" but this rule is not reciprocal. Such prescriptive statements or rules of choice, like what constitutes formality and informality as Irvine distinguished (above), need to be compared cross-culturally. Perhaps there are sets of social selectors, a finite number of options allowed, only certain types of outcomes, and comparable constraints. In section 5.3.3 below we will discuss some studies that have looked at the alternation rules that guide politeness in different societies as well as how the choice of pronoun to use in conversations influences whether an interaction is communicating (perhaps) power or solidarity.

In addition to alternation rules, sociolinguistic behavior is guided by **co-occurrence rules**. Co-occurrence rules deal with the predictability of later occurrences in the context of a choice made by an alternation rule. That is, they account for what happens when a component of the speech event changes. There are *horizontal* co-occurrence rules that operate most commonly when people who speak more than one language come into contact. They may speak a language with the syntax of one language and a lexicon from another. Such is the case with speakers of Pennsylvania German, who are bilingual in German and English. The rule is that sentences have German structure independent of the English lexicon, resulting in such utterances as *Di kau ist over di fens jumpt* or the line from the popular 1950s song *Throw Mama from the train a kiss*.

Vertical co-occurrence rules, unlike horizontal rules, do not apply to the entire component of a language's structure but specify "the realization of an item at each of the levels of structure of a language" (Ervin-Tripp 1972:233). Such rules account for such differences as those between casual and formal speech. To illustrate what a vertical co-occurrence rule is, consider the following violations of a number of them:

"How's it going, Your Eminence? Centrifuging o.k.? Also, have you been analyzin'
whatch'unnertookt'achieve?"

The most clear violation here is the juxtaposition of the formal title *Your
Eminence* with the rest of the discourse, which is casual. It is usually wrong to talk
casually to a cardinal—especially when using the cardinal's formal title (Your
Eminence). Once the formal address term is used, one expects that the /g/ will be
pronounced on *analyzing* (not *analyzin'*). Some semblance of appropriate talk to
a cardinal is retained with the final /g/s on *centrifuging* and on *going* in "How's it
going." But it is somehow off also even to use a question like "Centrifuging o.k.?"
without an introductory "Are you . . . ?" and the "o.k.?" is also too informal for
such a personage. The use of a technical word such as "centrifuging" in such an
elliptical construction is not usual either, and the slurrings in the phrase
"whatch'unnertookt'achieve" are clearly inappropriate. All of the **sociolinguistic
deviance** in this utterance points to what the appropriate language use would
otherwise be. This deviance may be seen as normal (communicatively competent)
if "one pictures a cardinal in a microbiology laboratory addressed by a janitor who
knows technical terms but cannot fully control formal syntax and phonology"
(Ervin-Tripp 1972:234).

Seeing sociolinguistic data as representing rule systems provides a means of
noting differences in speech style. Co-occurrence and alternation rules apply to
the speech of monolinguals when they use different social dialects in different
situations. There are rules for how to address a public meeting, for dealing with
an employer, for speaking during a bridge game. Alternation and co-occurrence
rules operate also in the speech of bilinguals and multilinguals in varying contexts.
We will see this below, as well as how such rules govern when to switch from one
language to another, when to mix languages, and when to use different varieties of
a single language.

5.2.2 Variability

William Labov's work represents a different approach to the study of *communicative competence*. Agreeing that a speech community ". . . is not defined by
any marked agreement in the use of language elements so much as by participation
in a set of shared norms" (1968:251), Labov bases his work on the idea that norm
changes may be seen as influencers and effecters of linguistic change. Labov's
doctoral dissertation (completed in 1964) investigated the relation of phonological
variation among speakers of English in New York City to social variation among
the same speakers. To illustrate his approach to the study of language and society,
we will consider what he found with regard to the use of /r/. Traditionally, New
Yorkers drop /r/ in final position and before consonants. They say /gɔːd/
homonymous with *god*, for /gard/ *guard* resulting in pronunciations such as "coast
god" for Coast Guard. This has led to the popular belief that "New Yawkahs have

no ahs." It was found, however, that in recent years it has become *prestigious* to pronounce /r/ rather than drop it. What Labov wanted to find out was, among native New Yorkers, who—in social and economic terms (that is, according to occupation, education, and income)—uses /r/ and who does not, when /r/ is retained and when it is dropped. His hypothesis was that "any groups of New Yorkers that are ranked in a hierarchical scale by nonlinguistic criteria will be ranked in the same order by their differential use of *r*" (1968:245). That is, what a person does with /r/ tells where that person fits into the New York City socioeconomic scheme of things.

This hypothesis was borne out. Further, Labov found that the more careful a person tried to be the more /r/ use appeared. In a summary of Labov's findings with respect to /r/, Burling (1970:94) noted, "people who are relatively high in the social scale use *r* a good deal more readily than do those lower down. To the extent that the higher classes set the standard, it is obviously prestigious to use the *r*."

In casual speech only the upper-middle class (the highest class) used /r/ with any regularity. Surprisingly, the lower-middle class in careful or formal speech used the prestigious /r/ with more frequency than the upper-middle class. Labov sees such "hypercorrect" behavior of the lower-middle class as a "synchronic indicator of linguistic change in progress" (1968:245). Burling points out with respect to this finding, "Sociologically, members of the second highest group [lower-middle class] are the ones who are classically supposed to be uncertain of their own position. In their uncertainty they may overcompensate in trying to demonstrate prestigious forms" (1970:94).

All subjects under forty years of age in the 1960s agreed that /r/ is prestigious whether or not they use it in daily speech, whereas among those over forty, some who used /r/ thought it was prestigious and some did not (Labov 1968:247). The prestige-linked reintroduction of /r/ in the speech of New Yorkers is a post-World War II development (that is, those under forty—now in 1990 under sixty— uniformly value its use), being carried forth as linguistic change largely through the values of the lower-middle class. By looking at /r/ and other phonological variables, Labov found that New York City is "a single speech community united by a uniform evaluation of linguistic features, yet diversified by increasing stratification in objective performance."

Since his initial work in the 1960s, Labov and his students have done a number of other studies in various speech communities demonstrating that the variable use of language is a reflection of community social structure. Further, his work has shown that language changes in the direction of *prestige*.

Labov's ideas have evolved, culminating in the view that ". . . sound changes are symbols of community—and that a rapid acceleration of change in the language occurs when excluded groups begin to share in the power" (Labov 1985:480). This theory explains why the people observed in New York City were more eager to use

/r/: they saw it as attached to *power*. Indeed the notions of power as well as prestige figure greatly in the options people take with regard to language use. Critical, too, is the need for contact between languages and language varieties if change is to be effected. We saw this in Chapter 3 when we discussed historical linguistics and the effects of contact on the form and function of languages that are geographically contiguous as well as genetically related.

Labov looks at *language change* as a synchronic rather than diachronic process (see Chapter 1 for a discussion of these terms). That is, he believes change in progress may be seen by looking at the variation that exists at a particular point in time in a single-speech community. Much of this more recent work has involved looking at the speech patterns of blacks and whites in the United States. Given his views on language change, one would expect that as blacks begin to join the middle class, they would begin to sound alike and speak a common dialect of American English. Instead, the opposite appears to be happening. Whereas "[b]lacks born in England sound English, blacks born in the United States sound black" (Labov 1985:479, as quoted by Quinn). What Labov found to be the reason for this difference is that segregation in the United States is increasing rather than decreasing. Labov observed that:

> There's a growing black middle class, we know. But the number of blacks who are isolated and poor is greater than ever—blacks who never see a white except as teacher or cop, or a performer on radio and television. (Labov 1985:479, as quoted by Quinn)

Labov's observations have caused him to revise prior thinking that language changes when people imitate prestige speakers. Instead, his view regarding why upper-working-class people such as teachers and politicians, and so forth, are at the cutting edge of language change is that these are the people in the community who have power. The variety of language such people use is referred to by Labov as a *local dialect*. This local dialect "becomes, in fact, the language of negotiation, a way of claiming local rights and privileges" (Labov 1985:480). Consistent in all of Labov's studies is the fact that sound changes appear to move regularly "out from the upper-working class into the classes above and below." Our language-use patterns come from the people we admire and from those "we have to be good enough to beat," not from radio and television announcers or from the teachers we have in the classroom. Ironically, the dialect we acquire may not be one we think of as prestigious or powerful, but it is nonetheless the form of language use we have worked out in order to be communicatively competent (acceptable) members of our speech community.

Labov expected that black speech would operate the same way and, thus, have an influence on the local dialect in areas with large Black populations. Working in Philadelphia, Labov found instead[1] that for Blacks the local dialect "had not become a way of claiming local rights and privileges." Labov found that street-wise people—those who needed to use the local dialect to get out of tight situations (as do street musicians or militants)—had moved in the direction of the standard dialect while the group with no necessary white contact had moved further away.

Labov found evidence of wider differences between Black English and Standard English than he had encountered before. For example, Blacks who do not need to communicate with whites on a daily basis use a narrative past-tense construction that no other dialect of English has. The marker of the past tense so used is {s}—yet another {s} morpheme to accompany the third person singular present tense /-s/ and the possessive /-s/ that are already used differently in Standard English and in the Black English Vernacular. Thus, in Black English the sentence "She takes your clothes out and lend them to people" the /-s/ on "take" is a past-tense marker indicating that the sentence is part of a story. When more than one verb is used only the first is in /-s/. Such a construction is new to English, though it is common in other languages. For example in Swahili, there is a morpheme {ka}, which is used in the first of a series of verbs indicating that the tense/aspect of the verb using it is the same as that in the preceding narrative and the actions to follow in the same sentence are seen as consecutive (and are not marked with any tense/aspect morpheme). Blacks who acquire upper-working-class status and who do not come into daily contact with whites thus do not pick up the local dialect. They achieve power and prestige in their own community—a community becoming increasingly more segregated. Labov found further that Blacks who neither identify with their own community nor negotiate their way on the streets will similarly not adopt the local dialect but instead adopt *network standard*, the dialect of English used by the media. The acquisition of network standard "is a claim to membership, rights, and privileges in a community larger than your city. Blacks have had some success in claiming national rewards—so network standard rather than local dialect seems to be a dialect that pays off" (Labov 1985:481).

The increasing social isolation of Blacks in the United States is likely to continue and result in increasing social problems. One solution, according to Labov, is to integrate schools across suburban lines so that inner-city Blacks will be in contact

---

[1]   One of Labov's major contributions to sociolinguistics is in the area of methodology. He has long been aware of the *observer's paradox*. The observer's paradox has to do with the effects of observation. According to Labov, "We want to know how people talk when they're not being observed—not thinking about language just using it." To Labov the solutions to this paradox "define the methodology for the study of language in context." In his own work, he has outlined procedures for conducting *sociolinguistic interviews* and *long-term observations* and for carrying out *rapid and anonymous observations*. See Labov (1971). In the study being discussed here, the person who gathered the data in Philadelphia was Labov's colleague Wendell A. Harris, known as Popcorn, a person accepted by a large cross section of the Black community there.

with suburban whites from their very early years on. Such a "solution" would affect the English of both Blacks and whites, opening the way for both groups "to shift as a whole, with the convergence that is the result of mutual influence" (Labov 1985:482). In the next section, as we discuss language contact from a cross-cultural perspective, the process Labov is advocating for the United States will become clear.

Because of the focus on linguistic rather than social variables Labov has been somewhat leery of the *socio-* prefix attached to the linguistic work he has done. Though moving beyond the more traditional levels of linguistic structure to encompass discourse as well, he sees his work as fundamentally language-based. He sees his concern as a general linguistic one. He is interested in the "forms of linguistic rules, their combination into systems, the coexistence of several systems, and the evolution of these rules and systems with time. If there were no need to contrast this work with the study of language out of its social context, I would prefer to say that this [is] simply linguistics" (Labov 1972:184).

Labov's approach to the study of linguistic variability focuses on *language* in context where ethnographers of communication/speaking focus on describing the *context* for varieties of language. Labov insists that data be gathered in a number of spheres. A chief insistence is that the linguist who traditionally relied on eliciting forms from a native speaker (often getting slow and pained repetitions of words in isolation as well as unnatural sentences) now records data through random but thorough observation. The idea is to find out how people talk when they are unaware that they are being observed (see also footnote 1 above). One way to do this is to record data obtainable through the mass media; for example, from speakers on interview programs or who call in to give opinions on talk shows. Similarly, the linguist can ask speakers to read selected passages to get their "formal" speech.

With such a sample of informants' styles it is possible to describe an individual speaker's varieties of speech as they covary with contexts. Once such data have been gathered it is possible to formalize the regularities in the styles of given members of a speech community. Gillian Sankoff proposed "a quantitative paradigm for the study of communicative competence." Sankoff assumed that speech-usage data (as gathered from a Labovian perspective) are statistically variable. In her proposal she distinguishes *categorical* from *variable* rules. Categorical rules are regular and depict what happens when people use language in prescribed rituals, during greeting sequences, in playing games, in performing insults, in singing praises, and in like events. Categorical rules are the kind that apply in specific speech events. In general unstructured situations of language use, she contends, it is still possible to discern regularities and to devise quantitative techniques to describe speech variability in everyday speech situations. To do this it is necessary to have data which adequately represent "the speech performance of members of [the] community" (1974:21). The speech community needs to be *stratified.* That is, an assessment needs to be made regarding what "geographic, social and sociolinguistic dimensions of variation" exist. Thus, the focus here is to determine what speech is variable (rather than what is regular as was the case with the ethnography of speaking) in relation to the stratified dimensions of variation within that community.

Labov (1972:237) defines a sociolinguistic variable as a linguistic feature that correlates with "some nonlinguistic variable of the social context: of the speaker, the addressee, the audience, the setting, etc." Variables may serve as **indicators** of social standing. This is the case of a linguistic feature which shows that a person belongs to a particular socioeconomic, ethnic, or age group being used the same way by all members of such a group. When indicators serve to order a social context, as we saw with /r/ as revealing membership in New York City's upper-middle class, then they are stratified. Indicators show **social stratification**.

Other linguistic variables, **markers**, on the other hand show **stylistic stratification**. People not in the New York upper-middle class may imitate such people by trying to use /r/ (often getting it wrong and overdoing it via being hypercorrect). The /r/ used that way is a **marker** showing that users are speaking in the upper-middle class style but not *indicating* that they actually belong to that class.

The types of study carried out by Labovian sociolinguists focus on describing the differences among the speech, writing, and gesture varieties within their contexts of use so that linguistic features are correlated with factors such as social-class differences, ethnic differences, sex differences, geographical location, and peer-group status. This type of study differs markedly from studies by ethnographers of speaking, who center on describing phenomena such as bilingualism, multilingualism, and use of different speech varieties in different situations (as we will see in the following section). Where the ethnographer of speaking wishes to describe language as a part of culture, the linguistic-variability researcher seeks to understand the "mechanism of linguistic change" through studying the social factors motivating linguistic evolution.

Labov (1972:326) holds that linguistic-variability studies will lead to an understanding of language change because language change operates in a social milieu. Not all scholars who deal with language change agree that social factors are as important as Labov feels they are. However, he illustrates his view by looking at sound change as occurring in the following way.

Change is first observed in an identifiable subgroup. It spreads to neighboring groups, carrying with it the prestige (or power or whatever social value it may have) from the originating group. Then the change becomes generalized in the originating group. New social groups move into the area of the originating group and reinterpret the change. "As the original change acquires greater complexity, scope, and range, it comes to acquire more systematic social value, and is restrained or corrected in formal speech (a marker). Eventually it may be labeled as a *stereotype,* discussed and remarked by everyone." Once stereotyped, the change—if high in social value (prestige, power)—may be adopted by the dominant dialect "at the expense of the other form." Reciprocally, if a change is negatively valued socially, it may "be stigmatized, corrected, and even extinguished" (Labov 1973:326). In Labov's solution to the social isolation of inner-city Blacks in the United States, he expects that a number of changes will take place from both originating groups— Blacks will acquire white forms and whites will acquire Black forms—resulting in a mixed form of English common to both groups.

5.2.3 Language in Contact: Bilingualism, Multilingualism, Diglossia, Codeswitching (Codemixing), Borrowing, and Style Shifting

As should be clear from preceding sections in this chapter, sociolinguistics frequently deals with speech communities where more than one language or language variety is spoken. Such communities represent situations of *language in contact* (Weinreich 1954:1). There are numerous types of language-contact situations and these will be the subject matter of this section. **Bilingualism** refers to the practice of using two languages alternatively. **Multilingualism** refers to the alternative use of three or more languages (Weinreich 1954:1). **Diglossia** is the practice of using "two or more varieties of the same language . . . under different conditions" (Ferguson 1959:325). **Codeswitching** is the term used to refer to using two or more languages or dialects in a single speech situation. Thus bilinguals and multilinguals codeswitch. Diglossics keep their varieties separate. In addition to these situations is the practice of **codemixing** wherein two or more languages or dialects are used in a single speech act. The example of Pennsylvania German discussed earlier (to exemplify a horizontal co-occurrence rule) represents codemixing.

All of these language situations that result from language contact involve deviation from the norms of each language (or dialect) used. Such deviation results from familiarity by members of the speech community with one or more other languages or dialects. Speakers have a tendency to transfer patterns from a first language to the other languages they learn as they learn them. Such instances of **interference** are of interest to some scholars of language in contact. To determine interference, the grammatical systems of the two languages involved are directly compared "in order to isolate points of difference" and there are "tests to determine individual speakers' ability to comprehend and produce grammatical sentences in the two languages" (Gumperz 1982c:168-169).

From a sociolinguistic (rather than **contrastive linguistic**) perspective, however, language use in contact situations is generally looked at in terms of which form of language is used in certain situations or with what impact on the message being conveyed. Fishman (1972:444-445) has referred to efforts to describe factors involved in linguistic choice as **situational analysis**. His view is that it is useful to find out what domains different languages and language varieties occur in. For example, where one language is used at home, another at work, another at school it is possible to assign "differentiated . . . role relations that are specifically crucial or typical of [the domain]" (p. 443) and associated with the language used there. It is also possible to correlate certain topics, settings, and participants with certain domains of language use.

Looking at language choices in terms of domains is not restricted solely to situations in which an individual speaks one or more languages, but may be carried out in situations where varieties of the same language are used in different situations. In such a case, situational analysis seeks to describe how the varieties compare (that is, to describe the interference through contrastive analysis) and to describe the domains (noting topics, setting, participants) in which the different varieties are used.

Charles Ferguson has labeled this result of language contact **diglossia**. A diglossic situation exists, for example, where there is a standard language and a regional dialect such that many speakers use their local dialect at home and with people from their area but speak the standard when communicating with speakers of other dialects, with people from other areas, or on public occasions (1959:325). Italian and Persian represent languages that have standard and regional varieties used in distinct domains. One of the language varieties where diglossia exists is referred to as High (H), the other as Low (L). H and L differ in both function and appropriateness depending upon the situation of use. Generally H is accorded more prestige, has a writing system, and is usually acquired formally (often through grammatical study). Other cases of diglossia exist in the case of classical and colloquial Arabic; High and Low German as mentioned briefly in Chapter 3. In English one can see a semblance of diglossia where children speak a regional dialect of the language at home but learn the standard at school.

The description of *codeswitching*, that is, using more than one language in one situation, presents problems somewhat different from those encountered in descriptions of other in-contact situations. It crosscuts situations of multilingualism, bilingualism, and diglossia. To analyze codeswitching, the linguistic choices themselves (codeswitches) made within speech situations need to be examined to see why people who share languages, dialects, or language varieties alternatively use one rather than another.

Blom and Gumperz (1972:433) feel that the setting, social situation, and social event in which switching occurs need to be described if an understanding of choice is to be achieved. This represents "an attempt to explain the natives' conception of their behavioral environment in terms of an ordered set of constraints which operate to transform alternate lines of behavior into particular social meanings."

There may be *situational switching* when participants redefine the social event in which their conversation is occurring. As Blom and Gumperz (1972:424–425) describe situational switching, it may occur when two business people meet (as might happen in New York City) "and begin a conversation in English; they may discover in the course of the conversation that they are both native speakers of French." This discovery redefines the speech situation as no longer one of business people meeting in New York but as one of two French people coming together on foreign soil. "They might then switch to French while keeping the topic of conversation the same."

In contrast to *situational switching* is *metaphorical switching*, in which the topic is changed, bringing about the use of another language (or variety). With metaphorical switching, the speech situation is not redefined. Beardsley and Eastman (1971) found speakers bilingual in Swahili and English would use Swahili when talking about education and English when talking about racial prejudice. It seems that the observed speakers went to primary school together in Tanzania, where they felt they had not encountered racial prejudice, so education was an appropriate topic in Swahili. Racial prejudice was more naturally discussed in English.

Within the general arena of *codeswitching* is also the practice referred to as *codemixing*. Codemixing involves using linguistic units (morphemes, words, phrases, clauses) from two or more languages or varieties within a sentence and within a speech situation. Where *codeswitching* has to do with the mixing of two languages intersententially, *codemixing* involves intrasentential switching. Bokamba (Bokamba and Eastman n.d.:4–5) provides examples of both phenomena in the utterance of a single speaker involving French and the Bantu language Lingala.

Codeswitching

Boni, Salomi, o-sil-i ko-zonga? (Lingala)
Well, Sally, are you already back?
Tu rentres comme ça sans me prévenir? (French)
You've come back, just like that, without letting me know?

Codemixing

Est-ce que o-tun-aki ye soko a-ko-zonga **le lendemain?**
Did you ask him/her if s/he will return the day after tomorrow?
(Lingala and French—French in boldface)

People who distinguish codeswitching and codemixing do so in order to find out what difference may exist as a result of the practice of embedding switches within sentences or alternatively using entirely separate syntactic structures. Codemixing, as the example above shows, involves using forms in the mixed languages inflected appropriately, given the rules for each language. Thus, the "day after tomorrow" has the appropriate French gender particle *le* and "he will return" has the appropriate Lingala [subject prefix + tense marker + verb] form from that language. Thus, codemixing differs from **borrowing**.

According to Gumperz, borrowing is a conscious process (codeswitching/mixing is not) of filling lexical gaps in the host (borrowing) language. Monolinguals borrow words from other languages when there is no word known to them for a particular concept in their own; bi- and multilinguals will borrow by learning vocabulary in one of their nonfirst languages for concepts they may not have used before. In Chapter 4 we discussed the idea of borrowing to some extent when we discussed the idea that people may have vocabulary from the language of their ancestors to refer to items such as food and clothing that represent their ethnicity. In a sense, the language one learns as a member of a social group—one's *social dialect*—is largely a borrowed set of lexical items giving one entry to the new environment. Gumperz has defined *borrowing* as:

. . . the introduction of single words or short, frozen, idiomatic phrases from one variety [or language] into the other. The items in question are incorporated into the grammatical system of the borrowing language. They are treated as part of its lexicon, take its morphological characteristics and enter into its syntactic structure. (1982a:66)

Borrowed items, generally, are used in the borrowing language as if they belong there. More importantly, borrowed items occur across large numbers of speakers in a speech community and with great frequency (Scotton 1987:14).

In contrast to borrowing, *codeswitching* phenomena represent an aspect of language contact that does not involve either the integration (or *embedding*—Joshi 1985:192) of linguistic elements into the other (or *matrix*—Joshi 1985:192) language/variety/style or repeated and frequent instances of use.

Code-shifting phenomena (shifting, mixing, borrowing) are used to negotiate power (Scotton 1986) and to reorganize the rights and obligations people in a speech community have with respect to each other. In the section above discussing the sociolinguistics of Labov, we observed that languages change for reasons of perceived prestige or power. The choices made within the context of codeswitching represent efforts by language users to achieve power and prestige, that is, to achieve status as communicatively competent members of a speech community (interacting appropriately using language so as to be respected among peers). In the next section we will discuss the idea that people tend to *accommodate* each other, try to be *polite*, and express camaraderie or group feeling—*solidarity*—with each other in using language. How they do so is by choosing the words, languages, and language varieties they use. To adjust to different people in different contexts people use *codeswitching*. To illustrate this adjustment consider **style shifting**. Scotton (1985) cites a number of interviews on television talk shows in which interviewers use an informal style while interviewees use a formal style: the person with the power *downshifts* while the less-powered ones *upshift* to avoid relaxing and giving out information they would rather withhold. What happens when the interviewee goes along with an interviewer's downshift is that the interviewer switches back again to formal usage and thereby wins. That is, style shifting involves the overt violation of *vertical co-occurrence rules* (see above, section 5.2.2, on *ethnography of communication*) for purposes of negotiating control of an interaction. When a person shifts to an informal style it is not necessarily to trivialize the response to a prior speaker (as is often the tactic of interviewers). However, it is also possible that style shifting from formal to informal speech serves to encode solidarity (Scotton 1986:15)—to help the other person relax. Exactly what effect language variety or style choices have on the way people are socially situated and what the words we borrow from other languages have to do with our relationship with speakers of those languages represents a good deal of the subject matter in the study of *language in contact*. As Scotton (1986:18-19) has observed:

> Code shifting [switching, mixing, style shifting, sustained borrowing] can encode both power and solidarity simultaneously, depending on the mix of other discourse features in the interaction. This is so because shifts are often to varieties which . . . symbolize a low degree of social distance between participants.

From this, she suggests the hypothesis that all shifting is "a strategy which increases the shifter's power relative to other participants, at least for the duration of the talk exchange" (p. 19). Thus when the acerbic interviewer Mike Wallace on the television journalism show "60 Minutes" utters such phrases as "That's *quite a charge*" or "They had promised that there was a *darn good chance*," a clever interviewee will "edit" him in the response so as not to be trapped. Edited replies might be "Yes, it's a strong statement" or "Very good chance they'd get their money" respectively ("60 Minutes" 8/9/81, cited in Scotton 1985:114). Thus these interviewees, appropriately leery of Wallace's style, covered themselves.

Studies of codeswitching phenomena suggest that it is overall interaction—"the larger discourse frame, not the addressee" (Scotton 1986:19)—that accounts for language choice. In sections 5.3.2 and 5.3.3 when we discuss Speech Accommodation theory and studies of Politeness, Power, and Solidarity from an applied sociolinguistic perspective, we will see that alternative approaches look at code choice as a matter of speaker's orientation to addressee. Codeswitching as such is more often examined from such a discourse perspective as suggested here.

There is also a growing feeling on the part of researchers of language contact that code choice is a matter of *language attitude*—codeswitches index a set of rights and obligations, holding between participants in conversations, that will call forth certain attitudes expressed by rule and obligation sets. It is possible to make unexpected or *marked* code choices to convey an attitude other than what the situation normally calls for.

Using notions of **markedness** (see Chapter 2 and Chapter 4 above as well), Scotton (1987) observes that decisions people make about language use (whether involving choice of style, language, or language variety) point out the rights and obligations they have as they converse with each other. The choices that invoke expected rights or obligations represent *unmarked* choices. Situational features (such as gender of participants, locale of exchange, or topic—the components of *speech acts*) will evoke unusual or *marked choices* representing a shift in roles and obligations. In different communities different situational features bring about codeswitching phenomena, yet any given community represents a single markedness theory on the part of its members. That is, communicatively competent members of a speech community share an understanding of the "consequences of their choice" (Scotton 1987:5). From a markedness perspective, codeswitchers make:

   (1) *sequential unmarked choices*—the same as Blom and Gumperz'
       situational switching; thus codeswitching occurs when participants
       redefine the situation.
   (2) *unmarked choices*—the usual conversational pattern among bilin-
       gual peers. Speakers use both languages.
   (3) *marked choices*—the speakers introduce a new style, language, or
       variety to indicate disidentification with the expected or in-place
       role and obligation balance.
   (4) *exploratory choices*—the speakers attempt to discover what code
       (language, style, language variety) will serve as the conversation
       norm (the *unmarked choice* for conversational sequences that will
       follow).

These type of codeswitching choices account for why in strict diglossic situations switching does not occur (each language variety keeps to its place). They also account for why switching takes place only where each variety *must* be someone's usual form of usage (and *unmarked choice*) and where both varieties are associated with social identities "positively evaluated from the exchange" (Scotton 1987:21):

> . . . this hypothesis predicts little switching as an unmarked choice between French
> and English for informal exchanges between French Canadians in Quebec Province
> who are bilingual in English. This is not because English is never associated with
> positive values by these Francophones, but rather because the identity indexed by
> English for informal exchanges with French Canadian peers is not valued. (22)

5.2.4 Language and the Study of Expressive Culture

With the advent of sociolinguistics, the field of *expressive culture* or *folklore* has shown the possibility of looking at the way people express themselves within their societies systematically. From much of what has been said in previous pages, it should be clear that sociolinguistics sees the grammatical structure of language as only part of the picture. Sociolinguistic interest extends to how language use *interacts* in cultural contexts. The subject matter of folklore study is clearly sociolinguistic in nature. Before sociolinguistics, the study of folklore followed along the lines of ethnography and descriptive linguistics as was discussed in Chapter 1. Scholars would go out to the field and bring home proverbs, stories, tales, and the like and present them translated to a reading public. What sociolinguistic awareness has done is bring forward the idea that expressive culture exists in context.

The methods and theories of sociolinguistics as discussed above (the ethnography of speaking, the study of variability, ideas about the nature and meaning of code choices in language-contact situations) apply to the study of song, dance, riddle sessions, proverb use, just as they do to the analysis of conversation. We saw above (Chapter 4) that people express an ethnic narrative style. Similarly, studies reveal that people move in patterned ways in society and that such patterns may extend from genre to genre. Ness (1987) looked at processions in honor of the Santo Niño (image of Jesus as a Boy King) in Cebu City, Philippines, combining a semiotic and sociolinguistic approach to her contextual data. She found that the performance process of the dancing informs the understanding of key cultural terms. For example, the terms for "movement" *lihok*, for "prayer" *pagampo*, and for "sacrifice" *halad* have a wider meaning within the daily life of Cebu City, a life extending from the way they are used in a ritual context. Phrasing (the way movements combine) used in the performance, the effort involved, and the way body parts are used provide a distinctive physical character associated with "prayer," "sacrifice," and "movement" behaviors in terms of the way body parts combine, the kind of effort put into movement, and so forth. Ness used the concept of "resilient phrasing" to exemplify a key mode of organizing action in Cebuano culture. Resilient phrasing appears in a vast array of domains such as political life, traffic patterns, and gestural style, and it also extends to conversation. Ness found that the structure of the Cebuano language also exemplifies this movement pattern. The Cebuano language uses a process of reduplication—in the form of doubling verb roots—to represent action done in a diminished but repetitive manner (that is, resiliently). Cebuano rhetorical style also has this pattern. Orators use repetition of short phrases to emphasize salient points. In the Santo Niño procession, movements of the hands and feet have a "staccato" look that reveals this pattern. Studies of movement are but one way to look at the patterned ways in which expressive activity correlates with social life.

Studies of the content and form of proverbs, stories, songs, and myth may be done sociolinguistically. Such studies of expressive culture (folklore, oral literature) in a social setting have been seen by Hymes (1964:291–294) to come under the rubric of "Speech Play and Verbal Art."

One of the earliest studies of this type was conducted by Murray Emeneau in the 1930s and reported in 1958. Emeneau went to India primarily to work on nonliterary languages in South India. He began his work with the Toda (Dravidian) people and discovered at the outset that one of the most valued aspects of their own language use was the language of their songs, representing a form of oral poetry (Emeneau 1958:316). What Emeneau found was that the poetry in songs functioned socially within Toda culture. In fact, Emeneau found that "every theme in Toda culture and every detail of the working out of every theme have been provided with one or several set patterns of words and turns of phrase for use in song" (318). Where Ness found a pattern of "resilient phrasing" that permeated Cebuano culture, Emeneau found that the Todas use three-syllable syntactic units in pairs. Each member of a pair matches its partner in structure but differs in content, and messages are gotten across via singing these couplets. To accommodate this feature, clan affiliations may have special three-syllable names for use this way. These sung poetic couplets are used most often at funerals to review the life of the deceased. Weddings form another context, while wife stealing represents a common subject as well. Beyond the expected arenas for using such a stylized form of expressive culture, there are also dairy-farming songs. In fact, songs in Toda culture are so pervasive that every Toda is a composer. All events of significance are remembered in a highly formalized way in the traditional phraseology of their songs. Where Ness saw Cebuano expressive culture as reflecting a general "resilience," Emeneau interpreted the pervasiveness of the three-unit paired songs as indicative of a general "closed" aspect in Toda lifeways. Toda culture is "marked by extreme elaboration of a smallish number of basic terms and . . . little of the detailed elaboration is not obligatory" (316). This obligation is reflected in their songs' having this single technique without variation in "accent, quantity, alliteration, rhyme"—relying solely on syllable count. Adding credence to this analysis of the culture as "closed" is the fact that songs are used for censorship purposes (322) as well as for entertainment. The term Emeneau uses, comparable to Ness's finding of Cebuano resiliency, is that the Toda poetic technique in songs is "enigmatic-elusive." Each song deals with a "single situation spoken of in terms of a generalization of Toda culture themes" (319).

In addition to studies looking at the context of expression as revealing a pattern of behavior that is society-wide, sociolinguistic approaches are also useful in the opposite way, that is, in revealing how what people do when they narrate, tell jokes, riddle, dance, or sing functions in the very act of constructing society. People learn the expectations of society and their place in it from the formulaic expressions of cultural world view that they are exposed to.

Steven Feld represents the way ethnomusicologists are beginning to look at their subject matter from a sociolinguistic standpoint. His work with the Kaluli people (of Papua New Guinea) indicates that "sounds" in Kaluli society are shared by animals, people, and nature: "Every Kaluli must become a competent maker, recognizer, user, and interpreter of natural and cultural sound patterns" (1984:389). Kaluli people acquire skill in "song, weeping, whooping, cheering, humming, drumming, bird call and animal identification, as well as environmental sound recognition" (389-390) whereas people in the West need only be communicatively competent verbally and/or gesturally. The common cultural ideal Feld finds involved in the construction of Kaluli culture may be seen in their concept "hard," a central metaphor that "links land, body, maturity, control, vitality, language, aesthetics, and social action" (390). Feld makes the point that in music, as we have been claiming is also the case in language, what is socially significant is marked. It appears likely, as more and more aspects of expression in society are examined in context, that each genre of cultural expression (dance, song, instrumental music, poetry, proverbs, riddles, tales, art forms) will point out salient cultural symbols and meanings. The idea that societies have "coherent" systems of cultural symbols is rapidly gaining acceptance, as Feld points out. The work of Feld, Ness, and Emeneau discussed here, demonstrating that pervasive cultural symbols emerge when expressive culture in its variety of forms is studied contextually, is in accord with Judith and Alton Becker's finding that such cultural symbols as metaphors ". . . gain power—and even cease being taken as metaphors—as they gain iconicity or 'naturalness' " (Becker and Becker 1981:203). That is, what appears to be metaphorical to a researcher may indeed be reality to the culture bearer. Feld feels that a society's sound structure reflects society's social structure, as Ness discovered social movement patterns to do as well.

In my own work with Swahili adult and children's songs (Campbell and Eastman 1984; Eastman 1986), the way in which world view is imparted through music has been highlighted. Children learn behavior appropriate to sex roles from the songs and dances in which they participate; young women learn what is expected of a new bride. The Swahili cultural form *ngoma* combines song context and dance form with social structure, especially with regard to "the reaffirmation of appropriate sex-role behavior, status, and values" (Campbell and Eastman 1984:467). We found by comparing the features of different *ngoma* types (the closest English translation for *ngoma* would be "happening" in the sense of the term as used in the 1960s) that rules of music use in Swahili society emerged. Different music-act components (analogous to speech-act components) interrelated, depending upon whether the *ngoma* is participated in by women only, by men only, or by both sexes. Indeed, we saw the Swahili music community as similar to a speech community insofar as at least one *ngoma* is known by every member of the community and the community as a whole manifests them all.

Other areas of expressive culture that covary with society much as language does include instances of ritual verbal protest. One such case is that codified in Trinidadian calypso songs (Saville-Troike 1982:37) and another is *rapping* in Black American culture.

Richard Bauman (1984) represents the range of behavior that is amenable to study using the approach that language use and society covary. He analyzed the storytelling that takes place at monthly dog-trading "markets" in Canton, Texas (south of Dallas). Using an ethnography-of-communication approach, Bauman describes the participants, hunter and trader, as "strongly associated with storytelling as subjects and performers, and both are major exponents of the widely noted American predilection for expressive lying" (1984:209). The *tall tales* they tell pit the honest narrator against the dishonest trader. In this genre of expressive culture it is expected that the person wanting to trade will tell a tale that is preposterous yet insist in the telling that it is fact. What occurs in the context of the structure and the overt lying (including exaggeration) is that the narrator by overstating the qualities of the dog to be traded reveals a knowledge of dogs and hunting and the trading process that provides that person with credibility. A good teller of tall tales reveals the kind of knowledge a potential trader would need to have and instills confidence in others that the dogs being traded are quality animals.

Dell Hymes (1981) has called for renewed interest in analyzing American Indian language texts as told in context. Many samples of text that were gathered years ago may have been altered to fit them for the printed page and certain stylistic features (such as repetition, remarks made by the audience, gestures and movements integral to the telling) may have been left out. Hymes's view is that the structure of texts is generally regular and phrases that translate into English as "And then," "Afterwards," "Finally," and the like actually serve to break up a text into verses that need to be analyzed as basic units of narrative structure. Hymes proposes analyzing texts in terms of lines, stanzas, and verses and correlating narrative structure with aspects of both social and linguistic structure.

Clearly, insights from sociolinguistics have provided a number of ideas that are applicable to the more general study of expressive behavior in context.

5.3 Applied Sociolinguistics

Because sociolinguistics deals with actual language use in actual social situations, efforts have been made since the late 1960s and early 1970s to put the results of sociolinguistic analysis into action. The general idea behind studies in applied sociolinguistics is that information about language use can be used to solve social problems. In what follows here we will look at two fields of study that have this goal in mind—*language planning* and work in the area of *speech accommodation*.

The kinds of social problems that may be solved by attention to language are often problems of misunderstanding that stem from language use. Applied-sociolinguistic studies assess situations of language use in order to make suggestions with regard to how to effect change. Peter Trudgill's *Applied Sociolinguistics* (1984) presents an edited collection of such assessments: instances of misunderstanding due to dialect differences among British English speakers; instances of sexual discrimination that are language based; ways the editing choices that newspeople make can result in misreporting; teachers' language attitudes that become bases for stereotyping children; and evidence that codeswitching and pidginization processes may help rather than hinder second-language learning. Much application of sociolinguistic ideas leads to arguments for intergroup models of second-language learning and appeal to "social psychological perspectives in analysing the issues of language and dialect contact, linguistic prescriptivism and nonstandard dialects" (Spolsky 1986:451—discussing an Edwards and Giles contribution in Trudgill 1984:119-158). This perspective will be the focus of section 5.3.2 below.

In the immediately following section our focus will be on *language planning*, which may be the most developed branch of applied linguistics (Spolsky, 1984:452). The term *applied sociolinguistics* refers to the activities whereby the results of research on language and society are used in other fields such as education, public policy, law, and the like (see Trudgill, 1984).

5.3.1 Language Planning[2]

The study of **language planning** focuses on the decision making that goes into determining what language use is appropriate in particular speech communities. It is concerned with the successful conduct and interpretation of language, given the goals of those communities. Once the choices available to a speech community are made clear, recommendations are made with regard to the kind of language policy a community might follow or adopt. For example, the United States has been thought of as a speech community—based on the assumption that all Americans share a knowledge for the rules and interpretation of at least one linguistic variety (see the Hymes definition of *speech community* in section 5.2.1 above). One result of the Bilingual Education Act of the late 1960s has been official recognition that many children are entering school in the United States with other-than-English as a first language. This Act is a case of language policy based on the analysis of the actual language situation in the country. As a result of that legislation it is possible for students to be educated in their first language while simultaneously learning English. Thus, in the United States, there has been an official shift in language-education policy. This shift has not been greeted with uniform support—as noted elsewhere:

---

2   Much of what is in this section is taken from Eastman 1983, especially from pp. 1-25 (Introduction and section 1.1).

A number of people oppose the policy of other-than-English in United States communities. They feel that such linguistic fragmentation will lead to political and social problems. The interplay of linguistic, political, and social issues is the stuff of which language planning is made. (Eastman 1983:3)

Language planning is deliberate and conscious, having to do with how people's ideas about language are coordinated. Planners in the United States are expected to be able to predict whether Americans will eventually accept or reject the idea of official linguistic diversity. Their predictions are based on data that indicate which language(s) are acceptable, salient, valued, prestige-laden, and powerful in which situations. That is, language planning uses the results of sociolinguistic analysis in order to suggest policy alternatives.

Spolsky (1986:453) further urges practitioners of language planning (and applied sociolinguistics in general) to be careful lest their approach be too narrow. The implication that *only* sociolinguistics has something to offer in the area of solving language problems (implicit in the term *applied sociolinguistics*) is to be avoided. Spolsky's point is that language planners and others need to look to the entire field of linguistics for help as well. We will see here that descriptive, structural, and generative linguistic approaches are all of use to planners, especially with regard to understanding linguistic differences and in *corpus* planning—in getting a language "in shape" to be planned. "Syntax, semantics, discourse analysis, social psychology, phonetics, and stylistics" scholars, as well as general sociolinguists, need to look "for the social relevance of their work" and choose "problems that are socially important" (Spolsky 1986:453). To some extent in previous sections we have already seen this need.

Perhaps the figure most associated with language planning is Joshua Fishman. Fishman sees his area of interest to be the *sociology* of language, emphasizing the social behavior aspect of sociolinguistics. Above we saw that the ethnography of communication had a situational focus and that the study of linguistic variability looked at the way actual linguistic forms correlated with social structure. To Fishman, the way language use and society interact includes the attitudes people have about language and the way they behave toward language and its users (1969:45). Information of use, then, in planning activity extends into how writing systems are created, how spellings are decided upon, and how official efforts to manipulate language may be guided (Fishman 1971a:365). Because of the fact that language planning requires the sanction of authority (usually political or educational), it may be seen to be the business of *political linguistics* as much as *sociolinguistics*.

Both socio- and political linguists often look at language as a social resource exploited by individuals and groups to influence personal and political outcomes. Sociolinguists are seen as taking a *micro* perspective in their focus on individual speakers who vary their linguistic repertoire to establish or adjust their identity and/or to enhance their power (Laitin and Eastman 1988). The recommendations for language policy that come from this perspective are based on actual use. The conversational analyses done by researchers interested in codeswitching phenomena (and the various aspects of power and prestige conveyed by shifting) and the insights from discourse analysis as discussed earlier in this volume provide valuable input to policy recommendations.

However, there is also a sense among planning researchers that a more macro perspective is also necessary if workable language plans are to be devised. That is, some consideration of the view of groups and nation-states is also needed. The idea here is that in a political context there are issues such as nation building or aspects of political economy that need to be considered along with social behavior. Laitin and Eastman (1988) explored the possibility that at this more *macro* level it may be possible to analyze situations of choice in a way that might complement *micro* analyses of language situations. At the macro level, we explored alternatives available to the government of Kenya respecting various ethnic groups in the nation with regard to what ought to be the languages of education,[3] of administration, of business, and of other functions. We hoped to come up with an overall analysis of the language situation in that country that might inform language-planning efforts.

What we found was that the micro and macro approaches reveal language choices made on different bases. The official government policy in Kenya is that Swahili is the national language and English and Swahili are both official languages (see below for definitions of these terms). Because of this duality it appears that as long as the government is in charge of schools and also requires forms to be filled out, licenses acquired, and the like, English will expand. Swahili is used in primary education while university lectures for the most part are in English. Thus, even though Swahili is the national language, it is not likely to be used in more diverse domains than it is now (on the Coast, in the streets).

Yet the data from language use at the *micro* level reveals the extensive use of street Swahili in the nation's capital to be an indication of a Kenyanized Swahili (with influences from a number of local languages via borrowing and codeswitching) growing "with the pace of the underground economy." The two approaches to analyzing a language-planning context (*micro* and *macro*) "have captured halves of the reality of the Kenyan language scene":

> To the extent that the Kenyan state exists, English will remain the language of elite mobility, the vernaculars will get local funding and support as media of instruction

---

3   The *macro* analysis was done using *game theory* to model likely group conflict in regard to language choice. The idea was that game theory can "demonstrate why certain social outcomes, which may look irrational to a policy analyst, are the conjunction of rational choices between groups that have divergent interests" (Laitin and Eastman 1988:12).

at lower levels of education, and Swahili will get (from party elites) strong moral but weak economic support. To the extent that the Kenyan state is weak and divided, its vibrant cities will develop a Kenyanized Swahili and perhaps a new vernacular which will express the language style of Kenyan urban society, and will be used increasingly by writers to reflect and challenge this new culture. (Laitin and Eastman 1988:19)

Decisions about what languages are written and spoken in sociopolitical contexts require that *extra-code* factors be seen as having equal importance with the languages themselves (355). If a speech community does not accept the purposes, goals, and recommendations of language use established by politicians and educators, then no matter how sensible it seems the plan cannot be successful.

Another key feature in language planning is the need to evaluate a policy after it has been in effect. Most choices made in language planning are matters of either language *maintenance* or language *shift*. In the Kenyan example above, we saw that the nature of political authority has an impact on the fate of languages in a nation. It appears that as speakers of minority languages gain "socioeconomic status and political visibility" their languages spread to "new functions and to majority-language speakers" (Heath and Laprade 1982:142). Thus people are able to maintain their first languages. But in situations where speakers of minority languages lack socioeconomic and political power it is likely that they will have to shift to the majority language to improve their position. When a minority language is maintained it affects the majority language. This is happening with Spanish in the United States where "formerly monolingual majority-language speakers are finding it advantageous to learn a minority language to enhance their political or socioeconomic roles and to achieve communication in a larger network within their own system" (*op.cit.*).

The point being made here is that *language planning*

. . . to be effective, must include other types of social planning, altering institutions and appointing change agents—educational, religious or political—to bring about changes in culture, material and nonmaterial, and systems of social interactions. (Heath and Laprade 1982:142)

Languages are allocated either officially or unofficially in terms of the functions they serve in the state or nation where they are used. In 1951 the UNESCO report on vernacular languages in education listed a number of functions languages serve. There are:

indigenous languages—what the original inhabitants of an area speak
lingua francas—languages used by people who do not share a first
    language, generally used for certain communicative purposes such as
    trade

first languages—what individuals acquire as children

national languages—languages of a political, social, cultural entity

official languages—what governments use to do their business

pidgins—mixed languages used by people of different language backgrounds

regional languages—common languages used by people of different language backgrounds who share a geographical area

second languages—acquired in addition to and after a first

vernacular languages—first languages of peoples socially or politically dominated by a group with a different language

world languages—used over wide areas of the world (also known as "languages of wider communication" or LWCs)

(UNESCO 1951:689-690)

The linguistic diversity represented by these language situations involves the interrelationship of language for wider communication purposes with what may be looked at as an aspect of ethnic identity, one's first language. Often language planning aims to reconcile first-language loyalty with the need of a speech community to operate efficiently and uniformly; but all planning must be sensitive to the cultural diversity reflected in such situations and by these diverse language functions when decisions are made as to what language will be a national language, a lingua franca, an official language, and the like.

Language plans involve both language *choice* and language *policy*. Policies need to be *formulated, codified, elaborated, implemented,* and *evaluated.* The key ingredient in policy formulation is the goal the planning authority has in mind. *Codification* has to do with the technical aspects of a policy. For example, if a policy is formulated that Swahili should become the language of higher education in Kenya, codification would involve finding out if this is what students and faculty want and making sure that teaching materials exist for both research and teacher-training purposes. *Elaboration* refers to the process of extending the codified policy (and language) to all arenas in which it will be used. If materials exist and teachers are trained but neither is in use the policy is doomed. *Implementation* refers to the process of monitoring an elaborated policy—this is usually handled in tandem with elaboration by some form of *language academy.* Indeed, this aspect of language policy is a problem in the Kenyan situation, where there is no official body (with power) charged with spreading Swahili as a national language. It is tacitly assumed that this is the job of the national university but there is no official clout brought to bear upon any recommendations that are made. To achieve a policy goal, people need to be intensely motivated both *instrumentally* and *sentimentally* to go along with it. That is, they need to see the language being promulgated as useful (politically, socially, and economically) and they have to have good feelings about it (not feel that their sense of self-identity is compromised by it).

So far, *evaluation* is an area in which language planning falls short. Little is known about how to measure the success or failure of a plan once it has been put into operation. Part of the problem stems from the fact that the variables involved are hard to quantify. What, for example, are the costs of learning another language or of being bilingual?

Language choices are often influenced by factors of *nationism* or *nationalism*. Nationistic choices enhance the degree of effective operation of a state while nationalistic ones enhance ethnic differences. The choice of Swahili in Kenya is a nationistic one intended to help "build the nation." Interestingly, at the micro level people themselves make nationalistic choices: using first languages at home, Swahili in the market, and English to fill out forms, go to a university, and conduct official and international business. The idea behind language choice is that selection should be based on an amalgamation of social, cultural, and psychological factors. In the Kenya case, nationistic goals prevailed yet the selection of Swahili to reach that goal rather than some other *vernacular* language was made after assessing such factors.

Language planning applies to written forms of language as well as to speech in context. In fact, the very act of writing involves planning. Decisions about how to represent a language (what kind of **script**) and what dialect of many will be the one to be written (what form of language will be *standardized*) are aspects of language planning. The development of systems for writing languages are often done by descriptive linguists who transform their phonemic analyses into *practical orthographies* by adapting their technical symbols in ways that native speakers will recognize as real in their language. It has become clear that what is most important about a writing system is not phonetic truth but rather acceptability—the people who will read and write need to like their alphabet, the way words are represented, and their punctuation system, as well as be able to use them. Readers may be familiar with the relatively recent orthographic reform in China wherein *Peking* has become *Beijing*. In this case, people wanted to replace one form of romanized spelling that did a disservice to pronunciation. The new *Pinyin* orthography allows Westerners reading it to come closer to what the language sounds like. The switch to Pinyin, a more phonetic alphabet, is also interesting because it was accompanied by social change—following the failure of Mao and his Cultural Revolution. Earlier efforts prior to the new regime failed. Scholars link language reform in general to social change and, indeed, predict likely failure in its absence (Fishman 1971a:360).

In Chapter 3 we discussed language change from a comparative and historical perspective. Language planning, similarly, is an approach to *language change* but represents an interventionist stance. Instead of observing what happens over time and comparing changes across languages, planners assess political, social, and economic situations and devise ways to effect change as a means for solving specific problems, allocating different functions to different languages, and doing things to languages that make change more likely. From the perspective of "doing things" to language there is *corpus* planning and *status* planning. Corpus planning deals with recommendations with regard to the language itself—its body (hence, *corpus*)—and includes what linguists generally do: devising orthographies, grammars, dictionaries, and the like. Status planning, on the other hand, deals with recommendations about the role of language in social and political contexts and is often in the domain of the political linguists and sociolinguists from their respective macro and micro perspectives. *Standardizing* a language is a form of corpus planning. *Nationalizing* a language is a form of status planning.

Other common language-planning objectives are *purification* (ridding a language of borrowings or influences from other languages no longer seen as hospitable); *revival* (bringing back a dead language or restoring an old language to its place of prominence in a community); *reform* (devising clearer spelling, simplifying vocabulary); *modernization* (admitting new vocabulary to express technological or other such ideas to the language).

To guide decision making with regard to language, language planners, in keeping with the subfield's interdisciplinary nature, often use ideas from planning in other areas. Ideas from cost-benefit analysis have been used to quantify certain language-planning variables. Decision-making theory, development studies, research on social relations, ideas from other-than-language planning, and even game-theory approaches are being used in order to come up with a research technique for examining language conflict and language change in sociopolitical contexts. For language planning it appears that what is needed most is an understanding of language conflict and language change from the national or state level in order to complement what sociolinguists have been able to find out about these phenomena in society. When both aspects of a language-planning context are understood, it is likely that progress can be made toward understanding the nature of rational language choices and how they can be consistently made.

Language planning occurs in a context of **language spread** or its opposite. Language spread is "the expansion of the uses or users of a language within a communications network" resulting from "the interaction of psychological, social, and linguistic factors" (Cooper 1982a:book jacket). Planners need to deal with factors of spread—of the sociolinguistic processes that have taken place and of language contact—as discussed above. This link with general sociolinguistics is, perhaps, why language planning is seen most specifically as *applied sociolinguistics*—its *political linguistic* aspect as well as its interdisciplinary nature, however, cannot be overstated.

5.3.2 Speech-Accommodation Theory

Where language planning as applied sociolinguistics implicates political linguistics and an overall interdisciplinary approach to language conflict, problems,
and change, **speech-accommodation** research "focuses on the social cognitive
processes mediating individuals' perceptions of the environment and their communicative behaviors" (Giles, Mulac, Bradac, and Johnson 1987:13-48).[4] That is,
it is a sociolinguistic approach that implicates *social psychology* (or a social
psychological approach to *psycholinguistics*). Where language planning needs to
consider the goals of nations/states (that is, of authority), speech-accommodation
theory (SAT) "purports to clarify the motivations underlying, as well as the currents
operating upon, speech shifts during social interactions and the social consequences
of these."

Where basic notions in language planning have to do with maintenance and
shift, speech accommodation is largely concerned with **convergence** and **divergence**. Speakers use convergence as a linguistic strategy when they "adapt to each
other's speech by means of a wide range of language features, including speech
rates, pauses and utterance length, pronunciations." Speakers diverge by emphasizing "vocal differences between themselves and others." As we saw earlier
in our discussion of codeswitching phenomena in situations of language contact,
shifts may be upward ("in a socially valued direction") or downward ("toward more
stigmatized forms"). In fact, the data of speech-accommodation theory is the same
as that analyzed by codeswitching and other researchers interested in language
contact. Whereas codeswitching is seen primarily as a matter of negotiating social
roles in a discourse context, speech accommodation is analyzed more as an
expression of psychological motives in an interpersonal context. To understand
this difference it is useful to consider the uses to which speech-accommodation
theory so far has been put.

For example, it has been found that the more a person's dialect diverges from
that of another the more that person's sense of social identity is distinct from that
of the other (Bourhis and Giles 1977). Conversely, when we converge to someone
else's dialect, that person may think we like him/her (Coupland 1985) or may think
that we are mimicking her/him; what emerges is the suggestion that our perception
of speaker intention "is crucial to specifying the consequence of both convergence
and divergence" (Giles, Mulac, Bradac, and Johnson 1987:13-48). Bell (1982)
observed that newsbroadcasters in New Zealand adjust their phonology according
to "the socioeconomic bracket they thought their listening audience derived from."

It appears that **convergence** and **mimicry** differ as a matter of degree: mimicry
involves adapting to another in terms of speech rate, pronunciation, *and* vocabulary

---

[4]   The discussion of speech-accommodation theory (SAT) in this section is for the most part a précis
     of Giles, Mulac, Bradac, and Johnson (1987), "Speech Accommodation Theory: The First
     Decade and Beyond."

(content) whereas convergence occurs in terms of speech rate and *either* phonology *or* content (Giles and Smith 1979).

Such notions of speech accommodation constitute applied sociolinguistics (and applied social psycholinguistics) when used to account for situations of interpersonal language conflict. The idea of **overconvergence** and its negative evaluation of mimicry is useful in understanding problems, for example those of patient-doctor communication (a physician may think it is friendly to talk to patients in what is thought to be their language whereas patients may feel that they are being talked down to). Speech-accommodation ideas are also useful in understanding problems of male-female communication as discussed above (Chapter 5, section 5.1.2), where we found that women (in societies of male dominance) converge toward their partners' behavior and that men do not (even in same-sex interactions), leading to the stereotypes each sex has of the other.

Strategies of convergence and divergence as psychologically based (rather than politically and economically based as is the case with maintenance and shift) may be seen to arise as a result of interpersonal motives. In the example given in our discussion of *style shifting*, efforts by interviewees to correct downshifts by interviewers would be seen in speech-accommodation terms as *disaccommodation* (Scotton 1985) in the interest of maintaining integrity. The essence of speech accommodation in terms of convergence and divergence is the "desire to extend our social influence through individual self-presentations" (Giles, Mulac, Bradac, and Johnson 1987:18). Commonly in Western societies "deep pitch, fast speech rate, standard dialect, and dynamic style are associated with perceived competence" and there is consequently a tendency to try to converge in that direction for power and prestige. It is no accident, from a speech-accommodation perspective, that Barbara Walters became the first woman in the United States to have credibility with the national news!

The emphasis in speech-accommodation theory on psychological aspects of language use calls on some of the ideas discussed in Chapter 4 with regard to *world view*. For example, for a person to accommodate (or disaccommodate) to another implies some acceptance of the idea that individuals have sets of beliefs or schemata about (1) what others they are talking to and the situation of talk, (2) whether one style is better or worse than another, (3) whether converging or diverging is most appropriate in view of the situation and intended recipient, and (4) how recipients will respond given their own schemata with regard to the speaker.

The idea of differing schemata on the part of speakers and recipients (hearers) has been applied to communication problems such as those experienced by people attempting to communicate across generations or by attempts at communication by nonschizophrenics with schizophrenics. Rutter (1985), for example, presented data suggesting that miscommunication between schizophrenics and others "may not arise so much because of any cognitive deficiencies on the part of schizophrenics so much as their social inability to take account of the role of their interlocutors" (Giles, Mulac, Bradac, and Johnson 1987:21).

Speech-accommodation theory, by making use of concepts derived from observations of interactional language use in a number of social contexts, much as is also the case with language planning, is not so much theory (thus far) as it is a descriptive metric allowing varied situations of language use to be compared.

Both SAT and language planning as applied sociolinguistics are somewhat controversial in that the practice of each is geared to the possibility of influencing social behaviors. As was mentioned in the section above on language planning, some attention needs to be given to exactly who are planners and accommodationists to be in a position to decide what ought to be. What are the ethics involved in manipulating language either nationally (or statewide) or interpersonally?

5.3.3 Politeness, Power, and Solidarity

Throughout this section on *applied sociolinguistics* we have seen that efforts to change language behavior have to do with assessments of motives at either a nation-state level or at an interpersonal level. In the scholarly literature this idea has also given rise to certain assumptions respecting general or universal aspects underlying communicative behavior that have had an implied impact. In earlier chapters we made small mention of the work of H. P. Grice in philosophy having to do with conversational *maxims* that people follow in the interest of effective communication. Essentially, people who enter into conversations with each other abide by what Grice (1975) calls the "cooperative principle"—that is, both speaker and hearer are assumed to want the conversation to work. Sometimes for certain reasons (often social, political, economic, or psychological) cooperation is not the pervasive goal of communication and maxims are flouted. When we discussed Labov and language change we saw that power and associated prestige are factors involved in change. Discussions of codeswitching research demonstrated how power and prestige in certain situations are a matter of negotiation accomplished through language use.

Results of pragmatic analysis (using Grice), codeswitching research, and linguistic-variability studies have all had an impact on applied linguistics. It remains in this section to address two more approaches that have had a practical application: **politeness theory** (again, as with language planning and accommodation, the label "theory" may be a bit strong) and studies of **address terms** from the perspective of whether pronoun choice encodes **power** or **solidarity**. Brown and Levinson (1978; 1986) theorize that people strive to minimize the likelihood of "face-threatening acts" (FTAs) when they talk to others. Further, they feel that in all cultures *politeness* is valued—though exactly what constitutes polite behavior in the interest of saving face (be the "face" our own or that of the person to whom we are talking) will differ in detail from culture to culture. Thus, from an applied sociolinguistic perspective, it makes sense to study what "politeness" means cross-culturally and how it is encoded cross-linguistically.

Similarly the decision, in languages that distinguish formal and informal pronouns, to say *tu* (informal second person singular—French) or *vous* (formal second person singular) to someone is a sociolinguistic choice depending upon whether the person to whom we are speaking is an intimate or not. We tend to *tu* our friends and *vous* our enemies. Switches in pronominal use, then, are good gauges of aspects of social relations. In English, where formal versus informal pronouns are not distinguished, the same effect may be seen in nicknaming—we can use a nickname or term of endearment to an intimate but not to a stranger or person we know slightly (even if the nickname is known to us). When we use a familiar term to another person we encode that the relationship we wish to express is one of *solidarity*; when we use a formal term of address or pronoun, we often express aspects of the *power* relationship that exists between us. We saw this earlier in our discussion of *rules of alternation*. In this section on applied sociolinguistics, we need to be reminded that such shifting notions as politeness, power, and solidarity are the effects of language use in context. To apply the results of sociolinguistics to problems of language, it is necessary to understand just how language and culture do interrelate as **strategic action**. This dynamic is critical to any effort to usefully apply the results of language and culture research.

5.3.4 Second-Language Acquisition and Bilingual Education

It is not my intention here to discuss the myriad research in the fields of second-language acquisition and bilingual education; rather I would like to point out how some of the work done in applied sociolinguistics (as discussed throughout this section) can be beneficial to those involved in teaching languages or teaching in bilingual programs. For example, speech-accommodation concepts would allow second-language learners to see that more than content is exchanged in language interaction. Research in the area of second-language acquisition has begun to take an interactionist stance. That is, there is a realization that people learning a second language are, in the process, interacting with other learners or with native speakers of that language (see Krashen 1982, and Krashen and Terrell 1983) and that aspects of the interaction itself need to be learned as well. This perspective has benefitted from the application of ideas of cooperation, accommodation, and negotiation as discussed in previous pages. Further, the way in which people cooperate, accommodate, and negotiate who they are, what status they have, and so forth are increasingly being seen as factors necessary in language acquisition. To be a communicatively competent member of one's first or second speech community means that one has a knowledge and understanding of the way that speech community is organized and how one fits into it.

From the perspective of bilingual education, ideas about the interactive nature of language do much to quell notions that people cannot express themselves in a second language. Whether a person learns is a matter of social and psychological as much as linguistic factors. While it is likely that learning in one's first language often succeeds, success is often a matter of having had a good home-school working relationship. Students perceive a continuity between what they do at school and what they talk about at home. When a different language is the medium of instruction for students, a different culture is generally also being imparted simultaneously.

We saw earlier that Labov's ideas for closing the widening gap between inner-city Black Americans and white middle-class Americans largely are a matter of both cultural and linguistic integration in the interest of having the two interact as one. Proponents of bilingual education need to consider the possibility that neither assimilation nor pluralism need necessarily be the macro-level language policy outcome for educators. People need to be able to get along both in society writ large and among their peers. In the process they work out their several social identities. Only where or when, for one reason or a series of reasons, individuals are cut off from access to certain members of their culture, from certain occupations, from certain social statuses—only then do they not acquire the language use (and cultural knowledge) associated with interaction with those people in those places. People who have many linguistic varieties at their disposal use their multi-"languages" "for the same communicative purpose for which one language is used" by people in unilingual contexts—that is, to get along in society (see Eastman 1984c:260). Recognition of the role of language choice within an interactional linguistic reality (as in an urban context) would seem to be an obvious application of sociolinguistic research in the interest of seeing that people do learn second languages and that people who are bilingual or multilingual maintain their language(s) and also receive an education.

5.4 Summary

In the preceding pages, we have seen that even when a language is shared in common, there are different rule systems depending upon the context of speech, who is talking, whether the situation is highly structured or casual, and other conditions. Again in Chapter 5, *markedness* as a concept applies. When situations other than usual obtain, we mark them (or mark participants in them) by language to highlight their social disjunction. Rules for what is appropriate, usual, and unmarked or invariable in particular social settings are sought by *sociolinguists*. These rules may be seen as statistical probabilities or as alternatives (choices) regarding what linguistic forms go together with what contexts of use. How people acquire the way to use language appropriately—that is, how they acquire *communicative competence*—is the concern in studies of child language *socialization*. What one says in a certain context is seen as a matter of decision making (choosing among alternatives) or of the negotiation of rules and obligations *vis à vis* others who dwell with us in a common *speech community*. As the situation and its associated events and speech-act components change, language also changes. Sociolinguistics provides a framework for examining aspects of culture hitherto difficult to deal with. Stories, songs, riddles, tales, and other folkloristic genres may be seen as speech acts associated with speech events and so described. The description of the appropriate use of language in culturally significant settings (those where folklore is performed, rituals enacted, or the like) is the concern of *ethnographers of speaking*. Symbols that pervade the organization of a society may be identified once the patterns of sound and meaning in context are analyzed.

It is *communicative competence*, as what constitutes the appropriate use of language in society, that unifies all approaches to the study of language and society discussed here: language socialization (Schieffelin and Ochs 1986a, 1986b), the ethnography of communication (Gumperz and Hymes 1972), and language-planning studies (Fishman 1968). Whether a certain aspect of language use is imbued with power or prestige (or encodes solidarity) in a speech community was seen to be the most important factor in language change (devices such as maintenance or shift, mixing or switching).

The fact that linguistic variability arises in the context of contact with speakers of other languages or language varieties was also made clear. Some people may be bilingual or multilingual; many may use different languages and dialects in different contexts (that is, they may *codeswitch*). Some people in urban multilingual areas may communicate by *codemixing*. The way linguistic elements (such as words, vowel pronunciations, and narrative constructions) are borrowed was also discussed along with the process of style shifting to accommodate to the perceived language and culture of those to whom we are speaking.

Throughout these pages, this volume has gone from looking at language (speech) in and of itself to looking at language (discourse) as the interaction of a general cognitive ability and specific social system (that is, as competence and *langue*) with its context of use (as performance and *parole*). It is no accident that Chapters 4 and 5 are the largest. A great deal of work by anthropologists trained in linguistics today looks at actual language use in cultural contexts. Nonetheless, such scholars, in order to look at language use productively, need to understand the principles of linguistic analysis and the history of approaches to the study of language. They need an understanding of the range of language types in the world, their similarities and differences, and the way languages change over time as well as how they are stratified in speech communities (the subject matter of Chapters 1, 2, and 3). The study of language in culture has been shown to range from the rather abstract (in regard to looking at language and culture as systems of thought or aspects of cognition) to the quite concrete (involving work in such applied fields as language-planning and speech-accommodation studies).

References

Abrahamson, David (1983). "Do Animals Think?" *National Wildlife* (Aug.-Sept.) 21/5:6-13.

Adamson, J. (1973). *Groucho, Harpo, Chico, and Sometimes Zeppo: A Celebration of the Marx Brothers*. New York: Simon and Schuster.

Agar, Michael H. (1986). *Speaking of Ethnography*. Sage Publications. (Qualitative Research Methods Series 2.)

Akmajian, Adrian, Richard A. Demers, and Robert M. Harnish (1984). *Linguistics: An Introduction to Language and Communication*. Cambridge, MA: MIT Press.

Anderson, Stephen R. (1985). *Phonology in the Twentieth Century*. Chicago: University of Chicago Press.

Bakhtin, M. M. (1981). *The Dialogic Imagination*, ed. M. Holquist. Austin: University of Texas Press.

Basso, Keith, and Henry A. Selby (eds.) (1976). *Meaning in Anthropology*. Albuquerque: University of New Mexico Press.

Bateson, Gregory (1967). "Cybernetic Explanation." *American Behavioral Scientist* 10(8):29-32.

Bateson, Gregory (1972). *Steps to an Ecology of Mind*. San Francisco: Chandler Publishing Co.

Baugh, John, and Joel Sherzer (eds.) (1984). *Language in Use*. Englewood Cliffs, NJ: Prentice-Hall.

Bauman, Richard (1984). "'Any Man Who Keeps More'n One Hound'll Lie to You': Dog Trading and Storytelling at Canton, Texas." In Baugh and Sherzer (eds.), pp. 198-210.

Bauman, Richard, and Joel Sherzer (eds.) (1974). *Explorations in the Ethnography of Speaking*. New York: Cambridge University Press.

Beardsley, R. Brock, and Carol M. Eastman (1971). "Markers, Pauses and Code Switching in Bilingual Tanzanian Speech." *General Linguistics* 11:17-27.

Becker, Judith, and Alton Becker (1981). "A Musical Icon: Power and Meaning in Javanese Gamelan Music." In Wendy Steiner (ed.), *The Sign in Music and Literature*. Austin: University of Texas Press, pp. 203-215.

Bell, A. (1982). "Radio: The Style of News Language." *Journal of Communication* 32:150-164.

Berlin, Brent, and Paul Kay (1967). "Universality and Evolution of Basic Color Terms," Working Paper #1, Laboratory for Language Behavior Research, University of California, Berkeley. And in *Basic Color Terms: Their Universality and Evolution*, University of California Press (1969).

Bernstein, Basil (1961). "Aspects of Language and Learning in the Genesis of the Social Process." *Journal of Child Psychology and Psychiatry* 1:313-324.

Bernstein, Basil (1964). "Elaborated and Restricted Codes: Their Social Origins and Some Consequences." In Gumperz and Hymes, eds., 1964:55-69.

Bickerton, Derek (1981). *Roots of Languages*. Ann Arbor, MI: Karoma Publishers, Inc.

Bissantz, Annette S., and Keith A. Johnson (compilers) (1985). *Language Files*. Reynoldsburg, Ohio: Advocate Publishing Group.

Bloch, Bernard, and George L. Trager (1942). *Outline of Linguistic Analysis*. Baltimore: Linguistic Society of America/Waverly Press.

Blom, Jan-Peter, and John J. Gumperz (1972). "Social Meaning in Linguistic Structure: Code-Switching in Norway." In Gumperz and Hymes, pp. 407-434.

Bloomfield, Leonard (1933). *Language*. New York: Holt, Rinehart, and Winston.

Boas, Franz (1929). "Classification of American Indian Languages." *Language* 5:1-7.

Bokamba, Eyamba G., and Carol M. Eastman (n.d.). "Urban Linguistics: A Cross-Linguistic Study of Codeswitching." Manuscript.

Bourdieu, Pierre (1977). *Outline of a Theory of Practice*. London: Cambridge University Press.

Bourhis, R. Y., and H. Giles (1977). "The Language of Intergroup Distinctiveness." In H. Giles (ed.), pp. 119-135.

Brass, Paul R. (1979). "Elite Groups, Symbol Manipulation and Ethnic Identity among the Muslims of South Asia." Paper presented to the Comparative Studies in Ethnicity and Nationality seminar (CSEN), February 20, 1979, University of Washington.

Brooks-Gunn, J., and W. S. Matthews (1979). *He and She: How Children Develop Their Sex-Role Identity*. Englewood Cliffs, NJ: Prentice-Hall.

Brown, Penelope, and Stephen Levinson (1978). "Universals in Language Usage: Politeness Phenomena." In Esther N. Goody (ed.), *Questions and Politeness: Strategies in Social Interaction*. Cambridge: Cambridge University Press, pp. 56-289.

Brown, Penelope, and Stephen Levinson (1986). *Politeness: Universals in Language Usage*. Cambridge: Cambridge University Press.

Brown, Roger (1958). *Words and Things*. New York: The Free Press.

Brown, Roger (1976). "Reference." In Memorial Tribute to Eric Lenneberg. *Cognition* 4:125-153.

Bruner, Jerome, R. R. Olver, and P. M. Greenfield, et al. (1966). *Studies in Cognitive Growth*. New York: John Wiley and Sons.

Burling, Robbins (1964). "Cognition and Componential Analysis: God's Truth or Hocus Pocus?" *American Anthropologist* 66:20-28; and in Tyler (ed.), pp. 419-428.

Burling, Robbins (1969). "Linguistics and Ethnographic Description." *American Anthropologist* 71:817-827.

Burling, Robbins (1970). *Man's Many Voices: Language in its Cultural Context*. New York: Holt, Rinehart, and Winston.

Bynon, Theodora (1977). *Historical Linguistics*. Cambridge: Cambridge University Press. Cambridge Textbooks in Linguistics.

Campbell, Carol A., and Carol M. Eastman (1984). "*Ngoma*: Swahili Adult Song Performance in Context." *Ethnomusicology* 27/3(Sept.):467-495.

Carmack, Robert H. (1972). "Ethnohistory: A Review of Its Development, Definitions, Methods, and Aims." *Annual Review of Anthropology* 1:227-246.

Carroll, John B. (ed.) (1956). *Language, Thought, and Reality: Selected Writings of Benjamin Lee Whorf*. Cambridge, MA: MIT Press.

Chomsky, Noam (1957). *Syntactic Structures*. The Hague: Mouton.

Chomsky, Noam (1962). "Explanatory Models in Linguistics." In Ernest Nagel and others (eds.), *Logic, Methodology, and the Philosophy of Science*. Stanford: Stanford University Press.

Chomsky, Noam (1964). "The Logical Basis of Linguistic Theory." In *Proceedings of the 9th International Congress of Linguists*. The Hague: Mouton, pp. 914-978.

Chomsky, Noam (1965). *Aspects of a Theory of Syntax*. Cambridge, MA: MIT Press.

Chomsky, Noam (1966). *Cartesian Linguistics*. New York: Harper and Row.

Chomsky, Noam (1975). *Reflections on Language*. New York: Pantheon Books

Chomsky, Noam (1981). *Lectures on Government and Binding*. Dordrecht: Foris Publications.

Chomsky, Noam, and Morris Halle (1968). *The Sound Pattern of English*. New York: Harper and Row.

Cohen, Rosalie A. (1969). "Conceptual Styles, Culture Conflict, and Nonverbal Tests of Intelligence." *American Anthropologist* 71:828-856.

Cole, P., and J. Morgan (eds.) (1975). *Syntax and Semantics*, vol. 3. New York: Academic Press.

Collins, Robert O. (1968). *Problems in African History*. Englewood Cliffs, NJ: Prentice-Hall, pp. 57-113.

Cooper, Robert L. (ed.) (1982a). *Language Spread: Studies in Diffusion and Social Change*. Bloomington: Indiana University Press in cooperation with the Center for Applied Linguistics, Washington, DC.

Cooper, Robert L. (1982b). "A Framework for the Study of Language Spread." In Cooper (ed.) (1982a), pp. 5-36.

Coupland, N. (1985). "'Hark, hark the lark': Social Motivations for Phonological Style Shifting." *Language and Communication* 5:153-171.

Courtenay, Beaudoin de (1895). *Versuch einer Theorie der Phonetischen Alternationen*.

Crane, L. Ben, Edward Yeager, and Randall L. Whitman (1981). *An Introduction to Linguistics*. Boston: Little, Brown and Co.

D'Andrade, Roy G. (1976). "A Propositional Analysis of U.S. American Beliefs about Illness." In Basso and Selby (eds.), pp. 155-180.

D'Andrade, Roy (1983). "A Folk Model of the Mind." Paper presented to Conference on Folk Models, Institute for Advanced Study, Princeton, NJ (May).

D'Andrade, Roy G., Naomi R. Quinn, Sara Beth Nerlove, and A. Kimball Romney (1972). "Categories of Disease in American-English and Mexican-Spanish." In *Multidimensional Scaling*, ed. A. Kimball Romney, Roger N. Shepard, and Sara Beth Nerlove. New York: Seminar Press, 2:9-54.

Davy, John (1969). "Chomsky Revolution." *London Observer* (August 10).

De Camp, David (1971). "Toward a generative analysis of a post-creole continuum." In Hymes (ed.) (1971), pp. 349-370.

Demuth, Katherine (1986). "Prompting routines in the language socialization of Basotho children." In Schieffelin and Ochs (eds.) (1986b), pp. 51-79.

De Valois, R. L., I. Abramov, and G. H. Jacobs (1966). "Analysis of Response Patterns of LGN Cells." *Journal of the Optical Society of America* 56:966-967.

De Vito, Joseph A. (1971). *Psycholinguistics*. Indianapolis: Bobbs-Merrill Co.

Dinneen, Francis P. (1967). *An Introduction to General Linguistics*. New York: Holt, Rinehart, and Winston.

Durkheim, Emile (1893). *The Division of Labor in Society*. New York: The Free Press (1964).

Eastman, Carol M. (1975). *Aspects of Language and Culture*. Novato, CA: Chandler & Sharp Publishers, Inc.

Eastman, Carol M. (1978). *Linguistic Theory and Language Description*. Philadelphia: J. B. Lippincott Co.

Eastman, Carol M. (1983). *Language Planning: An Introduction*. Novato, CA: Chandler & Sharp Publishers, Inc.

Eastman, Carol M. (1984a). *"Waungwana na Wanawake*: Ethnicity and Sex Roles in Islamic Coastal Kenya." *Journal of Multilingual and Multicultural Development* 5/2:97-112.

Eastman, Carol M. (1984b). "An Ethnography of Swahili Expressive Culture." *Research in African Literatures* 15/3(Fall):313-334.

Eastman, Carol M. (1984c). "Language, Ethnic Identity, and Change." In J. Edwards (ed.) (1984), *Linguistic Minorities, Policies and Pluralism*. New York: Academic Press, pp. 259-276 (Chapter 9).

Eastman, Carol M. (1985). "Establishing Social Identity Through Language Use." *Journal of Language and Social Psychology* 4/1:1-20.

Eastman, Carol M. (1986). *"Nyimbo za Watoto*: The Swahili Child's World View." *Ethos* 14/2:46-75 (Summer).

Eastman, Carol M. (1987a). "The Language of Housebuilding among Turkana Women." In M. Bender and F. Rottland (eds.), *Proceedings of the 3rd Nilo-Saharan Colloquium*. Hamburg: Nilo-Saharan Series.

Eastman, Carol M. (1987b). "Aspects of an African Constructed Environment: Language Use and the Nomadic Process." Paper presented at AAA Annual Meetings, Chicago, Illinois (Panel Title, The Anthropology of Space and Movement: Applied Cosmology).

Eastman, Carol M., and Thomas Reese (1981). "Associated Language: How Language and Ethnic Identity Are Related." *General Linguistics* 21/2:109-116.

Emeneau, Murray B. (1958). "Oral Poets of South India—the Todas." *Journal of American Folklore* 71:312-324.

Ervin-Tripp, Susan (1972). "On Sociolinguistic Rules: Alternation and Co-Occurrence." In Gumperz and Hymes (eds.), pp. 213-250.

Farris, Catherine (1988). "Language and Sex Role Acquisition in a Taiwanese Kindergarten: A Semiotic Analysis." Unpublished Ph.D. dissertation, University of Washington.

Feld, Steven (1984). "Sound Structure as Social Structure." *Ethnomusicology* 28/3(Sept.):383-409.

Ferguson, Charles A. (1959). "Diglossia." *Word* 15:325-340.

Fillmore, Charles (1971). "Verbs of Judging: An Exercise in Semantic Description." In Fillmore and Langendoen (eds.), pp. 273-289.

Fillmore, Charles, and D. Terence Langendoen (eds.) (1971). *Studies in Linguistic Semantics*. New York: Holt, Rinehart, and Winston.

Fishman, Joshua (ed.) (1968). *Readings in the Sociology of Language*. The Hague: Mouton. Humanities Press.

Fishman, Joshua (1969). "The Sociology of Language." In Giglioli (ed.), pp. 45-60.

Fishman, Joshua (1971a). "The Sociology of Language." In Fishman (ed.) (1971b), pp. 217-404.

Fishman, Joshua (ed.) (1971b). *Advances in the Sociology of Language*, vol. 1. The Hague: Mouton.

Fishman, Joshua (1977). "Language and Ethnicity." In Giles, ed. (1977), pp. 14-57.

Fishman, Joshua (1980). "The Whorfian Hypothesis: Varieties of Valuation, Confirmation and Disconfirmation." *International Journal of the Sociology of Language* 26:25-40.

Fishman, P. M. (1978). "Interaction: the work women do." *Social Problems* 25(4):397-406.

Fromkin, Victoria (1987). "The Lexicon." *Language* 63/1(March):1-22.

Fromkin, Victoria, and Robert Rodman (1983). *An Introduction to Language*, third ed. New York: CBS Publishing and Holt, Rinehart, and Winston.

Gazdar, Gerald, Ewan Klein, Geoffrey Pullum, and Ivan Sag (1985). *Generalized Phrase Structure Grammar*. Cambridge, MA: Harvard University Press.

Geertz, Clifford (1973). *The Interpretation of Cultures*. New York: Basic Books.

Gegeo, D. W., and K. A. Watson-Gegeo (1981). "Courtship among the Kuarafi of Malaita: an ethnography of communication approach." *Kroeber Anthropological Society Papers* 56-58:95-121.

Geohegan, William (1966). "Information Processing Systems in Culture." Paper presented at AAAS (Section H) Symposium on Mathematical Anthropology (Berkeley, 1966). And Working Paper 6, Language Behavior Research Laboratory. Berkeley, CA (January 1968).

Geohegan, William (1969). "Decision-making and Residence on Tagtabon Island." Working Paper 17, Language Behavior Research Laboratory. University of California, Berkeley, ERIC Microfiche Files.

Geohegan, William (1971). "Residential Decision-making among the Eastern Samal." Manuscript, Department of Anthropology, University of California, Berkeley, ERIC Microfiche Files.

Geohegan, William (1973). *Natural Information Processing Rules*. Monographs of the Language Behavior Research Laboratory. University of California, Berkeley, ERIC Microfiche Files.

George, Richard de, and Fernande de George (1972) (eds.). *The Structuralists from Marx to Lévi-Strauss*. Garden City, NY: Doubleday Anchor Books.

Giglioli, Pier Paolo (ed.) (1972). *Language and Social Context*. Harmondsworth: Penguin.

Giles, Howard (ed.) (1977). *Language, Ethnicity, and Intergroup Relations*. London: Academic Press.

Giles, Howard, R. Y. Bourhis, and D. M. Taylor (1977). "Towards a Theory of Language in Ethnic Group Relations." In Giles (ed.) (1977), pp. 307-348.

Giles, Howard, Anthony Mulac, James J. Bradac, and Patricia Johnson (1987). "Speech Accommodation Theory: The First Decade and Beyond." In McLaughlin (ed.), pp. 13-48.

Giles, Howard, and P. M. Smith (1979). "Accommodation Theory: Optimal Levels of Convergence." In H. Giles and R. St. Clair (eds.) (1979), *Language and Social Psychology*. Oxford: Basil Blackwell, pp. 45-65.

Givón, Talmy (1979). *On Understanding Grammar*. New York: Academic Press.

Gladwin, Christina (1976). "A View of the Plan Puebla: An Application of Hierarchical Decision Models." *American Journal of Agricultural Economics* 58:881-887.

Gleason, H. A. (1955). *Workbook in Descriptive Linguistics*. New York: Holt, Rinehart, and Winston.

Gleason, H. A. (1961). *An Introduction to Descriptive Linguistics*, revised edition. New York: Holt, Rinehart, and Winston.

Gleidman, John (1983). "Interview" (with Noam Chomsky). *Omni* (Nov.):1-8.

Goodenough, Ward H. (1957). "Cultural Anthropology and Linguistics." *Monograph Series on Language and Linguistics #9*. Washington, DC: Georgetown University Press.

Goodenough, Ward (1964). "Introduction," *Explorations in Cultural Anthropology*. New York: McGraw-Hill.

Goodenough, Ward H. (1981). *Culture, Language, and Society*, 2nd ed. Philadelphia: University of Pennsylvania.

Greenberg, Joseph H. (1968). *Anthropological Linguistics: An Introduction*. New York: Random House.

Greenberg, Joseph H. (1986). "On Being a Linguistic Anthropologist" Overview. *Annual Review of Anthropology* 15:1-24.

Greenberg, Joseph H. (1987). *Language in the Americas*. Stanford, CA: Stanford University Press.

Greenfield, Patricia Marks, and Jerome S. Bruner (1966). "Culture and Cognitive Growth." *International Journal of Psychology* 1:89-107.

Grice, H. P. (1975). "Logic and Conversation." In Cole and Morgan (eds.).

Gudschinsky, Sarah (1956). "The ABCs of Lexicostatistics (Glottochronology)." *Word* 12:175-210.

Gumperz, John J. (ed.) (1982a). *Discourse Strategies*. Cambridge: Cambridge University Press. Studies in Interactional Sociolinguistics 1.

Gumperz, John J. (ed.) (1982b). *Language and Social Identity*. Cambridge: Cambridge University Press. Studies in Interactional Sociolinguistics 2.

Gumperz, John J. (1982c). "Fact and Inference in Courtroom Testimony," in Gumperz (ed.) (1982b), pp. 163-194 (Chapter 10).

Gumperz, John J., Gurinder Aulakh, and Hannah Kaltman (1982). "Thematic Structure and Progression in Discourse." In Gumperz (ed.) (1982b), pp. 22-56 (Chapter 2).

Gumperz, John J., and Jenny Cook-Gumperz (1982). "Introduction: Language and the Communication of Social Identity." In Gumperz (ed.) (1982b), pp. 1-22.

Gumperz, John J., and Dell Hymes (eds.) (1964). *The Ethnography of Communication*. Special publication of *American Anthropologist* (66) (1964).

Gumperz, John J., and Dell Hymes (eds.) (1972). *Directions in Sociolinguistics: The Ethnography of Communication*. New York: Holt, Rinehart, and Winston.

Haas, Mary R. (1944). "Men's and Women's Speech in Koasati." *Language* 20:142-149.

Hansell, Mark, and Cheryl Seabrook Ajirotutu (1982). "Negotiating Interpretations in Interethnic Settings." In Gumperz (ed.) (1982b), pp. 85-94.

Harding, S. (1975). "Women and Words in a Spanish Village." In R. Reiter (ed.), *Towards an Anthropology of Women*. New York: Monthly Review Press.

Harris, Marvin (1964). *The Nature of Cultural Things*. New York: Random House.

Harris, Marvin (1968). *The Rise of Anthropological Theory: A History of Theories of Culture*. New York: Thomas Y. Crowell Company.

Harris, Zellig (1951). *Structural Linguistics*. Chicago: University of Chicago Press.

Heath, Shirley Brice, and Richard Laprade (1982). "Castilian Colonization and Indigenous Languages: The Cases of Quechua and Aymara." In Cooper (ed.) (1982a), pp. 118-148.

Herskovits, Melville J. (1962). *The Human Factor in Changing Africa*. New York: Alfred A. Knopf.

Hymes, Dell (ed.) (1964). *Language in Culture and Society: A Reader in Linguistics and Anthropology*. New York: Harper and Row.

Hymes, Dell (1967). "Models of the Interaction of Language and Social Setting." *Journal of Social Issues* 23:8-28.

Hymes, Dell (ed.) (1971). *Pidginization and Creolization of Languages*. Cambridge: Cambridge University Press.

Hymes, Dell (1972). "Models of the Interaction of Language and Social Life." In Gumperz and Dell Hymes (eds.), pp. 35–71.

Hymes, Dell (1974). *Foundations in Sociolinguistics*. Philadelphia: University of Pennsylvania Press.

Hymes, Dell (1981). *In Vain I Tried to Tell You*. Philadelphia: University of Pennsylvania Press.

Irvine, Judith (1984). "Formality and Informality in Communicative Events." In Baugh and Sherzer (eds.), pp. 211–228.

Jackendoff, Ray, and Fred Lehrdahl (1983). *A Generative Theory of Tonal Music*. Cambridge, MA: MIT Press.

Jakobson, Roman (1958). "What Can Typological Studies Contribute to Historical Comparative Linguistics?" In *Proceedings of the 8th International Congress of Linguists*. Oslo: University Press, pp. 17–25.

Jessell, Levic (1978). *The Ethnic Process: An Evolutionary Concept of Language and Peoples*. The Hague: Mouton.

Joshi, Aravind K. (1985). "Processing of Sentences with Intrasentential Code Switching." In David Dowty, L. Kartunnen, and A. Zwicky (eds.), *Natural Language Parsing: Psychological, Computational, and Theoretical Perspectives*. Cambridge: Cambridge University Press, pp. 190–204.

Kay, Paul (1966). "Comments on Colby" (from Paul Kay, "Comment," on B. N. Colby, "Ethnographic Semantics: A Preliminary Survey"). *Current Anthropology* 7(1966):20–23. In Tyler (ed.), 1969, pp. 78–79.

Kay, Paul (1969). "Some Theoretical Implications of Ethnographic Semantics." Working Paper 24, Laboratory for Language Behavior Research, University of California, Berkeley.

Kay, Paul, and Willett Kempton (1984). "What Is the Sapir-Whorf Hypothesis?" *American Anthropologist* 86(1):65–79 (March).

Kay, Paul, and Chad K. McDaniel (1978). "The Linguistic Significance of the Meanings of Basic Color Terms." *Language* 54:610–646.

Keesing, Roger M. (1979). "Linguistic Knowledge and Cultural Knowledge: Some Doubts and Speculations." *American Anthropologist* 81/1(March):14–36.

Keesing, Roger M., and Felix Keesing (1971). *New Perspectives in Cultural Anthropology*. New York: Holt, Rinehart, and Winston.

Kempson, Ruth (1977). *Semantic Theory*. Cambridge: Cambridge University Press.

King, Robert (1969). *Historical Linguistics and Generative Grammar*. Englewood Cliffs, NJ: Prentice-Hall.

Kirshenblatt-Gimblett, B. (ed.) (1976). *Speech Play: Research and Resources for the Study of Linguistic Creativity*. Philadelphia: University of Pennsylvania Press.

Klima, E., and U. Bellugi (1979). *The Signs of Language*. Cambridge, MA: Harvard University Press.

Kluckhohn, Clyde (1953). "Universal Categories of Culture." In A. L. Kroeber (ed.), *Anthropology Today*. Chicago: University of Chicago Press, pp. 507–523.

Kolata, Gina (1987). "Associations or Rules in Learning Language?" Research News, *Science* 237:(July 10):133–134.

Krashen, Stephen D. (1982). *Principles of Practice in Second Language Acquisition.* Oxford: Pergamon Press.

Krashen, Stephen D., and Tracy D. Terrell (1983). *The Natural Approach and Language Acquisition in the Classroom.* Oxford: Pergamon Press.

Kuhn, Thomas S. (1970). *The Structure of a Scientific Revolution,* 2nd edition. Chicago: University of Chicago Press.

Labov, William (1968). "The Reflection of Social Process in Linguistic Structures." In Joshua A. Fishman (ed.), 1968, pp. 240–251.

Labov, William (1971). "Some Principles of Linguistic Methodology." *Language and Society* I, pp. 97–120.

Labov, William (1972). *Sociolinguistic Patterns.* Philadelphia: University of Pennsylvania Press.

Labov, William (1973). *Language in the Inner City.* Philadelphia: University of Pennsylvania Press.

Labov, William (1985). Interview reported by Jim Quinn: "Linguistic Segregation." *The Nation* (November 9):479–482.

Laitin, David D., and Carol M. Eastman (1989). "Language Conflict: Transactions and Games in Kenya." *Cultural Anthropology* 4/1:51–72.

Lakoff, Robin (1975). *Language and Women's Place.* New York: Harper and Row.

Langness, L. L. (1987). *The Study of Culture—Revised Edition.* Novato, CA: Chandler & Sharp Publishers, Inc.

Laudan, Larry (1977). *Progress and Its Problems.* Berkeley and Los Angeles: University of California Press.

Lehmann, W. P. (1973). *Historical Linguistics: An Introduction.* 2nd edition. New York: Holt, Rinehart, and Winston.

Lehmann, W. P. (ed.) (1978) *Syntactic Typology.* Studies in the Phenomenology of Language. Austin: University of Texas Press.

Lévi-Strauss, Claude (1955). "The Structural Study of Myth." *Journal of American Folklore* 68:428–444; and Chapter 10, George and George (eds.), pp. 169–174.

Lévi-Strauss, Claude (1967a). *Structural Anthropology.* Trans. from French by Claire Jacobsen and Brooke Grundfest Schoept. New York: Basic Books.

Lévi-Strauss, Claude (1967b). "The Story of Asdiwal." In Edmund Leach (ed.), *The Structural Study of Myth and Totemism.* Association of Social Anthropologists Monograph (1967), pp. 1–47.

Li, Charles N., and Sandra A. Thompson (1978). "An Exploration of Mandarin Chinese." In Lehmann (ed.) (1978), pp. 223–266 (Chapter 5).

Linden, Eugene (1975). *Apes, Men, and Language.* New York: Saturday Review Press.

Lyons, John (1969). *Introduction to Theoretical Linguistics.* Cambridge: Cambridge University Press.

McLaughlin, M. L. (ed.) (1987). *Communication Yearbook 10.* Beverly Hills, CA: Sage Publications.

McNeil, David (1965). *Anthropological Psycholinguistics.* Unpublished manuscript. Harvard University.

Maltz, Daniel N., and Ruth A. Borker (1982). "A cultural approach to male-female miscommunication." In Gumperz (ed.) (1982b), pp. 195–216.

Mandelbaum, David G. (ed.) (1949). *Selected Writings of Edward Sapir in Language, Culture and Personality.* Berkeley: University of California Press.

Mandelbaum, David G. (ed.) (1949). *Selected Writings of Edward Sapir in Language, Culture and Personality.* Berkeley: University of California Press.

Martin, Laura (1986). "Eskimo Words for Snow: A Case Study in the Genesis and Decay of an Anthropological Example." *Research Reports* AA 88, pp. 418-423.

Martinet, A. (1955). *Economie des changements phonétiques.* Berne: Francke.

Mathiot, Madeleine (ed.) (1979). *Ethnolinguistics: Boas, Sapir, and Whorf Revisited.* The Hague: Mouton.

Montague, Richard (1974). *Formal Philosophy: Selected Papers of Richard Montague.* R. Thomason (ed.). New Haven: Yale University Press.

Murdock, George P. (1959). *Africa: Its People and Their Culture History.* New York: McGraw-Hill Book Co., pp. 271-274, 290-291.

Ness, Sally A. (1987). "The *Sinulog* Dancing of Cebu City, Philippines: A Semeiotic Analysis." Unpublished Ph.D. dissertation, University of Washington.

Newmeyer, Frederick J. (1986). "Has there been a 'Chomskyan Revolution' in Linguistics?" *Language* 62/1:1-18.

Nida, Eugene (1949). *Morphology: The Descriptive Analysis of Words,* revised edition. Ann Arbor: University of Michigan Press.

Nott, J. C., and G. R. Glidden (1854). *Types of Mankind.* Philadelphia: J. B. Lippincott.

Parkin, David (1974). "Language Switching in Nairobi." In Wilfred Whiteley (ed.) (1974). *Language in Kenya.* Nairobi: Oxford University Press.

Paul, Angus (1987a). "The Language of Language: Looking Outward for Practical Applications and Inward for Keys to the Mind." *The Chronicle of Higher Education* (July 15):4-5, 8-9.

Paul, Angus (1987b). Review of Joseph H. Greenberg, *Language in the Americas.* In "In Brief: Books," *The Chronicle of Higher Education* (July 15), p. 6.

Pei, Mario, and Frank Gaynor (1954). *Dictionary of Linguistics.* New York: Philosophical Library.

Perlmutter, David M. (ed.) (1983). *Studies in Relational Grammar.* Chicago: University of Chicago Press.

Peters, Ann M., and Stephen T. Boggs (1986). "Interactional routines as cultural influences upon language acquisition." In Schieffelin and Ochs (eds.) (1986b), pp. 80-96.

Philips, Susan U. (1976). "Some Sources of Cultural Variability in the Regulation of Talk." *Language in Society* 5(1):81-95.

Pike, Kenneth (1947). *Phonemics.* Ann Arbor: University of Michigan Press.

Pike, Kenneth L. (1967). "Language in Relation to a Unified Theory of the Structure of Human Behavior." The Hague: Mouton.

Pinker, S., and A. Prince (1987). "On Language and Connectionism: Analysis of a Parallel Distributed Processing Model of Language Acquisition." Occasional Paper #33. Cambridge, MA: Massachusetts Institution of Technology.

Poussaint, Alvin F. (1967). "A Negro Physician Explains the Negro Psyche." *New York Times Magazine,* August 20, pp. 52 ff.

Premack, David (1976). *Intelligence in Ape and Man.* Hillsdale, NJ: Lawrence Erlbaum Associates.

Premack, David (1981). "Language and Intelligence in Ape and Child." Public lecture, University of Washington, Seattle, May 15. Title also listed as "Cause and Intent in Ape and Child."

Radcliffe-Brown, A. R. (1924). "The Mother's Brother in South Africa." *South African Journal of Science* 21:542-555.

Radcliffe-Brown, A. R., and C. D. Forde (eds.) (1950). *African Systems of Kinship and Marriage*, "Introduction." London: Oxford University Press.

Radford, Andrew (1981). *Transformational Syntax*. Cambridge Textbooks in Linguistics. Cambridge: Cambridge University Press.

Randall, Robert A. (1977). *Change and Variation in Samal Fishing: Making Plans to 'Make a Living' in the Southern Philippines*. Ph.D. dissertation, University of California, Berkeley.

Randall, Robert A. (1987). "Planning and Cross-cultural Settings." In S. L. Friedman, E. K. Scholnick, and R. R. Cocking (eds.). *Blueprints for Thinking: The Role of Planning in Cognitive Development*. Cambridge: Cambridge University Press, pp. 39-95.

Ricks, Delthia (1987). "Apes can grasp words, say scientists." *The Seattle Times/Seattle Post-Intelligencer*, Sunday, August 16, p. A10.

Ricoeur, Paul (1979). "The Model of the Text: Meaningful Action Considered as Text." In Paul Rabinow and William Sullivan (eds.), *Interpretive Social Science Reader*, pp. 73-100. Berkeley: University of California Press. Originally published 1971 in *Social Research* 38(3) (Autumn):529-562.

Rinnert, Carol (1979). "Complexity of Class Inclusion in American English: The Many Kinds of 'Kinds of.'" In Mathiot (1979).

Romaine, Suzanne (1988). *Pidgin and Creole Languages*. London: Longman Group, Ltd.

Rose, Kenneth Jon (1984). "Can Animals Think? Surprisingly, They Can." *Science Digest* 92/2(February):58-61, 89.

Rudes, Blair A., and Bernard Healy (1979). "Is She for Real?: The Concepts of Femaleness and Maleness in the Gay World." In Mathiot (ed.) (1979), pp. 42-62.

Rumelhart, D. E., and J. L. McClelland (1987). "Learning the past tenses of English verbs: Implicit rules or parallel distributed processing?" In B. MacWhinney (ed.), *Mechanisms of Language Acquisition*. Hillsdale, NJ: Lawrence Erlbaum Associates, pp. 195-248.

Rutter, D. R. (1985). "Language in Schizophrenia: The Structure of Monologues and Conversations." *British Journal of Psychiatry* 146:399-404.

Sadock, Jerrold M. (1980). "Noun Incorporation in Greenlandic Eskimo." *Language* 56:300-319.

Sanches, Mary (1978-1979). "Brain Function Lateralization and Language Acquisition: The Evidence from Japanese." *Language Sciences* 1/1:35-49.

Sankoff, Gillian (1974). "A Quantitative Paradigm for the Study of Communicative Competence." In Bauman and Sherzer (eds.), pp. 18-49.

Sapir, Edward (1921). *Language. An Introduction to the Study of Speech*. New York: Harcourt Brace Jovanovich. Reprint 1955, Cambridge, MA: Harvard University Press.

Sapir, Edward (1931). "Conceptual Categories in Primitive Languages." *Science* 74:578.

Sapir, Edward (1951/1929). "The Status of Linguistics as a Science." In David Mandelbaum (ed.), *Selected Writings*. Berkeley: University of California Press. Original publication in *Language* 5:207-214.

Saporta, Sol (1974). "Language in a Sexist Society." Paper presented at the Modern Language Association, New York (December).

Saussure, Ferdinand de (1916). *Cours de Linguistique Générale (Course in General Linguistics)*. English translation: Philosophical Library (1954); McGraw-Hill Book Co. (1966).

Saville-Troike, Muriel (1982). *The Ethnography of Communication*. Baltimore, MD: University Park Press.

Schank, Roger, and Robert Abelson (1977). *Scripts, Plans, Goals and Understanding*. Hillsdale, NJ: Lawrence Erlbaum Associates.

Schieffelin, Bambi B., and Elinor Ochs (1986a). "Language Socialization." *Annual Review of Anthropology* 15:163-246.

Schieffelin, Bambi B., and Elinor Ochs (eds.) (1986b). *Language Socialization across Cultures*. Studies in the Social and Cultural Foundations of Language 3. Cambridge: Cambridge University Press.

Schneider, David M. (1968). *American Kinship: A Cultural Account*. Englewood Cliffs, NJ: Prentice-Hall.

Schumann, J. B. (1978). *The Pidginization Process. A model for second-language acquisition*. Rowley, MA: Newbury House.

Scotton, Carol M. (1983). "The Negotiation of Identities in Conversation: A Theory of Markedness and Code Choice." *International Journal of the Sociology of Language* 44:115-136.

Scotton, Carol M. (1985). "'What the heck, Sir': Style Shifting and Lexical Colouring as Powerful Language Features." In Richard L. Street and Joseph N. Cappella (eds.). *Sequence and Pattern in Communicative Behaviour* (1985). London: Edward Arnold (Publishers), pp. 103-119.

Scotton, Carol M. (1986). "Style-shifting and Language-shifting as Powerful Language Strategies." Paper presented at 1986 Minnesota Linguistic Conference (September 12-13).

Scotton, Carol M. (1987). "Code-Switching and Types of Multilingual Communities." Paper presented at 1987 Georgetown Round Table on Languages and Linguistics (March).

Seattle Post-Intelligencer (1985). "Science Briefs": "Pygmy chimp 'talks' say Atlanta scientists." June 25, p. C2.

Sells, Peter (1985). *Lectures on Contemporary Syntactic Theories*. Stanford, CA: Center for the Study of Language and Information.

Sherzer, Joel (1987). "A Discourse-Centered Approach to Language and Culture." *American Anthropologist* 89/2(June):295-309.

Sherzer, Joel, and Regna Darnell (1972). "Outline Guide for the Ethnographic Study of Speech Use." In Gumperz and Hymes (eds.), pp. 548-554.

Silberstein, Sandra (1988). "Ideology as Process: Gender Ideology in Oral Courtship Narratives." In Susan Fisher and Alexandra Todd (eds.). *Discourse and Gender*. Norwood, NJ: Ablex Publishing Co.

Silverstein, Michael (1976). "Shifters, Linguistic Categories, and Cultural Description." In Basso and Selby (eds.), pp. 11-56.

Spolsky, B. (1986). Review of Trudgill (ed.) (1984). *Applied Sociolinguistics. Language* 62/2(June):451-453.

Spradley, James P. (1970). *You Owe Yourself a Drunk: An Ethnography of Urban Nomads*. Boston: Little, Brown and Co.

Sturtevant, Edgar Howard (1917). *Linguistic Change*. Chicago: University of Chicago Press. Phoenix Edition (1965).

Swadesh, Morris (1955). "Towards Greater Accuracy in Lexicostatistic Dating." *International Journal of American Linguistics* 21:121-137.

Swadesh, Morris (1959). "Linguistics as an Instrument of Prehistory." *South-Western Journal of Anthropology* 15:20-35.

Swigart, Leigh (1984). "'86 the Gewertz, 2 More Rack': A Look at Restaurant Talk." Manuscript. University of Washington, Department of Anthropology.

Tannen, Deborah (1982). "Ethnic style in male-female conversation." In Gumperz (ed.) (1982b), pp. 217-231.

Terrace, Herbert S. (1979). *Nim: A Chimpanzee Who Learned Sign Language*. New York: Alfred A. Knopf.

Tiwary, K. M. (1968). "The Echo Word Construction in Bhojpuri." *Anthropological Linguistics* 10(4):32-38.

Todorov, Tzvetan (1981). "Bakhtin's Theory of the Utterance." In Richard T. de George (ed.), *Semiotic Themes*. Lawrence: University of Kansas (1981), pp. 65-78.

Troubetzkoy, N. (1937). *Grundzüge der Phonologie*. Travaux du Cercle Linguistique de Prague. VII.

Trudgill, Peter (ed.). *Applied Sociolinguistics*. London and Orlando: Academic Press.

Tsunoda, Tadanobu (1971). "The Difference of the Cerebral Dominance of Vowel Sounds among Different Languages." *The Journal of Auditory Research* 11:305-314.

Tsunoda, Tadanobu (1972). "An Audiological Difference between Right and Left Hemispheres." *Otologia* 18:58-66.

Tsunoda, Tadanobu (1973). "The Characteristic Pattern of the Cerebral Dominance for Vowel Sound Found in Japanese Second-generations." *Proceedings of the Japan Academy* 9:643-647.

Turner, Victor (1967). *The Forest of Symbols*. Ithaca, NY: Cornell University Press.

Tyler, Stephen (ed.) (1969). *Cognitive Anthropology*. New York: Holt, Rinehart, and Winston.

UNESCO (1951). "The Use of Vernacular Languages in Education: The Report of the UNESCO Meeting of Specialists, 1951" (Paris). In Fishman (ed.) (1968), pp. 688-716; also in *Monographs on Fundamental Education* 8.

Wasow, Thomas (1985). "Postscript." In Sells (1985), Chapter 5, pp. 193-214.

Watson-Gegeo, K. A., and D. W. Gegeo (1983). "*Fa'amanata'anga*: Family Teaching and Counseling in West Kwana'ae Child Socialization." Paper for conference on Talk and Social Inference, Pitzer College, Claremont, CA (October).

Weinreich, Uriel (1953). *Language in Contact: Findings and Problems*. Publications of the Linguistic Circle of New York, No. 1, pp. 1-6. Reprinted 1963. The Hague: Mouton.

Whorf, Benjamin Lee (circa 1936). "A Linguistic Consideration of Thinking in Primitive Communities." In Carroll (ed.), pp. 65-86.

Wissler, C. (1926). *The Relation of Nature to Man in Aboriginal America*. Oxford University Press.

INDEX